D0713531

The Jeffersonian Persuasion

EVOLUTION OF A PARTY IDEOLOGY

LANCE BANNING

Cornell University Press ITHACA AND LONDON

The Frederick Jackson Turner Award, presented annually by the Organization of American Historians, was won in 1977 by Merritt Roe Smith and Cornell University Press for *Harpers Ferry Armory and the New Technology: The Challenge of Change.* Cornell University Press has applied its share of the award toward production costs of *The Jeffersonian Persuasion: Evolution of a Party Ideology.*

First published 1978 by Cornell University Press.
Published in the United Kingdom by Cornell University Press Ltd.,
2-4 Brook Street, London W1Y 1AA.

International Standard Book Number 0-8014-1151-3
Library of Congress Catalog Card Number 77–14666
Printed in the United States of America
Librarians: Library of Congress cataloging information
appears on the last page of the book.

To my parents

Acknowledgments

N<small>INE</small> years in preparation, this book has loaded me with debts that I can never pay and left me with the special pleasure of awareness that, among historians, such debts are never called. John Murrin gave great blocks of time that he might have spent on his own projects to the careful supervision of a study that moved well beyond the bounds we had originally defined. John Pocock lent his mastery of early modern thought. The interest and participation of these scholars have been so complete that I have long since been unable to recall which thoughts and phrases may be theirs instead of mine. Others, too, have given freely of their time and care. Special thanks are due to Gordon Wood, Rowland Berthoff, John L. Thomas, William Willingham, Drew McCoy, and Richard Buel.

Financial help has also speeded the research and writing. Washington University granted a dissertation fellowship. The University of Kentucky gave a summer grant. The Nation Endowment for the Humanities made possible a final year of undistracted effort.

My largest debts, however, are harder to express: to a most uncommon laborer who did not live to see the product of this different kind of work; to Mom; and, most of all, to Lana, who taught and typed and kept my metaphors in check—and, happily, who loved.

L<small>ANCE</small> B<small>ANNING</small>

Lexington, Kentucky

Contents

The Jeffersonian Persuasion

EVOLUTION OF A PARTY IDEOLOGY

Introduction

LATE in his retirement, Thomas Jefferson gave part of his enormous energy to the preparation of his papers for posterity. In 1818, at age seventy-five, he wrote a preface for a collection of manuscripts and private memoranda dating, for the most part, from his tenure as George Washington's Secretary of State. The task of arranging the papers for the binder brought the politics of the 1790s sharply to his mind, and he expressed a hope that the collection would be seen as a documentary antidote to John Marshall's Federalist history of those years. Time had failed to temper his conviction that portentous issues had been at stake.

Jefferson insisted that the party struggles of the 1790s "were contests of principle between the advocates of republican and those of kingly government."[1] As he recalled the struggle, a faction of American monarchists, active since revolutionary days, had seized control of the federal government during the administrations of Washington and John Adams. These monarchists had exercised their powers in a systematic effort to replace the republican Constitution with hereditary forms. "Nothing rescued us from . . . liberticide . . . but the unyielding opposition of those firm spirits who sternly maintained their posts in defiance of terror until their fellow citizens could be aroused to their own

1. Summary and quotations from Paul Leicester Ford, ed., *The Works of Thomas Jefferson*, 12 vols. (New York: Putnam, 1904), I, 167–183. Spelling, punctuation, and typography have been modernized here and throughout.

danger, and rally, and rescue the standard of the Constitution."
Twenty-five years after the events, in the calm following his
party's triumph, Jefferson remained convinced that his election
had rescued the Republic from a real and potent threat.

In national mythology, there may survive a certain image of
the first years of our government as a time of harmony and steady
progress, when the heroes of the Revolution led the land in
dignity and peace. Historians know better. Every serious student
of the new American Republic has read the preface to the "Anas."
Most would readily agree that it repeated fairly and with little
change the accusation that Jefferson and his followers of the
1790s had made the central count in their indictment of
Federalism. Most would probably concede that both the party
leader and his friends believed the charge was justified. Countless
times, not just in public, but in letters to each other and even in
notations to themselves, Republicans insisted that what they opposed was nothing less than a conspiracy against liberty. The
very name they chose to characterize their party is evidence that
they believed republican government was at risk.

What to make of the Republican conviction is nonetheless
unclear. For there was, in the new nation, no influential group of
men who really plotted to reverse the Revolution. So insubstan-
tial was the Jeffersonian belief that many scholars have been
tempted to recognize it briefly, to note its strong appeal to voters,
and then to pass it quickly by. No one has made a full-scale effort
to comprehend the nature, sources, or importance of the party's
charge that the Republic was in danger. There, nonetheless, it
is—repeated in the speeches and the pamphlets and the private
correspondence so frequently and with such obvious conviction
that there is no denying it was somehow crucial to the party's
being. What, then, did they fear? What do we find if we attempt
to write their shorthand out? What role did their conviction play
in the development and conduct of the first Republican party?

These chapters try to reconstruct the Jeffersonian persuasion,
to understand the sources and the nature of the party's ideology,
and to trace relationships between the ideology and party growth

and actions. By "ideology" I mean the more or less coherent body of assumptions, values, and ideas that bound Republicans together as it shaped their common understanding of society and politics and lent a common meaning to events. I use the word in reference to a constellation of ideas—and not a formal "theory"—which made it possible for members of the party to perceive a pattern in the happenings around them, to define a group identity in terms related to that pattern, and to sketch a course of action that would make the pattern change.[2] I should be quick to say I do not think that all Republicans shared this ideology. Yet neither do I think it was confined to an elite. I think it possible to trace a process by which several score of men— many of them unknown even then—constructed a persuasion that was shared, in time, on every level of the party, linking lesser activists and many ordinary voters with the few men at the top. I think it possible to write about the party as a whole.

The effort rests, of course, on several assumptions and conclusions. Most importantly, perhaps, it rests on a conviction that we have to see the party's ideology in diachronic fashion for significant new insights to result. There has always been a tendency to think of the Republicans as progenitors, not heirs, to be interested primarily in the legacy they left. At best, this has produced a partial picture of their thought. At worst, it has resulted in a cloudy and anachronistic understanding of their own preoccupations and concerns. Accordingly, this study focuses on origins and process, on the evolution of the party's thought. And it insists that we must see Republicans as heirs.

There are no book-length studies of the thought of the Republicans as a party.[3] Brief summaries by authors principally con-

---

2. My conception of the development and function of ideology has been most strongly influenced by the various writings of J. G. A. Pocock, particularly *Politics, Language, and Time: Essays on Political Thought and History* (New York: Atheneum, 1971), and by Thomas S. Kuhn, *The Structure of Scientific Revolutions* (Chicago: University of Chicago Press, 1962). Also useful is Clifford Geertz, "Ideology as a Cultural System," in David E. Apter, ed., *Ideology and Discontent* (London: Free Press, 1964), pp. 47–76.

3. The closest approaches are Stuart Gerry Brown, *The First Republicans: Political*

cerned with other things are often the most useful guides, especially when they have been informed by thorough knowledge of
the context of contemporary writings and a careful concentration
on contemporary words. Close study of the documents permits
an author to avoid anachronisms and resist the inclination to
attribute to Republicans alone ideas that most of their opponents
also shared.[4] Yet summaries are not enough, nor do they usually
escape mistakes. The difficulty is that no examination of contemporary writings can suffice. Too many implications of contemporary phrases have been lost. In the preface to the "Anas," for
example, Jefferson explained his fears and justified his charges by
using phrases such as "mercenary phalanx," "British constitution," and "corruption." Such phrases fill the records of the
1790s. But contemporaries seldom paused for explanation. They
could and did speak volumes in a word, certain that their listen-
ers would understand the whole. Only recently have modern
readers found a door into the intellectual context that contemporaries shared. Only through an understanding of this context is
it possible to read the many paragraphs that often were implied
within a line.

The past few years have witnessed a reinterpretation of the
American Revolution.[5] This reinterpretation is a consequence of

---

Philosophy and Public Policy in the Party of Jefferson and Madison (Syracuse: Syracuse
University Press, 1954), which discusses party leaders only, and Donald H. Stewart,
The Opposition Press of the Federalist Period (Albany: State University of New York
Press, 1969), which does not deal with ideology in a systematic way. Richard Buel, Jr.,
Securing the Revolution: Ideology in American Politics, 1789–1815 (Ithaca, N.Y.: Cor-
nell University Press, 1972), a recent and ambitious effort to place party thought in the
broader context of the first party struggle, is based upon assumptions about the role and
nature of ideology which contrast sharply with my own.

4. Some of the better summaries can be found in John C. Miller, *The Federalist Era,
1789–1801* (New York: Harper & Row, 1960); Charles A. Beard, *Economic Origins of
Jeffersonian Democracy* (New York: Macmillan, 1915); and Adrienne Koch, *Jefferson
and Madison: The Great Collaboration* (New York: Oxford University Press, 1964).
Attribution of shared ideas to Republicans alone is noticeable in Brown and in Charles
Maurice Wiltse, *The Jeffersonian Tradition in American Democracy* (Chapel Hill: University of North Carolina Press, 1935). An inclination to interpret the Republicans
anachronistically is ubiquitous. Thus, Beard identified them as foes of property rights
and friends of human rights; Koch saw them as opponents of a crypto-totalitarianism;
and Wiltse interpreted Jefferson from the perspective of the New Deal.

5. Most importantly in Bernard Bailyn, *The Ideological Origins of the American*

better knowledge of the trans-Atlantic heritage of revolutionary thought. Historians have rediscovered an important group of eighteenth-century British writers whose influence in the colonies helped instigate the Revolution and launched the revolutionary generation on the course that led them to the Constitution. As yet, however, few historians have understood to what a very great degree this British heritage shaped the early national experience as well.[6] This book attempts to make a contribution to the later history of the universe of thought that shaped the Revolution. It argues that a constellation of inherited concerns gave rise to the Republican party and its foes. It seeks to trace the process. In doing so, it tries to show that the Republican persuasion was a great deal more coherent than has formerly been thought, and that it exercised a greater influence on the party's growth and conduct than has yet been recognized.

Early in the history of the new American government, opponents of administration policy began to see a pattern in events. Conditioned by the Revolution and its British sources, this perception soon impelled a thorough reconstruction of the eighteenth-century ideology from which it flowed. Throughout the 1790s, a Republican revision of British opposition thought served as the most important justification for the existence of the party and as the general framework for specific criticisms of administration plans. Developed very early, the ideology required a strict construction of the Constitution and helped to keep the party conflict within bounds. And yet it also taught that liberty and all the fruits of Revolution were endangered by a scheme to undermine the Constitution and subvert the social structure on

---

Revolution (Cambridge, Mass.: Harvard University Press, 1967), and Gordon S. Wood, *The Creation of the American Republic* (Chapel Hill: University of North Carolina Press, 1969). For a full bibliography, see Robert E. Shalhope, "Toward a Republican Synthesis: The Emergence of an Understanding of Republicanism in American Historiography," *William and Mary Quarterly*, 29 (1972), 49–80.

6. Important exceptions are John R. Howe, Jr., "Republican Thought and the Political Violence of the 1790's," *American Quarterly*, 19 (1967), 147–165; James M. Banner, *To the Hartford Convention: The Federalists and the Origins of Party Politics in Massachusetts, 1789–1815* (New York: Knopf, 1970); and Linda K. Kerber, *Federalists in Dissent: Imagery and Ideology in Jeffersonian America* (Ithaca, N.Y.: Cornell University Press, 1970).

which liberty must rest. This conclusion led Republicans to view the Federalist administrations' foreign-policy decisions as logical extensions of a plot. It prompted party members to interpret the repressive measures of the last years of the decade as the culmination of a liberticide design. And when the party came to power, the ideology of opposition days played a larger role in shaping policy than has usually been seen.

Recovering the party's thought, we will, of course, learn less than we might like to know about the new Republic. Ideology alone cannot explain the early party struggle. But better knowledge of the ideology can help us understand the speed with which Americans divided into parties after 1789. It can add a new dimension to our knowledge of the progress of the party quarrel and to our understanding of the violence of the dispute. It can also help us see the limitations of the party disagreement, the structure of the constitutional consensus within which the argument occurred. An understanding of this ideology can bring us far more closely into touch with the generation of the Founders, illuminating their most deeply felt concerns.

Part I

THE HERITAGE

The best instituted governments, like the best constituted animal bodies, carry in them the seeds of their dissolution; and, though they grow and improve for a time, they will soon tend visibly to their dissolution. Every hour they live is an hour the less that they have to live. All that can be done, therefore, to prolong the duration of a good government is to draw it back, on every favorable occasion, to the first good principles on which it was founded.

Bolingbroke

CHAPTER 1

Of Balanced Government

Histories were universal once, and it was customary to begin with the creation of the world. Today, most writers favor opposite extremes. Specialization is a necessary exchange for the proliferation of information, and 1789 is undeniably a useful and convenient point at which to separate two specialties in American history. The inauguration of a national government did mark an end and a beginning in several respects. For certain purposes, American historians have little need to look far backwards from that point. For other purposes, however, this late a start can prove a barrier to understanding. So can a concentration on America alone. The actions taken in the first years of the new Republic were not taken simply to resolve specific problems of that day. Developments were influenced every bit as much by the peculiar way in which specific problems were perceived.

When the first Federal Congress assembled in New York, its members meant to carry on a revolutionary effort which had preoccupied them since their youth. Those members' minds were not blank paper. They were fields well sown. To understand the harvest, we must start with what was planted in the heritage of 1789. The party conflict of the 1790s had intellectual roots that ran far deeper than the recent constitutional revision, back to the early eighteenth century and beyond.

I

There is a sense in which the intellectual sources of America's first party struggle should be traced to June 21, 1642. On that day, two months before the outbreak of the English civil wars, the crown returned its answer to a parliamentary list of nineteen propositions for reform. The propositions called for parliamentary control of the militia, parliamentary choice of royal councillors and judges, and parliamentary participation in religious reform. In its *Answer to the Nineteen Propositions*, the crown rejected these demands:

There being three kinds of government amongst men, absolute monarchy, aristocracy, and democracy, and all these having their particular conveniences and inconveniences, the experience and wisdom of your ancestors hath so molded this out of a mixture of these as to give to this kingdom . . . the conveniences of all three without the inconveniences of any one, as long as the balance hangs even between the three estates and they run jointly on in their proper channel . . . and the overflowing of either on either side raise no deluge or inundation. The ill of absolute monarchy is tyranny; the ill or aristocracy is faction and division; the ills of democracy are tumults, violence, and licentiousness. The good of monarchy is the uniting a nation under one head to resist invasion from abroad and insurrection at home; the good of aristocracy is the conjunction of counsel in the ablest persons of a state for the public benefit; the good of democracy is liberty and the courage and industry which liberty begets.

In this kingdom the laws are jointly made by a King, by a House of Peers, and by a House of Commons chosen by the people, all having free votes and particular privileges. [The laws entrust the administration of government and other great powers to the King, so that they will] draw to him such a respect and relation from the great ones as may hinder tumults, violence, and licentiousness. Again, that the prince may not make use of this high and perpetual power to the hurt of those for whose good he hath it, . . . the House of Commons (an excellent conserver of liberty, but never intended for any share in government or the choosing of them that should govern) is solely entrusted with the first propositions concerning the leavies of monies . . . and the impeaching of [officers who violate the law]. And the Lords, being trusted with a judicatory power, are an excellent screen and bank between the prince and people, to assist each against any encroachments of the other. . . .

Since, therefore, the power legally placed in both houses is more than sufficient to prevent and restrain the power of tyranny, and without the power which is now asked from us we shall not be able to discharge that trust which is the end of monarchy, since this would be a total subversion of the fundamental laws and that excellent constitution of this kingdom which hath made this nation so many years both famous and happy to a great degree of envy . . . our answer is *Nolumus Leges Angliae Mutare*.[1]

The "king's constitution," as this document would soon be called, abruptly changed the terms of English constitutional debate. Englishmen had customarily thought of king-in-parliament as an indivisible, organic whole.[2] Through years of mounting crisis, they had searched for a solution to their disagreements in the body of the ancient law. But the common law did not define the boundaries between the liberties of subjects and the powers of the king.[3] Slowly, advocates for Parliament had developed the idea that they were representatives of the nation, independent of the crown for their existence and authority. Gradually, they had approached an indistinct, but nonetheless important line that separates the concept of a limited monarchy, where the king acts sometimes in and sometimes out of Parliament, from the concept of a commonwealth, whose sovereignty can be thought of as divided among organs of government which hold their power from independent sources and operate in balance. Now, suddenly, the king himself had stepped across the line, descending from his traditional position as head of a political organism to justify his actions in more mechanistic terms. A royal veto was the proper course for one estate if it was seeking to preserve its

1. Relevant portions of the text are in Corrine Comstock Weston, *English Constitutional Theory and the House of Lords, 1556–1832* (New York: Columbia University Press, 1965), appendix 1.
2. For the earlier conception of the English state see W. H. Greenleaf, *Order, Empiricism, and Politics: Two Traditions in English Political Thought, 1500–1700* (London: Oxford University Press, 1964), chap. 2; E. M. W. Tillyard, *The Elizabethan World Picture* (London: Chatto & Windas, 1943); and Sir Thomas Smith, *De Republica Anglorum: A Dissertation on the Commonwealth of England*, ed. L. Alston (Cambridge: Cambridge University Press, 1906).
3. The fullest account of the debate is Margaret Atwood Judson, *The Crisis of the Constitution: An Essay in Constitutional and Political Thought in England, 1603–1645* (New Brunswick, N.J.: Rutgers University Press, 1949).

share of a balanced government from the encroachments of the other two.

Attempting to define the governmental functions of the three estates, insisting that the changes asked for by the Parliament would undermine the governmental structure, the *Answer to the Nineteen Propositions* called upon a very ancient theory to legitimate the English constitution. Classical political thinkers— Polybius especially, but also Plato, Aristotle, Cicero, and Plutarch—commonly distinguished three simple species of government, each having its peculiar virtue and its corresponding vice. In the Polybian formulation, which strongly influenced early modern thought, time transmutes the virtues into vices, and all the simple forms of government inevitably become corrupt. In time, a simple monarchy becomes a tyranny, in which the interests of the ruler, not the welfare of the people, guide the state. Tyranny inspires the great men to revolt, to found an aristocracy. But the rule of a few in the interests of all eventually becomes a selfish oligarchy, which drives the body of the people to resist. Democracy, in turn, gives rise to anarchy, which ends in the dominion of a single man. Corrupt form follows sound in a cycle that can never be escaped, unless by institution of a governmental structure mixing all three simple forms. A mixed constitution can combine the strength of monarchy with the wisdom of aristocracy and the virtue of democracy, while checking the instability and danger of injustice inherent in any simpler form.

It was not entirely novel in 1642 to describe the English constitution as a mixture. English humanists were familiar with the ancient theory as it appeared in classical sources or in its most influential modern version, Machiavelli's *Discourses on the First Ten Books of Livy*. Since the middle of the sixteenth century, several writers had employed it in accounts of English government.[4] Still, the theory took on new importance now.

4. Weston, pp. 9–23, and Z. S. Fink, *The Classical Republicans: An Essay in the Recovery of a Pattern of Thought in Seventeenth-Century England*, 2d ed. (Evanston, Ill.: Northwestern University Press, 1962), chaps. 1–2. For the influence of Machiavelli see Felix Raab, *The English Face of Machiavelli* (London: Routledge & Kegan Paul, 1964).

Sixteenth-century Englishmen had used the theory of mixed government to help explain the ways in which the monarchy was limited. To them, that theory did not justify the governmental structure or legitimate the conduct of its parts. During the constitutional crisis, the nation's interest had focused rather narrowly on explorations of the common law. Then, under pressure of the mounting disagreement between the Commons and the King, more familiar ways of thinking proved inadequate. The traditional languages of English politics, which legitimized the governmental structure as a product of an immemorial antiquity or linked it by analogy into a cosmic chain of being, could not explain an argument between the body of the nation and its head. Needing an alternative, Charles I's advisors summoned up an even older language, which seemed to promise some relief. They revivified the ancient theory, used it in a novel way, and lent to it the monarch's great prestige.[5]

Soon, parliamentary advocates were seizing on the crown's interpretation of the constitution to justify an armed resistance to the king.[6] The new conception rapidly took hold, and as events unfolded, classical and humanist ideas offered an increasingly important explanation for the revolutionary changes Englishmen were going through. Three years after Cromwell's dissolution of the Rump had severed the last link with the ancient constitution, James Harrington employed received ideas in a manner that was destined for a lasting influence on the English nation and its colonies as well.

II

The Commonwealth of Oceana, which appeared in 1656, urged the creation of an English mixed republic. Following the an-

---

5. Weston, especially pp. 23–29.
6. Henry Parker, "Observations upon Some of His Majesties Late Answers and Expresses," in William Haller, ed., *Tracts on Liberty in the Puritan Revolution* (New York: Columbia University Press, 1934), pp. 165–214; Philip Hunton, "A Treatise of Monarchy," in *The Harleian Miscellany* (London: Dutton, 1810), X, 321–371; and "A Political Catechism," which may also have been written by Parker and is reprinted as appendix 2 of Weston.

cients, Harrington rejected all the simple forms of government. With them, he argued that a mixture was required to force each member of society to attend to common interests and to take advantage of the natural distinctions among men:

> Twenty men . . . can never come so together but there will be such a difference in them that about a third will be wiser, or at least less foolish, than all the rest; these, upon acquaintance, though it be but small, will be discovered and (as stags that have the largest heads) lead the herd. . . . Wherefore this can be no other than a natural aristocracy diffused by God throughout the whole body of mankind to this end and purpose, and therefore such as the people have not only a natural but a positive obligation to make use of as their guides . . . not by hereditary right or in regard of the greatness of their estates only (which would tend to such power as might force or draw the people), but by election for their excellent parts.[7]

Reason, not passion, must rule the state. Reason is composed of invention and judgment. Invention, always solitary, must always be the function of one man or a few. Judgment, however, is strongest in a multitude.[8] Accordingly, a well-ordered commonwealth should be composed of a senate, where the aristocratic counselors of the people, acting as the wisdom of the state,

---

7. *The Oceana and Other Works of James Harrington, with an Account of His Life by John Toland* (London, 1771), p. 44. A modern edition of the works of Harrington is in preparation. Until it appears, students will find that Toland was an excellent editor and that none of the eighteenth-century editions of the works vary significantly from his first edition of 1700.

There is, as yet, no wholly satisfactory treatment of Harrington's thought. Chapter 4 of C. B. MacPherson, *The Political Theory of Possessive Individualism* (Oxford: Clarendon Press, 1962), misreads Harrington in order to fit him into the author's thesis. Charles Blitzer, *An Immortal Commonwealth: The Political Thought of James Harrington* (New Haven: Yale University Press, 1960), summarizes *Oceana* and collates it with the other writings. Largely sound, it adds little to a careful reading of Harrington, makes far too much use of the word "class," and advances a poor discussion of Harrington's sources. Though shorter, chapter 3 of Fink's *Classical Republicans*, which emphasizes the influence of Machiavelli and the image of Venice, may be more valuable. But the best starting point for an understanding of Harrington is the discussion of his historical thought in J. G. A. Pocock, "Machiavelli, Harrington, and English Political Ideologies in the Eighteenth Century," *William and Mary Quarterly*, 22 (1965), 549–563, and the same author's *The Machiavellian Moment: Florentine Political Thought and the Atlantic Republican Tradition* (Princeton: Princeton University Press, 1975).

8. Harrington, "The Prerogative of Popular Government," *Works*, p. 214.

will debate and propose legislation, and a popular assembly, where the representatives of the body of the people will judge between the senators' proposals. Separate the power of dividing from the power of choosing between the pieces, add a magistracy to act as the knife which executes the decision, and it will be as easy to organize a just and lasting government as it is for two serving girls to fairly divide a cake.[9]

With most other advocates of a governmental mixture, Harrington considered three different virtues necessary to a state: unity, wisdom, and attention to the common interest. Like the authors of the *Answer to the Nineteen Propositions*, he saw these virtues rising from a social base. Harrington, however, called himself a democrat. In Oceana, there would be no hereditary distinctions in society or government:

An equal commonwealth consists but of one hereditary order, the people, which is by election divided into two orders . . . and an unequal commonwealth consists of two hereditary orders . . . ; whence it comes to pass that the senate and the people in an equal commonwealth, having but one and the same interest, never were nor can be at variance, and that the senate and the people in an unequal commonwealth, having two distinct interests, never did nor can agree.[10]

Harrington insisted that the few of a mixed republic must not be nobles. They should hold their place in government by popular election and sit both in the senate and the other house. Yet Harrington was trying to rebut the advocates of single-chamber rule, as well as to combat the friends of a hereditary second house. Like Aristotle, he identified two separate social groups, and he insisted on a place for natural aristocracy. Athens fell, he said, because she lacked an aristocracy, because the functions of her government were entirely in the people's hands. Without an aristocracy, a commonwealth must be "altogether mechanic," and mechanics are

so busied in their private concernments that they have neither leisure to study the public nor are safely to be trusted with it. . . . An army may as

9. "Oceana," ibid., pp. 43–45.
10. "Prerogative of Popular Government," ibid., p. 244.

well consist of soldiers without officers . . . as a commonwealth . . . of a people without a gentry. . . . There is something first in the making of a commonwealth, then in the governing of it, and last of all in the leading of its armies which . . . seems to be peculiar to the genius of a gentleman. . . . That, I say, which, introducing two estates, causes division or makes a commonwealth unequal, is not that she has a nobility, without which she is deprived of her most special ornament and weakened in her conduct, but when the nobility only is capable of magistracy or of the senate.[11]

Nobles must not hold a special place by virtue of their birth alone. The few who bear the talent and the wisdom of a state are best distinguished by their greater leisure. They are "such as live upon their own revenue in plenty, without engagement either to the tilling of their lands or other work for their livelihood."[12] Still, good estate will normally accompany good birth, and the senate of Oceana was to be composed of those worth at least £100 per year.[13]

A division of society into two distinguishable orders of men was a fundamental tenet of the classical republican theory of mixed government.[14] The possibility of conflict between the two orders, which Harrington admitted in his discussion of the serving girls, required that each be given an appropriate, rigidly defined, and carefully guarded share in legislation. Each would thus command the means of self-protection, and neither could be tempted to pursue its separate interests at the expense of the common good. Each order would contribute its distinctive virtue to the public, and the public would be safe against the selfishness of either one. The state might stand indefinitely against the ravages of human nature, which time would otherwise set loose.

In form and in its effort to achieve perfection, *The Commonwealth of Oceana* was utopian. Most of its length was given to an explanation of elaborate devices that might offer further checks

11. "Oceana," ibid., pp. 53, 124–125, 128; "Prerogative of Popular Government," ibid., p. 254.
12. "Oceana," ibid., pp. 124–125.
13. Ibid., pp. 78, 91–92.
14. *The Politics of Aristotle*, trans. with intro. and notes by Ernest Barker (New York: Oxford University Press, 1962), especially III, xi.

on selfish inclinations and protect the constitution from decay. To Harrington, however, the work was not an exercise, nor was it grounded in deductive reason. Harrington believed that history had presented England with a set of social circumstances that left no other option than a classical republic, and here he made his most important contribution to political ideas.

After the collapse of Rome, in Harrington's account, nearly all of Europe came to be governed in the interests of one man or a few. A few owned nearly all the landed property and distributed it to other people by way of dependent military tenures. Controlling most of the land and holding an exclusive right to bear arms in their own cause, this feudal nobility could dictate the form of government. Since pure aristocracy was too contentious to survive, the government that naturally arose on this structure of ownership was the "Gothic" system of limited monarchy. Gothic government was inherently unstable, involving a perpetual struggle between the king and the nobles, who retained enough power to check any single individual or to pull him down from the throne. This led to its destruction in England. Beginning with Henry VII, English monarchs purposefully tried to increase the strength of the commons, so that they could act as a counterbalance to the nobility. The kings destroyed the nobles' right to dispossess their larger tenants and to retain personal forces of armed bodyguards, while allowing them to sell their property and move to court. The monarchs also threw the vast lands of the Church on the market. As a result, the people gradually acquired most of the land in nondependent tenures. Unwittingly, the princes had unleashed a force capable of sweeping away the monarchy as well as the lords. The conduct of the Stuarts was all that was required to make the commons try their strength and seize a place in government appropriate for those who own the land.[15]

Drawing a principle from these events, Harrington maintained that governments cannot continue to be stable unless authority resides with those who hold the power of the state, which rests

15. "Oceana," *Works*, pp. 57–72.

on landed property.[16] If one man owns a large enough proportion of the land, the natural form of government will be a monarchy. If a few men do, the natural form will be the Gothic system. But where the people own the land, a commonwealth will be the natural result. Unnatural force can be imposed, but that will necessarily produce one of the inherently unstable, degenerate forms of government. Ultimately, either the government must be brought to accord with the balance of property or the balance of property must be brought to accord with the government.[17]

In the idea of the balance of property, Harrington believed he had discovered the engine that turns the never-ending wheel of governmental revolutions. In consequence, he thought he could present an empirical system of politics as sound and as complete as Harvey's system of anatomy. Venice was his model for a range of technical devices that might guard the superstructure of a government from decay. The principle of the balance, applied in the form of an agrarian law, could protect the state from shifts in the ownership of land, which might undermine its foundation. Together, this variety of laws would make it possible to build a kind of polity that older theories had denied: a commonwealth that would be capable, at once, of immortality and increase.[18]

Harrington was strongly influenced by the Machiavellian idea that commonwealths must choose between stability, which is best preserved in states where aristocracy is dominant within the mixture, and the power necessary for expansion, present only where the people are predominant and where the citizens com-

---

16. Unlike his eighteenth-century followers, Harrington did not believe that personal property could be a foundation for lasting power, except in states that lived by commerce. Money "may now and then stir up a Melius or a Manlius, which, if the commonwealth be not provided with some kind of dictatorian power, may be dangerous, though it has been seldom or never successful; because to property producing empire it is required that it should have some certain root or foothold, which, except in land, it cannot have" ("Oceana," pp. 37–38). "An army is a beast that has a great belly and must be fed; wherefore this will come to what pastures you have, and what pastures you have will come to the balance of property" ("Oceana," p. 38).

17. "Oceana," ibid., pp. 36–38. The clearest statement of the idea of the balance is, however, "A System of Politics," ibid., pp. 465–468.

18. "Oceana," ibid., pp. 32–34.

prise the military forces of the state.[19] At the foundation of his thought—and prior to the division of the body of the citizens into the many and the few—was an Aristotelian concept of the citizen as independent man, whose virtue is expressed both in the government and in a citizen militia. Society contains both heads of households, whose ownership of land enables them to act upon their own in politics or serve themselves in arms, and men who cannot live upon their own and so must be dependent on the will of those who can. Dependent for their livelihoods, servants cannot act with freedom in the other aspects of their lives. Unable to dispose their virtue freely, obligated to the will of others, servants are not citizens. And citizens alone, as Machiavelli said, possess the absolute commitment to the commonwealth that makes a citizen militia superior to any other sort of military force.[20]

Harrington envisioned an almost boundless future for his newly modeled England, a vision which resulted from this neoclassical conception of the unity of economic with political and military power.[21] Discovering the principles that promised the construction of a stable polity, he also found that it was in the English commonwealth alone of modern states that history had arranged for landed property to be distributed among a group of men so large that they could be identified with the people as a whole. As long as this peculiar distribution of the land could be maintained, this vast body of citizens, properly organized for both political and military action, could wield a power unknown since the greatest days of ancient Rome.

Harrington dedicated his masterpiece to Oliver Cromwell, hoping to persuade the Protector to act as the classical legislator of a free commonwealth. Between 1656 and 1660, he untiringly

19. Machiavelli, "Discourses on the First Ten Books of Titus Livy," in *The Chief Works and Others*, trans. Allan Gilbert, 3 vols. (Durham, N.C.: Duke University Press, 1965), bk. I, chap. 6.
20. Machiavelli's praise of militia and strictures on mercenary armies pervade both the *Discourses* and *The Prince*.
21. We owe recognition of the role of this classical conception in Harrington's thought to Pocock, "Machiavelli, Harrington, and English Political Ideologies," especially pp. 549–583. Its persistence is a major theme of *The Machiavellian Moment*.

explained and defended the principles of his great work.[22] Although his writings failed to move the Lord Protector, they did assure wide knowledge of his neoclassical ideas. There were ten recognizable followers of Harrington in the Parliament summoned by Richard Cromwell on January 27, 1659. Led by Henry Neville, these classical republicans entered the debate on the creation of a second house, urging that it should be organized as an elected body and confined to the task of preparing legislation, rather than created as a hereditary body with the power of veto.[23] Between November 1659 and February 1660, Harrington's ideas were also disseminated from the popular Rota Club, which met at Miles' Coffee House in London. Here, to the amusement and instruction of many passers-by, Harrington presided in person over the arguments and balloting of members such as Neville, Sir William Poulteney, John Aubrey, Cyriac Skinner, and the one-time Leveller, John Wildman.[24]

These efforts had few practical results. Long afterward, in America, some of Harrington's specific proposals would be written into law, notably the secret ballot and rotation in office. In the last years of the Interregnum, though, the English were determined on a restoration of the monarchy and House of Lords. Harrington's immediate contribution was in the realm of political thought. Here he offered an impressive vision of a great society and a free and lasting government. He advanced this vision in the context of a carefully prepared interpretation of the fundamental course of English history and a thorough argument from comparative historical experience. He seized upon the skeleton that had appeared in the *King's Answer*, fleshed it out, and stood it upright on the ground prepared by its greatest ancient and mod-

22. For the controversy over *Oceana* see Fink, pp. 85–89 and J. G. A. Pocock, "James Harrington and the Good Old Cause," *Journal of British Studies*, 10 (1970), 30–48.

23. Fink, p. 86; J. F. Russell-Smith, *Harrington and His Oceana: A Study of a Seventeenth-Century Utopia and its Influence in America* (Cambridge: Cambridge University Press, 1914), pp. 80–84.

24. Russell-Smith, pp. 101–105, 108; Fink, pp. 87–89. Pocock's "Harrington and the Good Old Cause" discusses the broader immediate influence.

ern advocates. The power of this brilliant synthesis, no less than the prestige of the "king's constitution," helps explain the striking impact of the theory of the balanced constitution on eighteenth-century minds. For more than a hundred years after the Restoration, a Harringtonian language would determine the directions of English and American political debates.

III

When the monarchy returned to England, Harrington was imprisoned for a time. Another famous commonwealthman, Sir Henry Vane, was executed in the aftermath of a trial in which he boldly rested his defense on the *Answer to the Nineteen Propositions*.[25] Nevertheless, the theory of the mixed and balanced constitution soon acquired a virtually unchallenged hold. By the eve of the American Revolution, the theory was so solidly entrenched and seemed so characteristically British that one of its best-known proponents could forget its ancient roots.

William Blackstone began his description of the English constitution by asserting that the ancients had distinguished only three simple species of government, according to whether the sovereign (or legislative) power resided in one man, the many, or a few. Each of these forms has weaknesses as well as virtues, he continued. However,

as with us the executive power of the laws is lodged in a single person, they have all the advantages of strength and dispatch that are to be found in the most absolute monarchy; and as the legislature of the kingdom is entrusted to three distinct powers entirely independent of each other, . . . as this aggregate body, actuated by different springs and attentive to different interests, composes the British Parliament and has the supreme disposal of everything, there can be no inconvenience be attempted by either of the three branches but will be withstood by one of the other two. . . .

Here then is lodged the sovereignty of the British constitution, and lodged as beneficially as is possible for society. For in no other shape could we be so certain of finding the three great qualities of government [wisdom, virtue, and power] so well and so happily united. . . . Like

25. Weston, pp. 83–86.

three distinct powers in mechanics, they jointly impel the machine of government in a direction different from what either, acting by itself, would have done, but at the same time in a direction which constitutes the true line of the liberty and happiness of the community.[26]

Writing in 1765, Blackstone was giving his assent to an explanation of English stability and happiness which had become the common property of the British political nation. Through Montesquieu and Jean Louis de Lolme, the theory of the balanced constitution was beginning to achieve an international renown.[27] Ideas about mixed government had been firmly planted in the Interregnum years, if in a rather contradictory form. Then, Restoration thinkers had worked their way around the contradictions to achieve a constitutional consensus which, by Blackstone's time, had become the necessary starting point for governmental thought.[28]

Shortly after the Restoration, ideas about mixed government were seriously discussed in the circle of influential men concerned with the colonization of America. The Fundamental Constitutions of Carolina, drafted by John Locke, may well have been the earliest effort on the part of the men associated with Anthony Ashley Cooper, soon to be first Earl of Shaftesbury, to incorporate the thought of Harrington, who had resisted the re-

26. William Blackstone, *Commentaries on the Laws of England*, ed. John Taylor Coleridge, 4 vols., 16th ed. (London: Strahan, 1825), I, 49–50, 154–155.

27. Weston discusses the theory of mixed government as it appeared in Blackstone's *Commentaries*, Montesquieu's *Spirit of the Laws*, De Lolme's *Constitution of England*, and the works of Edmund Burke, pp. 123–137. I would emphasize even more strongly than she does Montesquieu's adherence to the theory of mixed government. His reformulation of concepts in the direction of a theory of separation of powers and checks and balances was of great importance. To my mind, however, it is doubtful that he thought of the separation of powers as something to be treated apart from mixed government. In *The Spirit of the Laws*, separation of legislative and executive functions *means* the placing of distinct functions in the hands of different orders. However, all later writers were influenced by the peculiarities of Montesquieu's formulation, and, with De Lolme (1775), separation of powers had become something very close to a different theory of government.

28. In what follows I have combined Weston's discussion, which concentrates too exclusively on the influence of the *King's Answer*, with portions of the story to be found in Fink and in Pocock's article, emphasizing that this concept of the constitution was only the centerpiece of a vast conceptual structure of neoclassical and Harringtonian ideas.

vival of the ancient constitution, with an allegiance to the three estates. On this effort to combine republican ideas with a traditional commitment to the older order the eighteenth-century synthesis would rest.[29]

Issued in 1669, the Fundamental Constitutions sought to establish a stable "Gothic" government in the new world. Under their provisions, three-fifths of the land of Carolina would be distributed to freeholders, who would elect from among themselves one house of the legislature, assuring safety to the people. Two-fifths of the land would be granted to hereditary nobles, whose privileges and titles would depend on their continued ownership of vast tracts of land. The nobles would comprise a second house of the legislature, and they would dominate the great council, which was to act as the executive and propose legislation for resolution by the houses. This governmental organization would be guarded by the secret ballot and by agrarian laws designed to maintain the original balance of land ownership. Following the comments Harrington had made concerning property and empire, the proprietors of Carolina may have hoped that a colonial constitution with a carefully conditioned place for a hereditary aristocracy would insure the continued dependence of the colony on the government at home.[30]

The Fundamental Constitutions never really went into effect.

---

29. Although he does not discuss the Fundamental Constitutions, Pocock has pointed to the restatement of Harrington's ideas in Shaftesbury's circle beginning in 1675, "Machiavelli, Harrington, and English Political Ideologies," pp. 558–562. Russell-Smith offers the fullest account of Carolina, although he sees the Fundamental Constitutions as a straightforward application of Harrington's principles, pp. 157–161. The text of the document is in Francis Newton Thorpe, ed., *The Federal and State Constitutions, Colonial Charters, and Other Organic Laws*, 7 vols. (Washington, D.C.: Government Printing Office, 1909), V, 2772–2786.

30. After 1675, acceptance of a Harringtonian version of the theory of mixed government in England can be documented from other sources. Still, it is interesting to note that there were attempts to apply Harrington's principles in all the proprietary colonies in which William Penn acquired an interest: West Jersey (1676), East Jersey (1683), and Pennsylvania (1682). The ballot, rotation, and agrarian laws were all employed, though never in such elaborate combination as in Carolina. Like the Fundamental Constitutions, all these frames of government had short lives and small impact in America. They can all be found in Thorpe, vol. V. See also Russell-Smith, pp. 161–164, 167–179.

They seem to have exerted no great influence on contemporary thought. And yet the intellectual effort that informed this plan of government may have prepared the way for an appeal to Harringtonian ideas that did have lasting impact. In 1675, involved in a dispute over privilege between the houses of Parliament, Shaftesbury warned that any weakening of the House of Lords could lead to the destruction of mixed government in England, as it had in other states, His speech, along with pamphlets written by his friends, clearly associated the health of the English constitution with reliance on militia and with the presence of a social balance appropriate for its support.[31]

Four years later, Shaftesbury was once again involved in an important confrontation between the branches of the English government, guiding a committee of the Commons which quoted the *King's Answer* in its arguments against the royal power to pardon in cases of impeachment. Published in quantity and distributed throughout the country, the committee's *Narrative and Reasons* helped assure wide knowledge of the "king's constitution." During the next few years, it also helped to stimulate a flurry of new publications in which the theory of mixed government was more extensively discussed.[32]

Between 1679 and 1683, John Locke and Algernon Sidney independently prepared rebuttals of Sir Robert Filmer's Tory classic, *Patriarcha*. Both were primarily concerned with questions of the proper origins and limits of a government, not with its structure. But Sidney, unlike Locke, left no doubt where his preference would lie. Published in 1698 from a manuscript he had been working on when he was seized for treason, Sidney's *Discourses concerning Government* insisted that "there never was a good government in the world that did not consist of the three simple species of monarchy, aristocracy, and democracy." This, Sidney argued, was the government that God had given to the Hebrews, the government of long-lived Venice and the greatest

---

31. Pocock, "Machiavelli, Harrington, and English Political Ideologies," pp. 558–562.

32. Weston, pp. 93–112.

ancient states. More just in peace, mixed governments were at the same time best equipped for war, since all the citizens would have an interest in the outcome. Mixed governments were also least susceptible to decay.[33]

Sidney was a theoretical republican. His commonwealth principles cost him his life. Still, the *Discourses* showed that he had moved some way toward an acceptance of hereditary nobility and an identification of England and other "Gothic" polities as stable forms of government:

> In all the legal kingdoms of the North, the strength of the government has always been placed in the nobility, and no better defense has been found against the encroachments of ill kings than by setting up an order of men who, by holding large territories and having great numbers of tenants and dependents, might be able to restrain the exorbitance that either the kings or the commons might run into.[34]

With Harrington, Sidney insisted that "no man, whilst he is a servant, can be a member of a commonwealth, for he that is not in his own power cannot have a part in the government of others."[35] He seems to have been reconciled to hereditary nobility, in part, because of the extraordinary landed independence of the lords. The lords' lands linked their interests with the lesser gentry's and qualified their house to guard the liberties of all.

Perhaps it was a similar attraction to the landed independence of the lords that lay behind another classic treatise of these years. Henry Neville never gained an eighteenth-century reputation that might have earned his work the fame accorded Sidney's. Though Neville was a famous old republican, rumored to have had some part in writing *Oceana*, he never found it necessary to

33. Algernon Sidney, *Discourses concerning Government*, 3d ed. (London: A. Millar, 1751), II, xvi, xxi, xix. Following Machiavelli more closely than Harrington had, Sidney doubted that any government could be immortal and chose a commonwealth for increase over a commonwealth designed for preservation. Fink, chap. 6, is a good discussion. See also Caroline Robbins, *The Eighteenth Century Commonwealthman: Studies in the Transmission, Development, and Circumstances of English Liberal Thought from the Restoration of Charles II until the War with the Thirteen Colonies* (Cambridge, Mass.: Harvard University Press, 1959), pp. 41–47.

34. *Discourses*, p. 384.

35. Ibid., p. 79.

become a martyr to the good old cause. Yet *Plato Redivivus* was a crucial contribution to the integration of the thought of Harrington with the mystique of the ancient constitution.[36] Neville's reconciliation to mixed monarchy goes far to help explain John Toland's statement, in the preface to the works of Harrington, that "the English government is already a commonwealth, the most free and best constituted in the world."[37]

Plato Redivivus called on Harrington's ideas to deal with the Exclusion Crisis. Neville saw that to insist on York's exclusion from the throne would lead to civil war. To bar a Catholic, he tried to demonstrate, would be, in any case, no better than a stopgap. The underlying cause of arguments between the people and the court was

the breach and ruin of our government, which having been decaying for near two hundred years, is in our age brought so near to expiration that it . . . can no longer . . . carry on the work of ordering and preserving mankind. . . .

Government is broken . . . because it was founded upon property and that foundation is now shaken; . . . you must either bring property back to your old government and give the king and lords their lands again or else you must bring the government to the property as it now stands.[38]

The fundamental cause of present troubles was the uncomprehending, but inevitable, uneasiness of a people whose political power no longer corresponded to their share of the property.[39]

So far, this explanation seemed to follow Harrington, who had denied that mixed monarchy could be restored, now that the

36. Fink's interpretation of Neville, chap. 5, is his weakest treatment of a classical republican. His theme leads him to concentrate on the question of Neville's republicanism, which is peripheral to his importance. Robbins' perspective gives her better insight into Neville's importance. Pocock's article calls *Plato Redivivus* the "key work" in the process of identifying England as an example of a classical Harringtonian mixed constitution, p. 569. My discussion is similar to that in *The Machiavellian Moment*, pp. 417–422.

37. *Works of Harrington*, p. x.

38. Caroline Robbins, ed., *Two English Republican Tracts: Plato Redivivus or, A Dialogue concerning Government (c. 1681) by Henry Neville [and] An Essay upon the Constitution of the Roman Government (c. 1699) by Walter Moyle* (Cambridge: Cambridge University Press, 1969), pp. 153–159, 81, 152.

39. Ibid., pp. 132–148.

commons held the largest portion of the land in nondependent tenures. At first glance, so did Neville's plan to solve the problem with an increase in the powers of the people at the crown's expense, a measure necessary to adjust the government to the people's greater share of property. Yet Neville quickly disavowed any opposition to the monarchy, asserting that the present government, with few repairs, could last for ages more.[40] Critics saw that these "repairs" would make the king an English Doge, requiring that the monarch exercise important powers only on the advice of councils appointed by Parliament. But it was equally significant that the repairs would not include an abolition of hereditary rights.

Harrington had argued that there would be a constant and unavoidable conflict of interests in any government founded on two hereditary orders of men. Neville disagreed. Perhaps his definition of the problem—"a disunion of the people and the governors"—directed his attention to the image of the lords as an intermediary power, which derived from the *Answer to the Nineteen Propositions*.[41] In any event, he seems to have identified the hereditary nobility of the *King's Answer* with the few of *Oceana*. To weaken the nobility, he wrote, would be to rob the people of their champions and make them slaves. It would remove the wisdom necessary in the preparation of legislation. "If we had no such peerage now, yet we should be necessitated to make an artificial peerage or senate."[42] Having retreated from Harrington's position far enough to grant that a hereditary aristocracy could play the role of the few in a mixed commonwealth, Neville took a new stand under the protection of the ancient constitution, revising Harrington's historical account so that the ancient Gothic polity of England had been a stable state in which a dominant nobility checked both king and people in the interests of all.[43] The English polity had always been a common-

40. Ibid., pp. 172–178.
41. Ibid., p. 79.
42. Ibid., pp. 87, 130.
43. Ibid., pp. 144–145.

wealth. The virtues of a classical republic need not be seen as incompatible with lords and kings.

Plato Redivivus marked the culmination of an intellectual adjustment in which the theory of mixed government, in its Harringtonian formulation, assumed perhaps the leading place among the ways in which the English constitution could be understood. By 1685, when James II took the throne, it was possible for Englishmen to see their state as a classical, mixed commonwealth. English freedom could be explained, the constitution justified, by means of an empirical argument that identified the English system with most of the great and lasting states of ancient and modern times. It was possible, indeed, to think of the balanced constitution as a form of government that could be legitimized by immemorial usage, having served the nation since the Goths.

During these years, to be sure, the theory of the balanced constitution was advocated mostly by the Whigs. Yet the triumph of Whiggery in 1688 seems to have assured the rapid triumph of the Whiggish theory. At the time of the Glorious Revolution there was another flood of reprintings of works derived from the *King's Answer*, and the idea that England was a mixed government was a commonplace in original writings of the time.[44] During the reign of William III, it was adopted by many Tories as well. The years from 1697 to 1702 saw fierce partisan warfare in Parliament and the press. But the writers led by Charles Davenant and recruited by the Tory leader, Robert Harley, battled with the Whigs on a field enclosed and limited by a common allegiance to the mixed constitution.[45]

Early in the eighteenth century, the theory of mixed government began to serve most Englishmen as the most important legitimation of their form of government. In intimate association with classical and Machiavellian concepts of social change, citi-

44. Weston, pp. 113–123.

45. The story of the pamphlet wars of these years, which saw "Old Whigs" such as Toland and Trenchard enlisted among the Tory writers, is told in Frank H. Ellis' introduction to Jonathan Swift, *A Discourse of the Contests and Dissensions between the Nobles and the Commons in Athens and Rome* (Oxford: Clarendon Press, 1967).

zenship, and civic virtue, which had been transmitted to the eighteenth century through the works of Harrington, the theory rested at the base of an entire language of politics. Like the paradigms in scientific thought described by Thomas Kuhn, this neoclassical language soon established limits for political debates. It also helped define a set of issues that would prove the most important focus for political disputes until the influence of the democratic revolutions made it possible, once more, for Englishmen to question their commitment to the ancient constitution.[46]

46. Unshakable allegiance to the ancient constitution until the French Revolution is the thesis of Weston's *English Constitutional Theory and the House of Lords*. In fact, it is quite difficult to find any republicans at all in England between 1700 and the American Revolution. Even Robbins' Old Whigs, many of whom retained a theoretical attachment to a mixed republic, usually believed that there were no differences worth a disturbance between the English constitution and a republic. Two examples might be added to the statement of Toland. "Our own constitution . . . is the best republic in the world . . . ; our government is a thousand degrees nearer akin to a commonwealth . . . than it is to absolute monarchy" (*Cato's Letters*, 4 vols., 3d ed. [London, 1733], no. 37). "I do not think it worth while to hazard any considerable commotion for the sake merely of changing the constitution from limited monarchy to republican government" (James Burgh, *Political Disquisitions*, 3 vols. [London: E. & C. Dilly, 1774–1775], I, 9).

CHAPTER 2

Of Virtue, Balance, and Corruption

A neoclassical legitimation of the English constitution had its origins in revolutionary turbulence and civil war. For Machiavelli, too, the classics had suggested intellectual tools for grappling with a period of chronic instability and rapid change. From Aristotle forward, balanced constitutions had been praised because they seemed to offer most resistance to the universal tendency of governments toward degeneration and decay. Concern for the stability of constitutional arrangements was a necessary corollary of classical and neoclassical ideas.[1]

In Restoration England, then, the theory of the mixed and balanced constitution developed hand-in-hand with a preoccupation with political decay. As in the revolutionary years, the constitution was defined in terms of balance because there seemed to be a danger that its equilibrium would be disturbed. Thus, the very men who laid the groundwork for the eighteenth-century constitutional consensus also helped to generate a lasting fear of constitutional decline. Throughout the eighteenth century, in England and America alike, this fear would both provoke and justify determined opposition to the men who led the state.

I

After 1660, English sovereignty resided in the king-in-

---

1. "The maintenance of a constitution is the thing that matters. . . . Legislators should therefore direct their attention to the causes which lead to the preservation and the destruction of constitutions. . . . They must leave their state with a body of laws . . . which will include, above everything else, all the elements of preservation" (*The Politics of Aristotle*, trans. with intro. and notes by Ernest Barker [New York: Oxford University Press, 1962], VI, v, 1–2).

parliament again. Ministers of state were more than technically the "servants" of the king, who long retained the power to dismiss as well as to appoint them. But the crown could not determine policy without cooperation from the Commons and the Lords, who could upset, if not select, the government. In practice, the direction of affairs soon came to center in the ministry, which acted as the bridge between the branches, and the power of the ministry depended partly on effective use of patronage or "influence." Among the parliamentary backbenchers, there were always some who normally desired to aid the crown. Others voted with the ministry because of party ties or factional connections. Still others sat for boroughs that were in the pocket of the government at election time. But ministers could also call upon additional inducements in the form of governmental offices or pensions for their parliamentary supporters. Patronage and governmental influence in elections, which made it possible for ministries to exercise a certain measure of executive control of Parliament, were one of the foundations for the great stability of eighteenth-century England.[2] Yet the use of these techniques, the rise of cabinet direction of the state, was also an essential starting point for eighteenth-century oppositions.

The Earl of Danby was the first great minister to employ executive influence in a systematic way. By the time of Danby's ministry, the foreign policy of Charles II and the Catholicism of his brother James, the heir-apparent to the throne, had aroused intense suspicions of the crown.[3] But criticism had to be directed at the royal ministers, not at the king himself. The king's conventional immunity to opposition, the growth of ministerial influence, and the impact of James Harrington's ideas combined to further new developments in Restoration thought.[4]

2. J. H. Plumb, *The Growth of Political Stability in England, 1675–1725* (London: Macmillan, 1967).

3. For the development of an opposition after 1673 see David Ogg, *England in the Reign of Charles II*, 2d ed. (Oxford: Clarendon Press, 1955), chap. 15, and Keith Feiling, *A History of the Tory Party, 1640–1714* (Oxford: Clarendon Press, 1924), pp. 154–174.

4. J. G. A. Pocock located the origins of "Country" ideology in a revision of Har-

Harrington had seen close links between political and military power. Oceana was to be defended by a citizen militia. A monarchy, by contrast, had to depend on a feudal nobility, with its ranks of armed dependents, or on a professional army. The Earl of Shaftesbury, who had recently assumed the leadership of opposition to the court, must have had these thoughts in mind when, on October 20, 1675, he urged the House of Lords to defend their traditional prerogatives from a challenge by the Commons:

My Lords, 'tis not only your interest but the interest of the nation that you maintain your rights; for, let the House of Commons and gentry of England think what they please, there is no prince that ever governed without a nobility or army: if you will not have one, you must have the other, or the monarchy cannot long support or keep itself from tumbling into a democratical republic.[5]

Shaftesbury's warning was repeated and explained in an anonymous pamphlet published later that same year, *A Letter from a Person of Quality to His Friend in the Country*.[6] The author of the letter, probably John Locke, discerned in recent legislation the outlines of a scheme for introducing arbitrary government and a popish church. This scheme, he argued, would be capped by the creation of a permanent military force, an end plainly prefigured in attempts to "debase and bring low the House of Peers."

For the power of peerage and a standing army are like two buckets [on a balance], the proportion that one goes down the other exactly goes up; and I refer you to the consideration of all the histories of ours or any of our neighbor Northern monarchies to see whether standing forces, military and arbitrary governments, came not plainly in by the same steps that the nobility were lessened.[7]

---

rington's ideas by the men around Shaftesbury, "Machiavelli, Harrington, and English Political Ideologies in the Eighteenth Century," *William and Mary Quarterly*, 22 (1965), 549–563. My account combines Pocock's findings with portions of the story to be found in other authors.

5. Published in *State Tracts: Being a Collection of Treatises . . . Published in the Reign of Charles II* (London, 1693), p. 59.

6. Ibid., pp. 41–56.

7. Ibid., p. 55.

The *Letter* praised the "Country Peers" for putting obstacles in the way of the design, but it also pointed out that scheming ministers had already gotten much of their program through Parliament with the aid of executive influence:

> The officers, Court Lords, and bishops were clearly the major vote in the Lords' House; and [ministers] assured themselves to have the Commons as much at their dispose when they reckoned the number of courtiers, officers, pensioners . . . [and] the Church and Cavalier Party, besides . . . [the hopes they could offer] of honor, great employment, and such things.[8]

Two years later, Andrew Marvell saw a smiliar conspiracy against free government. For proof, he emphasized a foreign policy that favored France, but he hinted at the frightful role intended for the army, and he cautioned that the House of Commons could not be relied on to check the ministerial design. Nearly a third of the Commons had offices at court or in the government or military forces. Another third of the members, "hungry and out of office," could be "bought and sold."[9]

Shaftesbury, Marvell, and the "Person of Quality" all sought to justify their opposition to court policies by arousing traditional fears of Catholicism and arbitrary government. They warned of a conspiracy to introduce these evils by means of military force. But they implied a great deal more. With the aid of the idea that standing armies were a standing threat to liberty, they could identify the "Gothic" states of modern Europe as classical, mixed commonwealths.[10] This association made it possible for them to summon up a body of ideas about the vulnerabilities of balanced governments, molding a coherent explanation of a grave, contemporary danger and placing their resistance on the firmest constitutional grounds.

Mixed governments, the Restoration thinkers knew, were sub-

8. Ibid., p. 44.
9. "An Account of the Growth of Popery and Arbitrary Government in England," in *The Complete Prose Works of Andrew Marvell*, ed. Alex B. Grossart (privately printed, 1875), III, 323–328.
10. A complete analysis of the idea of the standing army as the fulcrum for revision of Harrington's ideas is in Pocock's article.

ject to a range of dangers. Harrington had argued that an alteration in land ownership had undermined the Gothic polity of
England. He had been led to this analysis, he said, by hints he
found in older writings.[11] Aristotle taught that great extremes of
property produce degenerate forms of government, that a nation
of farmers could best support a democratic polity.[12] Machiavelli
had insisted on the incompatibility of a republic with a feudal
nobility, whose private followings made them intractable to public control.[13] Harrington had built upon these comments to explain the revolutionary changes of his time. The destruction of
dependent tenures had released the private armies of the nobility,
on which both lords and monarchy had rested. Owning their
own land, the commons followed their own will, and they would
not submit to hereditary rule.

Changes in the social order could undermine a balanced government. So could moral changes in the body of its citizens.
Long before the Baron Montesquieu, it was an axiom that commonwealths must rest on public virtue. "Virtue" meant a
willingness and an ability to put attention to the common good
ahead of selfish ends. A nation in which individuals or groups are
bent on private gain and personal pursuits will sink into anarchic
chaos or fail to guard its freedom from tyrannical designs.[14]

A general collapse of public morals will not occur spontane-
ously, however. Individual virtue has close ties to social health,
and that is tied, in turn, to proper governmental structure. Most
of the masters taught that depravity of morals is a product and a
symptom of a change within the government. Most looked
within the government for the sources of more general decay.
Harrington had traced destruction of dependent tenures to
specific actions of the English kings. Harrington had also written

11. *The Oceana and Other Works of James Harrington with an Account of His Life by
John Toland* (London, 1771), pp. 39–40.
12. *Politics*, IV, xi; VI, iv, 1–10.
13. "Discourses on the First Ten Books of Titus Livy," in *The Chief Works and
Others*, trans. Allan Gilbert, 3 vols. (Durham, N.C.: Duke University Press, 1965), I,
xvii, lvi.
14. Ibid., I, xvii, xviii.

that "the people . . . are never subject to any other corruption than that which derives from their government."[15] Similarly, Machiavelli had discussed depravity of manners as the last, irretrievable stage of political degeneration, when the corruption of the rulers has spread among the people as a whole.[16]

"Corruption" was a central term in neoclassical discourse, a term that linked a number of specific threats into a single process of decay. "Corruption" might refer to bribery, embezzlement, or other private use of public office, much as it does today. For seventeenth- and eighteenth-century thinkers, though, the word most often brought to mind a fuller, more coherent, and more dreadful image of a spreading rot. A frequent metaphor compared corruption to organic cancer, eating at the vitals of the body politic and working a progressive dissolution. The word could call attention to the tendencies of social change. It could suggest depravity of morals. It always carried, too, at least a hint of its original, more technical definition: the degeneration of a proper government into a more illiberal, less stable form.

Proponents of mixed government began with the assumption that, whenever they are able, men will seek their private interest at community expense. As Machiavelli put it, legislators must assume that "men are evil."[17] Founders of a state must favor balanced constitutions as the only governments that make it difficult for any man or group to concentrate on selfish ends. In commonwealths alone, each man or social group must seek cooperation from the rest of the society in order to secure a selfish good. Each citizen and group will have a necessary place in government. No one can be subjected to another. And freedom from another's arbitrary will was what was meant by liberty.[18]

Of course, man's fundamental nature would not change upon

15. *Works*, p. 178.
16. *Discourses*, I, xvii, xviii.
17. Ibid., I, v.
18. "Liberty solely consists in an independency upon the will of another, and by the name of slave we understand a man who can neither dispose of his person nor goods but enjoys all at the will of his master" (Algernon Sidney, *Discourses concerning Government*, 3d ed. [London: A. Millar, 1751], p. 12).

the institution of a balanced government. Men would continue to seek the power to fulfill their personal ambitions, and there would still remain a way in which that power could be had. Few of the masters thought a balanced state could be immortal. They hoped the parties to the governmental mixture would exert themselves to guard their portions of the power (and protect the balance of the state), but they expected each to also try to enlarge its share of the power at the others' expense. Success in any such attempt could be defined as technical corruption, since it would cause the government increasingly to approximate one of the simpler, unmixed forms. In terms less familiar to its early-modern advocates, mixed government required divided sovereignty. Corruption was the process by which a single party to the mixture sought to seize an undivided sovereignty for itself.

A fear of constitutional degeneration, progressive in its nature and productive of a range of threats to liberty and moral health, was unavoidable once Englishmen identified their state as commonwealth. The theory of mixed government arose from a concern with temporal stability, and it was grounded in assumptions that induced its proponents to anticipate disturbance of the balance on which liberty must rest. In Renaissance and ancient writers, praise of balanced government was commonly connected with an imagery of governmental cycles and constitutions subject to inevitable decay. Balanced structures could resist the normal tendency to dissolution, but it was difficult to see them as immune. Balances could not grow stronger. An equilibrium could be altered only for the worse. Accordingly, the crucial task for friends of liberty in balanced states would be to keep a constant vigil, to concentrate on frequent efforts to restore an always fragile, always threatened system.[19]

Danby's critics plainly followed this old logic, though they modified tradition far enough to take into consideration some

19. Machiavelli estimated that a mixed state, to avoid the corruption that invariably accompanies time, would have to be forced back to its original foundations (or balance) at least every ten years. This re-founding might be required by its own institutions or might happen through chance. *Discourses*, III, i.

conditions that their teachers had not faced. Classical and humanist proponents of mixed government had given only brief consideration to corruption as it might affect a balanced state. Aristotle reasoned that mixed polities could be expected to decline in the direction of the simple form of government which dominated an imperfect mixture. If the many held the largest share of power, for example, popular encroachments on the other parts of government would bend the state in the direction of democracy.[20] Similarly, Machiavelli said that threats to the original equilibrium could be expected either from the many or the few.[21] Neither of these masters thought in terms of a society composed of three estates, so neither of them contemplated dangers that might issue from the one. And both expected threats to be straightforward and direct.

Shaftesbury was responding to the kind of threat that Aristotle had in mind when he urged the House of Lords to defend their traditional prerogatives against encroachments by the other house, against a challenge by the many to the powers of the few. But Shaftesbury was less concerned with dangers coming from the Commons than he was with threats that emanated from the court.[22] These threats were not direct, but subtle. The Restoration critics saved their deepest worries for a new variety of evil, which would seem a growing danger in the century to come.

The critics of the 1670s saw cause to fear direct attempts against free government, because they were convinced that English freedom had already been impaired. A standing army, in their view, had been the classic instrument for ultimate destruction of mixed states. It was also one of several agencies of influence. It posed more distant dangers because it was already part of a design by which the ministry intended to control all parts of government and reduce the balanced constitution to a

20. *Politics*, V, vii, 5–7, 11.
21. *Discourses*, I, v.
22. See Ogg, pp. 530–533. A useful discussion of the relationship between the Shaftesbury Whigs' political objectives and their ideology is B. Behrens, "The Whig Theory of the Constitution in the Reign of Charles II," *Cambridge Historical Journal*, 7 (1941), 42 ff.

sham. Parliament was filled with army officers and others who held governmental posts or pensions. These pensioners and placemen would not jeopardize their livelihoods by voting against the wishes of the crown. Through them, accordingly, the ministry had found a way to weaken the resistance of the other parts of government to its designs. Rather than encroach directly on the powers of the Commons or the Lords, it would determine their decisions. Given a sufficient number of its creatures, the court could clearly rule without effective checks. Three heads would be reduced to one.

The theory of mixed government required a distribution of political authority among distinctive governmental parts. Theorists had always been concerned to place the proper power in the proper hands. The *Answer to the Nineteen Propositions*, for example, had explained why the executive authority, requiring unity and strength, was given to a single man; why a leading role in legislation and taxation was granted to the Commons; and why the House of Lords was qualified to hold an intermediary place. The crown rejected Parliament's demands because they would have meant participation by the Commons in the exercise of functions poorly suited to the character of such a body, as well as limitations on the king's ability to hold his independent place in government. In other words, when ancient theory was adopted by the English, the insistence that mixed government involve cooperation by three parts, each independent of the others and each possessed of powers suited to its nature, took on clearer definition. The English theory called both for a mixture of peculiar virtues and for a separation of distinctive governmental powers.[23]

The writers of the 1670s could have appealed to the *King's*

23. Probably the best study of the origins of the theory of the separation of powers is in the early chapters of M. J. C. Vile, *Constitutionalism and the Separation of Powers* (Oxford: Clarendon Press, 1967). More detailed is the similar discussion of W. B. Gwyn, *The Meaning of the Separation of Powers: An Analysis of the Doctrine from its Origins to the Adoption of the United States Constitution* (New Orleans: Tulane University Press, 1965). Both studies, though, are analytical rather than developmental in their approach.

Answer to support their attack on influence. For even Charles I had treated Parliament as a device for checking kings who might abuse their awesome powers. Ministerial agents in the Parliament gave the executive a share in functions it was never meant to exercise, violating the integrity and character of the other branches of the government and threatening the liberty that rested on the independent interaction of distinctive parts. In their attack on influence, Shaftesbury and his allies appealed to an old English habit of stressing the polarity between the crown, always seeking to enlarge its powers, and the nation, whose liberties depended on the ability of its representatives to resist the crown's aggressions. The new conception of the constitution imparted new dimensions to the standing argument between the "Country" and the "Court."

The new attack on influence also called upon another set of neoclassical ideas, which powerfully appealed to England's landed gentry. Implicitly, it echoed Harrington's belief that commonwealths were only possible where citizens lived on their own estates. To Restoration critics and their heirs, landed property was more than evidence of a stake in society. For citizens and for their representatives alike, ownership conferred a certain independence, and an independent will was a prerequisite for political participation. Dependent men were not full citizens, if citizens at all. Not free themselves, they could not be trusted with the liberty of others. They were corrupt, and their corruption threatened all the rest.

Again, Harrington provided guidance, offering a detailed explication of devices that could guarantee that legislatures would fulfill their function of mirroring the interests of the people. In Oceana, representatives would hold their places briefly and sink back from time to time into the whole from which they came. Short terms of office, ineligibility for reelection in successive terms, and a rotation in office of one-third of the members each year would make it certain that the representatives could not acquire a separate interest of their own. Harrington insisted also on a secret ballot. In elections, the ballot would free each citizen to vote according to his own perception of his needs.[24] In the legislature, the same device would defeat the workings of faction, which might otherwise encourage partial interests. Harrington believed that legislatures would be fully representative only when there was an identity of interests between their members and the people as a whole. Election by the people was the first prerequisite for this identity, but it was not sufficient by itself. It was necessary, too, that each elector and each of the electors' representatives cast every vote according to the dictates of his own, unguided will.

While Harrington said little of corruption, it was possible to see in his discussion a complete examination of the points at which corruption could enter the legislature of a mixed state. Reversing his requirements for responsibility, it was necessary to condemn long terms of office, lack of a provision for rotation, interference with the independent choice of the electors, and legislative factions. All of Harrington's requirements for responsibility would influence British thought. The critics of the 1670s concentrated on the need for legislative independence.

. Harrington had indicated that a legislator could be trusted just so long as he remained in every sense a citizen, affected equally with all the rest by his decisions. Similar demands were at the heart of the attack on ministerial influence. Representatives whose salaries depended on the crown could not be independent freemen. They were servants of the court. Their livelihoods were chained to the success of an employer whose fundamental interests were not only different from, but often hostile to, those of the landed body of the nation.[25] Equally, the followers of Danby's church-and-king persuasion were a faction with a special interest which distinguished them from the people as a whole. Together,

24. *Oceana*, p. 51.
25. Harrington himself had expressed some hostility to the court, remarking that, in England, "men of country lives have been entrusted with the great affairs, and the people have constantly had an aversion to the ways of the court. Ambition, loving to be gay and to fawn, has been a gallantry looked upon as having something in it of the livery; and husbandry, as the country way of life, . . . as the best stuff of a commonwealth" (*Oceana*, p. 33).

though, these party men and creatures of the court could control both houses of the Parliament on behalf of the executive. Only the form of a balanced government remained in England—slight security for gentlemen in their liberties or estates.

II

Originating in the 1670s, a neo-Harringtonian critique of ministerial influence and corruption became the standard rhetoric of eighteenth-century English oppositions.[26] A legislative program to combat corruption appeared with equal speed. There were repeated efforts to protect the independence of Charles II's Parliaments. A bill to exclude placemen failed in 1675. Dissolution prevented action on another in the first Exclusion Parliament. In the next, members unanimously passed a resolution against accepting governmental offices.[27] Concern with influence was less relevant in the succeeding reign, when outright despotism seemed to have arrived, but it appeared again soon after James II was deposed. The years from 1689 to 1702, a time of reconstruction, realignment, and fierce party combat, witnessed new developments in governmental practices and in the opposition's criticism of the change. The rising cost of parliamentary elections, growing governmental influence in the

---

26. There is no longer any need to demonstrate the central place of this critique in eighteenth-century British thought. That has been fully done in Pocock's writings, in Corrine Comstock Weston, *English Constitutional Theory and the House of Lords* (New York: Columbia University Press, 1965), and in Caroline Robbins, *The Eighteenth Century Commonwealthman* (Cambridge, Mass.: Harvard University Press, 1959), the work which initiated much of the current interest in this English minority tradition. It has been further buttressed by Isaac Kramnick, *Bolingbroke and His Circle: The Politics of Nostalgia in the Age of Walpole* (Cambridge, Mass.: Harvard University Press, 1968), and studies that demonstrate the persistence of the same critique into the age of the American Revolution: Ian R. Christie, *Wilkes, Wyvill, and Reform: The Parliamentary Reform Movement in British Politics, 1760–1785* (London: Macmillan, 1962), and Herbert Butterfield, *George III, Lord North, and the People, 1779–1780* (London: G. Bell & Sons, 1949). It has seemed necessary, nonetheless, to offer a brief examination of the growth of opposition thought. More is known about persistence of the opposition language than is known about its content, and a tendency to think we understand it better than we do has encouraged a neglect of facets that would come to have a crucial influence in the United States.

27. Plumb, pp. 45–52.

boroughs, and an increase in the number of governmental officers provoked a standard set of opposition demands. Before 1694, while William ruled without regard for party, the Whigs sought triennial and place bills. Later, as the Whigs secured control of government, Tories led by Robert Harley cooperated with a remnant of "Old Whigs" in a continuing demand for frequent parliaments, exclusion of parliamentary placemen, and confinement of parliamentary membership to men of substance. Landed qualification and place bills narrowly failed in 1694 and 1696. Much of the "Country" program was briefly realized in the Act of Settlement in 1701.[28]

Meanwhile, much elaboration of the criticism of corruption went forward among partisans in the pamphlet wars that accompanied the parliamentary struggles. "Old Whigs" republished several seventeenth-century classics and added new sophistication to the condemnation of the role of mercenary forces, building into "Country" eschatologies a standard place for standing armies.[29] Opposition writers also emphasized depravity among the people.[30] By 1701 the elements for a consistent opposition ideol-

28. Ibid., pp. 129–147; Feiling, pp. 275–277, 286–289, 315–316; and David Ogg, *England in the Reigns of James II and William III* (Oxford: Clarendon Press, 1955), pp. 337–338, 468–469. I have consistently preferred "Country" or "opposition" to alternative labels for this eighteenth-century tradition. "Old Whig" or "radical Whig," which may be more familiar, seem inaccurate descriptions for a program and an ideology that Tories also clung to. I prefer to save the label "Whig" for the political party and for the compact theory of the origins and proper limitations of a government.

29. The "Old Whigs" are discussed at length in Robbins, chap. 4, and Kramnick, chap. 9, where their criticism of the changing social order is emphasized. Among the most important early treatises in opposition to the standing army are Andrew Fletcher, "A Discourse of Government with relation to Militias," in *The Political Works of Andrew Fletcher* (London: Bettesworth, Hitch, & Davis, 1737); [John Trenchard and Walter Moyle], *An Argument Showing that a Standing Army Is Inconsistent with a Free Government and Absolutely Destructive to the Constitution of the English Monarchy* (London, 1697); and Robert Molesworth, *An Account of Denmark as It Was in the Year 1692* (London, 1694). See also [John Trenchard and Thomas Gordon], *Cato's Letters, or Essays on Liberty, Civil and Religious, and other Important Subjects*, 4 vols., 3d ed. (London, 1733), letters 94–95: "All parts of Europe which are enslaved have been enslaved by armies, and it is absolutely impossible that any nation which keeps them amongst themselves can long preserve their liberties."

30. "If any man think that this evil of advancing officers for personal respects, favor, or corruption is not of great extent, I desire him to consider that the officers of state, courts of justice, church, armies, fleets, and corporations are of such number and power

ogy had all appeared, along with an extensive program to restore the threatened balance of the constitution.

Cato's Letters were the product of the first maturity of opposition thought, appearing in the *London Journal* between December 1720 and July 1723. Collected in four volumes, republished many times throughout the eighteenth century, this series celebrated freedom and contrasted English happiness with the tyranny and popery that afflicted nearly every other spot on earth. To their praise of liberty, however, the authors joined sharp fears for its survival in its only home. "Cato" was a pseudonym intended to recall the champion of Roman virtue in the days of its decline. With most men of their time, John Trenchard and Thomas Gordon identified self-interest as the spring of human action. Because they did, they praised mixed monarchy as a necessity for happiness and freedom, but they also feared that a mixed state would be a constant target for subversion and military rule. *Cato's Letters* brought the elements of opposition thought together with the theory of a social compact into a synthesis that won them unmatched popularity and created lasting bonds between the Whiggish theory of the origins and necessary limitations of a government and neoclassical ideas about its proper form and ultimate degeneration.[31]

"Cato" doubted that the liberties of a free people could be openly attacked, but he feared their subversion underhand.[32] Men at court—for the executive has always been the most impor-

---

as wholly to corrupt a nation when they themselves are corrupted" (Algernon Sidney, *Discourses concerning Government*, 3d ed [London: A. Millar, 1751], pp. 220–221). Compare "An Essay upon the Balance of Power," in *The Political and Commercial Works of . . . Charles Davenant*, ed. Charles Whitworth, 5 vols. (London: Horsfield et al., 1771), III, 299–301.

31. "Cato's" fear of power has often been remarked, but the "Country" aspects of his thought have often been neglected for an emphasis on his contractual philosophy. Robbins emphasizes libertarianism in her discussion, pp. 115–125. Another example is David L. Jacobson's introduction and selection of letters for *The English Libertarian Heritage* (Indianapolis: Bobbs-Merrill, 1965). Jacobson offers a fine sampling of "Cato's" Whiggish letters, but inclusion of letters 40, 60, 70, and 85 would have produced a more balanced picture. The synthesis of Whig and neoclassical ideas is set forth most clearly in letters 60 and 85.

32. Letter 17.

tant source of danger—can threaten liberty if they can first corrupt the other branches of the government, making it a tyranny
in fact if not in form.[33] Indeed, they had succeeded all too well in
England. Governmental offices, promises of ministerial favor,
pensions, and luxurious entertainments had seduced the people's
representatives.[34] Liberty would still be safe, if the body of the
people were still pure. Yet parliamentary influence was but one
of many symptoms of a growing evil. Court money was employed in parliamentary elections, purchasing the representatives
and debasing the electors: "the little beggarly boroughs" were
"pools of corruption."[35] Conspirators at court, "knowing that
dominion follows property," sought to enrich themselves and
impoverish the people, squandering the great sums raised by
growing taxes on their creatures and dependents. To distract the
country from its plight, they waged expensive wars and encouraged the divisiveness of parties. By their prodigal example, they
promoted "a general depravity of manners," loosing men from
old restraints, reducing them to want. They did not fear, but
rather hoped, for discontent and disaffection, for disturbances
would give them an excuse to maintain a standing army, which
was the universal instrument for introducing tyranny.[36]

By the time of *Cato's Letters*, it is clear, opposition thinkers had
discovered in the concept of corruption a device that made it
possible for them to organize a sweeping condemnation of the
course of recent English history and a constitutional legitimation
for resistance to the court. Combining the ideas of Harrington
with the denunciation of court influence, they warned of a progressive dissolution of the institutions and the social habits that
supported English freedom. Opposition ideology identified a
conspiracy of diabolical design and frightening proportions, with
its head at court and its hands in every pocket in the kingdom. It
could connect the fare at a court dinner with bribery in the

33. Letter 70.
34. Letter 61.
35. *Cato's Letters*, III, 18–19.
36. Letter 17. For the historical role of armies see letters 94, 95.

boroughs or the votes of an army officer in the House of Lords. It pictured a disease that started in the government and spread inevitably to every facet of the nation's life. It traced the source of nearly every evil of the age to the development of ministerial rule.

Not surprisingly, therefore, the condemnation of corruption proved a valuable resource to Viscount Bolingbroke when his connection undertook a war upon Sir Robert Walpole, under whom the ministry's direction of the government became a work of art.[37] Bolingbroke had been a Tory minister and sometime Jacobite. Trenchard and Gordon were radical Whigs. Like "Cato," though, Bolingbroke insisted that the only real distinction was the one between the Country and the Court, adding his strong voice to the condemnation of court influence, war, high taxes, and a standing army.

The most important incidents of Bolingbroke's campaign were his *Remarks on the History of England* and *A Dissertation on Parties*, both of which began as letters to *The Craftsman*, the vehicle of the newspaper war on Walpole in the early 1730s.[38] Together these two works proposed a history of English liberty from Saxon to contemporary times. They managed to link a Harringtonian account of the rise of the commons with the myth of an ancient Saxon constitution.[39] Their fundamental purpose was to show that it is possible for a government to be a faction, concerned with partial ends, and to attribute all of England's historical disruptions to a factious administration of its affairs. The argument was focused on a criticism of corruption. Corruption was historically the means to selfish ends for factious governors. Since the shift in the balance of property and the settlement of

37. Kramnick's *Bolingbroke and His Circle* offers a fine and full discussion of opposition thought in the age of Walpole. An excellent discussion of the Tory leader is H. T. Dickinson, *Bolingbroke* (London: Constable, 1970).

38. Both are in *The Works of the Late, Right Honorable Henry St. John, Lord Viscount Bolingbroke*, 5 vols. (London: David Mallet, 1754). For their publication see Kramnick, pp. 24–28.

39. Bolingbroke accomplished this by postulating an imperfect imposition of feudalism on the ancient constitution at the Conquest. The great themes of modern history then became for him the rise of the commons from their feudal dependence and a consequent restoration of ancient, Saxon freedom.

1689, it had become the only threat of consequence. Whig and Tory were historical distinctions that the present ministry encouraged in order to prevent a union of the country in opposition to its schemes.[40]

Like "Cato's," Bolingbroke's opinion of the power of self-interest affected all he said about the origins and proper form of governments. "The notion of a perpetual danger to liberty," he wrote, "is inseparable from the very notion of government."[41] Limited, divided government can offer some protection from the interested assaults of men in power, but power will inevitably encroach on liberty's domain. The danger grows as power is placed in fewer hands for longer lengths of time. Thus, we may prefer a monarchy to a democracy for its superior stability, but monarchy will necessarily increase the danger of oppression.[42] Here, more than in republics, men must see that liberty can only be preserved by frequent restoration of the original principles of the government. And this continual re-founding will take place no longer than the people can retain a libertarian spirit.[43]

Since Saxon times, in Bolingbroke's account, the English had preserved a proper spirit, so that neither factious governors nor foreign conquerors could destroy their freedom. Henry VII might have established an absolutism, if he could have prevented the rise of the commons while he reduced the great. Instead the commons gained the property the lords had lost and achieved the independence that came with it. Much of the ancient Saxon freedom, threatened since the Conquest, was restored.[44] More years of struggle were required against the Stuarts, but the

40. Kramnick points out that Bolingbroke also objected to parties because he believed that allegiance to a group violates the necessary independence of the individual in much the same way as would the acceptance of a place (p. 153).

41. "Remarks on the History of England," *Works*, I, 280.

42. Ibid., p. 284.

43. Kramnick remarks the clear influence of Machiavelli and compares Bolingbroke's idea of a patriot king to Machiavelli's legislator (pp. 163–169). For a fuller discussion of Machiavelli's influence see part 4 of Herbert Butterfield, *The Statecraft of Machiavelli* (New York: Macmillan, 1956).

44. To this point, I have been summarizing the "Remarks."

Glorious Revolution put an end to any danger of an open imposition of arbitrary rule.[45]

Still, English freedom was not safe. The danger had become more subtle, but was no less frightening on that account. While it was no longer possible to govern without Parliament, it had become possible to obtain a Parliament that could be governed. Because the Revolution failed to secure "freedom of elections and the frequency, integrity, and independency of Parliaments," factious rulers had been able to concoct more underhanded ways to reach their ends:

I do not imagine that an army would be employed . . . directly and at first against the nation and national liberty. . . . To destroy British liberty with an army of Britons is not a measure so sure of success as some people may believe. To corrupt the Parliament is a slower but . . . more effectual method, and two or three hundred mercenaries in the two houses . . . would be more fatal to the constitution than ten times as many thousands in red and in blue out of them. . . . No slavery can be so effectually brought and fixed upon us as parliamentary slavery.[46]

Of course, conspirators at court could not succeed in their designs against the constitution unless a slothful and luxurious people concurred in the loss of liberty by reelecting representatives who betray them.[47] But this they may well do. Growing revenues and higher taxes make it possible for ministers to create a horde of officers, who fill the Parliament and exercise a rising influence in elections. The civil list provides vast funds for the corruption of Parliament, and the practice of anticipating revenues creates additional supplies. In fact, the means available to ministers have grown to such a great extent in recent years that the crown has now, through influence, powers just as great as it once had by prerogative.[48] The fate of English liberty depends on a union of good men against the progress of corruption.

Bolingbroke was probably the finest spokesman for the

45. This is the thesis of letters 1–9 of the "Dissertation on Parties."
46. "A Dissertation on Parties," *Works*, II, 137.
47. Ibid., letters 12–17.
48. Ibid., letters 18–19.

eighteenth-century oppositon, as Walpole was its classic villain. Bolingbroke, however, was a Tory and a Deist, while Walpole was a statesman under whom most Englishmen could be content. The criticism of corruption did not reach its widest audience until the period of the American Revolution, when stronger stirrings of reform gave rise to James Burgh's *Political Disquisitions.* Published in 1774 and 1775 under the influence of the Wilkesite agitation, this treatise would supply a theoretical foundation for the program of the Yorkshire Association.[49] The author's sympathy for the colonials assured a good reception in America as well. There the work acquired a rank near that of *Cato's Letters* among the opposition tracts.[50]

Burgh's reputation seems remarkable to modern tastes, for the *Political Disquisitions* was so huge and ponderous that few men, surely, ever read it through. Those who opened it, however, got a thorough education in the opposition point of view. The author's method was to pry into the sources and support each point with long strings of quotations from his predecessors. In three large volumes, he set down every argument that he could find on the evils of ministerial influence, along with an account of the repeated efforts to defeat it. The work was little less than an encyclopedia of opposition thought.

Burgh's own ideas were not extremely novel. A theoretical republican, who nonetheless refused to quarrel with mixed monarchy,[51] he can be distinguished from Bolingbroke or "Cato"

---

49. The "Country" character of the reform movement of the years after 1760 is discussed in Christie, *Wilkes, Wyvill, and Reform,* in Butterfield's *George III, Lord North, and the People,* and in Weston, pp. 146–160. Robbins also discusses the reformers of this period at length in chap. 5.

50. See Robbins, pp. 364–368, and Oscar and Mary Handlin, "James Burgh and American Revolutionary Theory," Massachusetts Historical Society, *Proceedings,* 73 (1961), 38–57.

51. "In the short, the too short period of the republic . . . we see what may be expected from a set of un-bribed, un-biased men assembled together to consult for the public good without fears and without hopes from a bribing court and free from the incumbrances of . . . kings or houses of peers. . . . I write in this seemingly republican strain not that I have the least thought of suggesting the necessity or propriety of changing the form of government in Britain from regal to republican–though the latter is undoubtably preferable to the former, supposing a state to be settling its form of government–but to caution kings and lords not to bring on . . . their own exclusion"

mainly by his more horrendous picture of the progress of corruption:

Ever since I have been of age to distinguish between good and evil, I have observed that . . . the men in power have pursued one uniform track of taxing and corrupting the people and increasing court influence in Parliament, . . . while the constitution was drawing nearer to its ruin and our country lay bleeding. . . . I know of scarce any evil we have escaped by the Revolution, popery excepted, that is not in a fair way of being brought back upon us by corruption.[52]

Opposition thinkers always warned that tyranny was making giant strides. Burgh was convinced that the conspirators had actually achieved their end. The court had secured complete control of a majority in Parliament, making England "a licensed tyranny instead of a free government."[53] It was not sufficient, then, to stop with an appeal to Parliament and the electors, as other oppositionists had done. Liberty was lost, and its restoration would require the formation of popular associations determined—by pressure if possible, but by extra constitutional action if necessary—to secure annual parliaments, an exclusion of placemen and pensioners, and an eradication of the rotten boroughs.[54]

Some Englishmen (and more colonials) were coming to believe that corruption had already spread so thoroughly among the people that England was no longer capable of a reform. Burgh disagreed, but he admitted that the time was running out, and he exhorted the remaining men of virtue to concentrate on parliamentary reform:

There is scarce such a thing under the sun as a corrupt people where the government is uncorrupt; it is that and that alone which makes them so. . . . Our governors . . . lead the people to laugh at religion and conscience; they play at cards on Sundays instead of countenancing the public worship of their Maker; they have made adultery a matter of

---

(J.B., Gent., *Political Disquisitions, or an Inquiry into Public Errors, Defects, and Abuses*, 3 vols. [London: E. & C. Dilly, 1774–1775], II, 18).

52. Ibid., I, 402.
53. Ibid., 360.
54. Ibid., III, 434. Most of volume I, along with book 1 of volume II, is concerned with the corruption of Parliament.

merriment; they cheat at play whenever they can; they lead their inferiors into extravagance and dissipation by encouraging public diversions more luxurious and debauched than all that ever the orientals exhibited; . . . they are the first and most extensive violators of the laws themselves have made; they are the destroyers of the constitution, for by openly bribing electors and members and by leading both clergy and laity into dissimulation and perjury, they destroy the virtue of the people, without which no constitution ever stood long.[55]

A depraved people; a large standing army: these marked the level of the danger. But the scheme hinged ultimately on Parliament. "The principle of the British government is an independent House of Commons. If that be safe, all is safe. If that be violated, all is precarious."[56]

III

"Cato," Bolingbroke, and Burgh were the most eloquent proponents of an ideology that occupied a central place in eighteenth-century British thought, headmasters of a school in which five generations of less able advocates were trained. From the Restoration to the French Revolution, English arguments were bounded by a constitutional consensus. Through all those years, all loyal oppositions justified their presence by starting with the charge that men in power were conspiring to subvert the balanced constitution. This was the only way their opposition could be placed on loyal, yet absolutely fundamental grounds.

It would be possible, however, to emphasize consistency too much. Shaftesbury would have recognized the danger Burgh described, but opposition thought had not been static through the hundred years in which it organized concerns and shaped a program of reform. On the contrary, it had been the most important apparatus through which English thinkers comprehended changes in the nation's life. Changing in response to changing times, opposition thought encompassed several new ideas and worked some major alterations in political and social goals.

55. Ibid., II, 375; III, 179–180. All of volume III, book 1, is concerned with the extent of corruption among the people.
56. Ibid., I, 363.

Throughout the eighteenth century, for example, the most rigorous examinations of the English constitution were written by the opposition thinkers, as prefaces to their critiques. Fear of executive influence led the oppositionists to phrase their discussions of the constitution so that it increasingly appeared that what was balanced in the English government was, not so much the three estates, as liberty and power. Identifying liberty with Parliament and power with the court, opposition tracts portrayed the constitution as a battlefield where liberty was constantly besieged by the executive. With ever-rising voice, they called for restoration of a legislature free from the executive and its assaults. They talked increasingly in terms of the necessity for separation of these governmental parts.

Montesquieu and other great philosophers made contributions to the formulation of a finished theory, but the change did not appear by way of vaulting leaps from one great thinker to another. No one had to seize upon ideas implicit in the concept of mixed government. No one had to build upon ideas submerged beneath an older language.[57] Opposition rhetoric had long been moving the whole complex in a new direction, and, for many years to come, no clear distinction would be made between a demand for "a separation of powers" and the older call for "an end to ministerial influence." The meaning was essentially the same.

Close examination of the changing opposition language suggests that "Country" thinkers made a number of important contributions they have not received full credit for. Denunciations of corruption, to take one more example, grew more strident through the years, despite the periodic passage of place and pension acts. It was a fundamental tenet of the opposition argument that corruption must increase with time, and nearly every opposition writer thought the threat was greatest in his day. But

57. Both Gwyn and Vile see the emergence of a theory of separation of powers in this way. While their books make a valuable contribution to our analytical understanding of both the old and newer theories, it is questionable whether they present a genuinely developmental history of the new idea.

this was poorly calculated to confirm the public's faith in monarchy. "Cato" said that liberty might be safer in a mixed republic. Bolingbroke and Burgh affirmed the same, each in stronger terms. Meanwhile, the opposition also ceased to hope that the great properties of the Lords would make their house an independent bulwark against corruption. When they did not ignore the upper house, later opposition writers seem to have assumed that it was captured by the court, and this conclusion may have been related to a subtle and concurrent change of mind about the people's representatives. Early in the eighteenth century, the opposition's emphasis on landed qualifications and place bills reflected a preeminent concern for independence in the representatives. A desire for independent representatives persisted through the years. Still, as oppositionists increasingly directed their attention to the problem of the boroughs and the growing influence in elections, the desire for independent representatives was partially displaced by a demand for electoral reform and closer responsibility of the representatives to their constituents. These shifts of emphasis were changes of degree, not kind, and yet they seem to indicate that oppositionists were moving in a democratic and republican direction. British peoples had good reason to resist republican conclusions. Certainly, few British thinkers went so far in that direction as did Burgh. Yet there is room to wonder if the implications of the opposition arguments were lost—on Englishmen or on their fellow subjects overseas.

These possibilities can only be suggested here, to indicate that there is more to learn from further study of the eighteenth-century oppositon. But one development within the changing language was undeniably important on both sides of the sea, although it has attracted less historical attention than it might. The clearest pattern in the growth of opposition thought is obvious. To the original and always central criticism of ministerial influence in Parliament later critics added condemnations of the standing army, influence in elections, and corruption of the manners of the people. Soon, the language was complex enough to shape discussions of a vast array of social ills. It had become an instrument for seizing on and shaping a coherent understanding of all sorts of change. As such, it came to organize a bitter criticism of the methods of finance that had appeared in the aftermath of the Glorious Revolution, methods that the oppositionists denounced as "government by money."[58] Criticism of the new finance became a staple part of Country thought.

Although the origins of this attack are far from clear, it certainly was far advanced by 1701, when Charles Davenant published *The True Picture of a Modern Whig*. This work was an electioneering tract in which the noted economic thinker criticized the Whigs, who had been recently deposed, by means of a dialogue between Whiglove and Double. Double, an unprincipled new man, instructs an honest Whig in the techniques by which a grasping crew has profitted at public expense. The pamphlet deals, for the most part, in accusations that a party seeking little more than private gain has fleeced the public and would betray it absolutely in order to gain more. Along the way, however, Davenant advances what was possibly the earliest analysis of the role of new financial institutions in a ministerial conspiracy to undermine the country's freedom. Double claims to have performed a special service to his party by proposing the creation of the Bank of England and the New East India Company:

For what had become of our party if it had not been for these projects? It is true we have run the nation head and ears in debt by our funds and new devices, but mark what a dependence upon our noble friends this way of raising money has occasioned. Who is it sticks to them but those who are concerned in tallies and the new stocks?[59]

In a second part of the dialogue, published after the election, Double has occasion to explain the scheme more fully. He confesses that the Whigs could have financed the recent war without resorting to extensive loans and piling up huge debts. While this

---

58. For the origins and workings of the eighteenth-century system of public finance see P. G. M. Dickson, *The Financial Revolution in England: A Study in the Development of Public Credit, 1688–1756* (New York: St. Martin's Press, 1967).

59. *Political and Commercial Works*, IV, 146–147.

alternative would doubtless have been better for the country, it would not have been so good for them. A long-term debt requires high interest rates, which gain a ministry strong friends. "Remote funds . . . are the bravest things that ever were invented for enriching private men out of the ruin of the public." Yet private profit for the monied friends of ministers was only one dimension of the scheme. The Whigs required a shield against a parliamentary enquiry into the management of the war, and there were disciplined and fearless soldiers in this "army of men with their pockets full of bank bills, East India stock, malt and lottery tickets, exchequer bills, bankstock" and so on. In Parliament or without, these seasoned troops would follow any ministerial command. Their fortunes were inextricably connected with the ministry's ability to maintain (and to manipulate) the new financial institutions. So close, indeed, was the connection between the ministry and its monied friends that the Whigs were planning now, by doubling the national debt, to make it possible for their adherents to entirely overwhelm the landed interest. While public debts enriched the monied class, they impoverished the country gentlemen who had to pay the bill. Eventually, as Double saw with glee, the landed men would be unable to compete in parliamentary elections, and the monied creatures of the court would hold the places necessary to deliver total power to the Whigs.[60]

Davenant was possibly the first to list the new finance among the evils in the opposition catalogue. His explanation of the danger was systematic and complete. But it was Bolingbroke who integrated the attack most fully with the broader criticism of corruption, according it a central place in his critique.[61] Though Walpole's great opponent had no love for placemen, pensioners, or officials who used influence in elections, he believed that these

60. Ibid., 210–216.
61. This is a major theme for Kramnick. Since this writing, moreover, Drew McCoy has directed my attention to Roger Durrell Parker, "The Gospel of Opposition" (Ph.D. dissertation, Wayne State University, 1975). This exhaustive study of the criticism of the new financial order, developed independently of mine, contains a wealth of information and confirms the crucial role of Davenant and Bolingbroke.

were threats of ancient vintage which had never been sufficient to corrupt the spirit of the people. Because the danger posed by the financial system hit directly at the habits of the people, it exceeded all the older threats.

After the Revolution, Bolingbroke explained, ministers established the civil list and began to borrow in anticipation of revenues. Over the long term, this practice boosted taxes more than would have been required had revenues kept pace with annual expenses. Larger taxes meant new hordes of tax collectors, additional dependents for the government, and growing opportunities for officers to use their influence in elections. Long-term debts mortgaged the body of the people for the benefit of the ministry and its monied supporters. The system of anticipating revenues spread habits of extravagance throughout the nation, raised disgusting jobbers to high places, and reduced more honest men to poverty. The spread of poverty induced dependence and depravity in growing numbers of the people. Luxury and avarice, influence and dependence, bred every other form of immorality until the people were in danger of becoming universally corrupt. And universal immorality could have no other consequence than absolute destruction of the nation's freedom.[62]

Bolingbroke and Davenant presented the most systematic criticism of the new financial institutions, but hostility to the effects of the financial revolution was by no means the preserve of Tories. *Cato's Letters* were inspired by the South Sea Bubble, which provoked their authors to a general condemnation of the new financial order and its consequences for society and government. Trenchard and Gordon denounced exclusive companies for the way they altered the balance of property and served the designs of ambitious statesmen by combining monied men into a unified, directed body able to exert irresistible pressure on the government. Monopolies disrupted social order by opening great gaps between the rich and poor, breeding influence and corrup-

---

62. Letters 18 and 19 of the "Dissertation of Parties" present the systematic attack on the new finance. See Parker for a full discussion.

tion and subverting the conditions that supported English freedom. Criticism of the new finance became a standard theme for all whose thought derived from neoclassical assumptions.[63]

Condemnation of the modern structure of finance—the long-term debt, the sinking fund, and the privileged corporations—naturally appealed to the inarticulate suspicions and misgivings of a people who were largely agricultural and unfamiliar with the mysteries of public credit. Country gentlemen were understandably outraged by spectres such as Double, who had risen from the very bottom of society by jobbing paper stocks while landed property was burdened by the taxes necessary to finance the growing debt. Traditional hostility to monopolies was exacerbated by the opposition's image of a group of monied men well organized against the landed interest. In anticipation of American developments, however, it must be emphasized that the attack on "government by money" involved a good deal more than an appeal to prejudice and agrarian misunderstandings. In its neo-Harringtonian concern for the balance of property and in its careful connection of the monied interest with a designing ministry, the criticism of the new finance was a coherent part of an extensive and well integrated ideology. This ideology was not essentially concerned with differences between agrarian and commercial interests. It focused not on commerce, but on government finance. It was preoccupied with the defense of balanced government.

Opposition fears were undeniably reactionary. With little serious distortion, they can be characterized as a hysterical response to most of the developments that built a modern English state. The new financial institutions can be seen, in hindsight, as prerequisites for the Industrial Revolution. Public credit was the

63. Attacks on stockjobbing, projects, and exclusive companies are scattered throughout *Cato's Letters*, but Trenchard and Gordon are most systematic in letter 91. Even James Burgh, who was less an advocate for the gentry than other opposition writers, regretted the increased influence made available to ministers by the new finance, and he added to the opposition blacklist the practices of awarding governmental contracts with an eye on the parliamentary influence of the bidders (*Political Disquisitions*, I, 275–278).

foundation for the international power of eighteenth-century England. Ministerial influence, the bullseye in the opposition target, was seen by other politicians as an indispensable technique for helping to secure cooperation between the branches of the government. It was the cornerstone for a political structure that made a country once known for volubility a model of ordered freedom for eighteenth-century Europe.

No wonder, then, that opposition arguments had little impact on the practical affairs of eighteenth-century England. As time went by and men grew used to the new institutions, the fear of standing armies tended to become a rhetorical convention. The opposition came to understand that borrowing and public debts were indispensable for modern European wars. Men who fought corruption out of power wielded patronage in office. But it is not unusual for men to take advantage of conventions they do not believe—or even to adopt a different set of principles when faced with new responsibilities. And their "apostasy" may not convert their former friends. There always were some men, the "Country" part of Parliament, who feared corrupting power all the more because they never wanted or expected to employ it. In America, peculiar circumstances opened an enormous field of influence for the same ideas.

CHAPTER 3

Of Revolution

COLONIAL Americans were Englishmen—not simply in a formal sense, but deep in the recesses of their personal identities and modes of thought. Indeed, there is a sense in which they came to be more English as the eighteenth century passed. The maturation of the colonies, which made them more like older countries than they once had been, was speeded and conditioned by deliberate imitation of the motherland in nearly every aspect of the people's lives.[1] Ironically, the problems that resulted in a war for independence originated at a time when the provincial pride in being British had never been so great. Colonial Americans began the Revolution with a fierce determination to defend accepted institutions and a powerful commitment to received ideas.

As Englishmen, the eighteenth-century colonists participated fully in contemporary adulation of the mixed and balanced constitution. To them, as to the Englishmen at home, the governmental system of the motherland was the foundation for a happiness and freedom that made the British peoples an excep-

1. For "Anglicization" as a major theme of the colonies' eighteenth-century development—an idea that has begun to attraction wide attention—see John M. Murrin, "Anglicizing an American Colony: The Transformation of Provincial Massachusetts" (Ph.D. thesis, Yale University, 1966); Rowland Berthoff and John M. Murrin, "Feudalism, Communalism, and the Yeoman Freeholder: The American Revolution Considered as a Social Accident," in Stephen G. Kurtz and James H. Hutson, *Essays on the American Revolution* (Chapel Hill: University of North Carolina Press, 1973), pp. 256–288; and Jack P. Greene, "Search for Identity: An Interpretation of the Meaning of Selected Patterns of Social Response in Eighteenth-Century America," *Journal of Social History*, 3 (1970), 189–224.

tion in a world of misery and power unadulterated with restraints. For all their lack of a nobility or court, most colonists
were also used to thinking of their own provincial governments
as mixed and balanced systems. The constitutional consensus
held on both sides of the ocean, determining political concerns
and offering a universe of thought within which Englishmen
could judge the workings of their institutions.[2] Within this
common universe, the revolutionary generation got its education
in the principles of social health and governmental structure.
Revolution started as an effort to defend accepted constitutional
arrangements, and the revolutionary process never lost touch
with the heritage from which it came.

The colonists, however, were never fully English. In England
the preoccupation with corruption in society and state was always a minority concern. Its greatest advocates were intellectuals, who played no role in government and often hired their pens
to politicians who could use them. Opposition notions had the
most appeal to independent country gentlemen, who lingered in
the backwash of an age in which position in society and government might well depend on a connection with one of the parliamentary "interests"—groups who attached themselves to men of
weight and bargained their collective power for ministerial
favors. After 1760 great men such as William Pitt, Charles Fox,
and even George III felt some attraction to the "Country" program. There was widespread agitation for reform. But opposition notions had little practical effect. Few really feared the
imminent collapse of English liberty. At heart, most of the men
who counted were content to operate within the normal structure.

In the colonies the situation was far different. There, for a
variety of reasons, the eighteenth-century critics found a more
receptive audience among the great and small alike. There, as
crisis came upon the empire, the opposition writers would acquire an influence that could not be matched by any other au-

2. The theory of the balanced constitution was "so pervasive as to constitute less an
idea than a reflex. As such it colored all aspects of political and constitutional thought"
(Bernard Bailyn, *The Origins of American Politics* [New York: Knopf, 1968], p. 23).

thors, affecting thought on levels that could shape perceptions of the world and alter practical affairs. The influence of an opposition understanding of events led the Americans to revolution. Opposition ideology, as much as any other force, gave purpose and direction to the revolutionary movement. It helped define America. It molded institutions. It created a perspective and a vision that would guide the revolutionaries' conduct through the remainder of their lives.[3]

I

Colonial Americans displayed an early and voracious appetite for opposition works. *Cato's Letters* were still appearing in the *London Journal* when James Franklin printed excerpts in the *New England Courant.*[4] Quickly, the collection became the most popular political work in colonial America.[5] Other opposition treatises had similar appeal. Booksellers made the most important tracts available soon after their appearance, advertising opposition books as often as they did the works of Locke.[6] English

3. Two of the most brilliant historical studies of our generation, Bernard Bailyn, *The Ideological Origins of the American Revolution* (Cambridge, Mass.: Harvard University Press, 1967), and Gordon S. Wood, *The Creation of the American Republic, 1776–1787* (Chapel Hill: University of North Carolina Press, 1969), established the central influence of British opposition thought on revolutionary ideas and conduct. This chapter is based primarily on these two studies as supplemented by Pauline Maier, *From Resistance to Revolution: Colonial Radicals and the Development of American Opposition to Britain, 1765–1776* (New York: Knopf, 1972), and the many books and essays discussed in Robert E. Shalhope, "Toward a Republican Synthesis: The Emergence of an Understanding of Republicanism in American Historiography," *William and Mary Quarterly,* 29 (1972), 49–80.

4. Bailyn, *Ideological Origins,* p. 43; Gary Liddle Huxford, "The Old Whig Comes to America: A Study in the Transit of Ideas" (Ph.D. thesis, University of Washington, 1963), p. 146. On July 7, 1722, Benjamin Franklin reprinted "Cato" on freedom of speech in defense of his brother, who had been incarcerated for his writings.

5. Clinton Rossiter was probably the first to show that Locke was no more influential in the colonies than Sidney, Bolingbroke, Burgh, or Trenchard and Gordon. *Seedtime of the Republic: The Origin of the American Tradition of Political Liberty* (New York: Harcourt, Brace, & World, 1953), p. 141. But the importance of the discovery was not fully recognized until the appearance of Caroline Robbins, *The Eighteenth Century Commonwealthman* (Cambridge, Mass.: Harvard University Press, 1959).

6. H. Trevor Colbourne, *The Lamp of Experience: Whig History and the Intellectual Origins of the American Revolution* (Chapel Hill: University of North Carolina Press,

radicals made sure that their colonial friends were well supplied with recent writings and with eighteenth-century printings of the older classics. No colonial library was complete without its copies of the seventeenth-century standards and the major opposition works.[7]

Perhaps colonials were first impressed with the radical libertarianism of the opposition writers, finding useful their defenses of free speech, freedom of the press, and religious toleration. Perhaps the opposition authors' domination of the press assured them a colonial influence larger than they exercised at home. Yet it is also probable that colonists were naturally attracted to the "Country" strands in opposition thought. The facts of their colonial situation were responsible, in part, since there were unavoidable tensions between local and imperial desires. Traditional suspicions of the executive were heightened in America by its semiforeign character. Moreover, the colonial executives had usually retained a set of formal powers that the crown no longer exercised in England, such as the legislative veto and the right of prorogation. Hemmed in between colonial assemblies and the government at home, the royal governors had less authority in point of fact than English ministries could wield; but to the colonists their powers seemed unduly great. Closely watching these executives, Americans were sensitive about their liberties and more than ordinarily susceptible to opposition stories of the constant danger posed by swollen power.[8]

1965), pp. 117–120 and appendix 2; Huxford, p. 123 and chap. 5. Although the *Political Disquisitions* appeared almost simultaneously in England and America, the ready availability of imports meant that American presses seldom printed their own editions of opposition works.

7. Colbourne, pp. 9–16 and appendix 2.

8. It is the thesis of Bailyn's *Origins of American Politics* that the tension between the executives' great apparent authority and their actual weakness accounts in large part for the endemic political turmoil of colonial America. Colonial apologists and executive officials alike rationalized this instability in the usual terms of English political debate, as a result of faction or of executive influence. Bailyn's argument can appear illogical, since the colonial executives' lack of a sufficient influence to insure stability paradoxically contributed to the acceptability of the rhetoric about corruption, and Bailyn's findings should probably be modified in the manner indicated below. Still, his points are carefully made and seem a valuable contribution.

Through the first half of the eighteenth century, it is true, colonials had few occasions for attacks on influence. By nature, criticism of corruption was a weapon of minorities, who customarily employed the claim that influence had perverted the expression of the people's will in order to reconcile their inferior legislative status with the claim that they spoke for the majority. But the first half of the eighteenth century was a time when a majority in most colonial assemblies was united in an effort to imitate the House of Commons in its seventeenth-century struggle to reduce the role of the prerogative. It was a time, accordingly, when the patronage of governors seemed less important than their formal powers and representatives were less concerned with influence than they were with better distribution of responsibilities among the governmental parts.[9] In America, attacks on influence seldom proved of major use before mid-century. Even then, they were of most importance in colonies where the executive had actually contracted close relations with a legislative party: Massachusetts, Maryland, New Hampshire, and New York.[10]

Still, the criticism of executive influence was not the whole of opposition thought. It was the core of an elaborate ideology concerned with civic virtue, balanced government, and social health. While the critique of influence entered relatively late into colonial debates, the impact of the opposition writers was sufficient long before that time to put Americans on the alert for all the subtle

9. Jack P. Greene, "Political Mimesis: A Consideration of the Historical and Cultural Roots of Legislative Behavior in the British Colonies in the Eighteenth Century," *American Historical Review*, 75 (1969), 350–351. For the peculiarities of the American situation see also Paul Lucas, "A Note on the Comparative Study of the Structure of Politics in Mid-Eighteenth-Century Britain and the American Colonies," *William and Mary Quarterly*, 28 (1971), 301–309.

10. Greene, "Political Mimesis," but I am also indebted to John M. Murrin for the observation that Bailyn's own evidence for the widespread use of opposition critiques in America before 1763 is taken primarily from New York during the 1730s and 1750s, from Pennsylvania in the 1750s, and from Massachusetts in the middle years of the century. In all these cases, it was a weapon of a minority unable to gain control of the assembly. See also Richard L. Bushman, "Corruption and Power in Provincial America," in *The Development of a Revolutionary Mentality* (Washington: Library of Congress, 1972). Bushman seems to show conclusively that the criticism of executive influence played no important role in political controversies in Massachusetts before 1740.

signs of constitutional disease: standing armies, patronage, and popular disinterest in the public good. No doubt remains about the impact of the opposition works. Influential colonists repeatedly recommended the writings and principles of the classical republicans and their eighteenth-century admirers.[11] In newspapers and pamphlets, on nearly every occasion for serious political dispute, they quoted and plagiarized the opposition works.[12] At minimum, the colonists were deeply influenced in their understanding of themselves as British citizens and in their comprehension of the course of modern history by opposition thought.

It would be difficult, in fact, to overemphasize the impact of the opposition works. In an age that thought it possible to comb the past for lessons applicable to the present, history was an important pursuit. History, for most colonists, meant the classic tales of Roman greatness and decline, often in one of the modern translations that were projects of the opposition writers and vehicles for their own ideas.[13] History also meant the great Whig classics, which interpreted the Glorious Revolution as the culmination of an effort to recover ancient Saxon liberties and as the point from which those liberties had steadily declined.[14] The colonists' reading of history reflected and reinforced a sense of the fragility of liberty to which they testified on every side. Their selections from the classics, their choice of British histories, and their tastes among contemporary controversialists all revealed a fascination with political and moral decay.

Americans have periodically been seized with a conviction of the depravity of their times. Fear of declension plainly marked

11. Z. S. Fink suggested that the attractiveness of these authors was sufficient to permit us to call the Americans the last of the classical republicans. *The Classical Republicans*, 2d ed. (Evanston, Ill.: Northwestern University Press, 1962), pp. 189–190.

12. Bailyn, *Ideological Origins*, pp. 43–45, 52–54. More examples can be found in Huxford, chaps. 5–8, and Colbourne, chaps. 4–8.

13. Colbourne, pp. 21–25 and *passim*; Bailyn, *Ideological Origins*, pp. 25–26, 41–42. Particularly popular were Gordon's translations of Sallust and Tacitus, both of which he used to discourse on the dangers of corruption.

14. Colbourne, chap. 3.

the middle years of the eighteenth century. The countryside was changing as population grew more dense and growing commerce wove a tighter network of dependencies through larger portions of the land. The harmony of simpler times (part real and part imagined) was threatened by the new complexities and by the more acquisitive behavior that developed in response to rising opportunities. Many were alarmed by challenges to older values, and many were accustomed, through the heritage of Calvinist theology, to a rhetoric of declension and decline.[15] As politics displaced theology among the colonists' concerns, Americans were easily attracted to the opposition prophets of political collapse. In the course of the eighteenth century, America's place in the world and its mission in history were being redefined in political terms, and eighteenth-century Jeremiahs often saw the people's loss of virtue as declension from a political ideal.[16]

There were both positive and negative attractions in the opposition works. As eighteenth-century colonists sought models for a more mature society—and found one in their imitation of the motherland—they may have seen in opposition ideology some compensation for provincial immaturity. Unburdened by the hierarchical dependencies of Europe, untempted by the old world's luxuries, the colonies could easily be seen as a uniquely favorable setting for the cultivation of civic virtue. A land of

15. In "Rhetoric and Reality in the American Revolution," *William and Mary Quarterly*, 33 (1966), 1–32, Gordon S. Wood suggested that the appeal of opposition ideology might point to the existence of serious tensions and strains within colonial society, recommending a reexamination of social and economic interpretations of the coming of the Revolution. Two recent reexaminations are Kenneth A. Lockridge, "Social Change and the Meaning of the American Revolution," *Journal of Social History*, 6 (1973), 403–439 and Jack P. Greene, "The Social Origins of the American Revolution: An Evaluation and Interpretation," *Political Science Quarterly*, 88 (1973), 1–22.

16. An interesting discussion of the reinforcement of political by religious concepts of the decline of virtue is Edmund S. Morgan, "The Puritan Ethic and the American Revolution," *William and Mary Quarterly*, 24 (1967), 1–43. A most important discussion of this connection and of the changing concept of mission is Nathan O. Hatch, "The Origins of Civil Millenialism in America: New England Clergymen, War with France, and the Revolution," *William and Mary Quarterly*, 31 (1974), 407–430.

independent farmers, free from feudalism and as yet relatively undistracted by commerce and finance, America almost defined the neoclassical ideal. It was a less mature, but also purer, England. As such, however, it had to fear an English fate. Freedom and civic virtue, the English writers taught, were delicate and short-lived flowers, extinct in most of Europe and faring none too well at home. The influence of the opposition writers may have operated in the colonies to build a half-unconscious pride. It worked more certainly to build an apprehension of a crisis and to reinforce a fear of cultural collapse.[17]

II

Revolutions usually begin with social conflict. Wars for independence follow the emergence of a separate sense of nationality. In both respects, America was quite peculiar. Social strains would shape the progress of the Revolution, but they were not sufficient to explain its start.[18] The colonists were proud of being British, and crisis came upon the empire suddenly, just when provincial loyalty to Britain had been reinforced by brilliant victory in war with France. With very little warning, in response to taxes that imposed no grievous burden and were levied to provide for their defense, the colonists sprang literally to arms. They had accumulated grievances against imperial policy in the years since 1759,[19] but nothing in their objective situation seems satisfactorily to explain their violent response. The colonists did not react to tyranny in 1765. What provoked them was a fear of tyranny's approach.[20]

17. For the ambivalent effects of the redefinition of America's character see Bailyn, *Ideological Origins*, pp. 80–84, 138–143; Wood, *Creation of the American Republic*, pp. 93–114.

18. In separate recent studies, cited in note 15, Jack P. Greene and Kenneth Lockridge both reach this conclusion. Other recent studies overwhelmingly confirm the dominant opinion that the Revolution did not issue from domestic change or controversy over who should rule at home, although it may have given reign to both.

19. Bernhard Knollenberg, *Origins of the American Revolution, 1759–1766*, rev. ed. (New York: Free Press, 1965).

20. See Wood, *Creation of Republic*, pp. 3–5, where he quotes Edmund Burke: "They augur misgovernment at a distance and snuff the approach of tyranny in every tainted breeze." Since the appearance of Edmund S. Morgan, "The American Revolu-

A satisfying explanation must begin with recognition of the force of the colonial commitment to British principles of government, together with a knowledge of the special influence of an opposition understanding of the world. Because the colonists were British, they rose up to insist that taxes should be levied only by consent. They were determined to defend a principle and practice that defined the British nation on both sides of the sea. Because they were especially attracted to an opposition understanding of the world, the colonists were quick to see the British effort to secure a revenue in virtually apocalyptic terms. Steeped in stories of the universal flight of freedom from the world, the colonists were ready to imagine speedy ruin.[21] Educated in the principles of political pathology, they were convinced that tyranny could be successfully resisted only at the start, and they were readily inclined to find the sources of political and social evils in deliberate conspiracies by men who occupied positions from which liberty had always been besieged.

There were real dangers to the colonies in the reorientation of imperial policy which became apparent after 1763. Real hardships were involved in some of the new measures. But there were even greater dangers to the empire in the way in which the colonists interpreted events. From all their favorite British writers, the colonists had heard that a corrupting cancer was destroying English freedom. Never having lived in England—or seeing it as visitors from simpler and more uniformly prosperous lands—the colonists were always more inclined then Englishmen at home to take the oppositionists in earnest.[22] And as the crisis swelled, events conspired to lend a growing credibility

---

tion: Revisions in Need of Revising," *William and Mary Quarterly*, 14 (1957), 3–15, predominant historical opinion has denied that eighteenth-century colonists were discontent within the empire and insisted that the rhetoric of the resistance to the change in British policy was something more than camouflage for other, "harder" things. This interpretation seems stronger in the light of growing emphasis on the degree to which the colonists identified themselves as Britons and in the light of new insistence that, in stressing the centrality of ideology, we stress the primacy of men's perceptions of the world, not their abstract or rational commitment to ideas.

21. Bailyn, *Ideological Origins*, pp. 94–95.
22. Ibid., pp. 135–137, 85–92.

to opposition warnings of the progress of corruption in the motherland. Colonial resistance stiffened government's resolve; repression led to more resistance. Eventually, the colonists concluded that the danger to their liberties and way of life was so profound that separation from the empire was their only safe recourse.[23]

Independence was a difficult decision. Colonists were loyal to the crown and generally content within the empire. Their leaders knew how easily a revolution could produce excess, and they were well aware that it would not be easy to construct appropriate alternatives to the imperial relationship. Independence would imply American republics, and eighteenth-century thinkers had grave doubts about the feasibility of governments without hereditary parts.[24] Resistance was originally intended to defend the British constitution, not destroy it.[25] At every stage of their long struggle, the radicals faced strong resistance. They did not secure their end until events in the villages and on the battlefields made separation an accomplished fact. Nevertheless, the logic of an opposition understanding of events led the Americans inexorably toward independence. No less importantly, it led them toward a definition of themselves that they could not complete without a revolutionary effort to transform their world.

Loyal to the empire, the colonists were hesitant, at first, to trace their discontents to any fundamental dislocation in the British system. Some blamed the change in British policy on the malevolence of royal governors or customs agents, who had misinformed the ministry at home. Determination to resist went hand in hand with an assumption that Parliament was innocent of any ill intent and would defeat the ministerial measures. Par-

23. This and the succeeding paragraphs on the coming of the Revolution supplement Bailyn with Pauline Maier's *From Resistance to Revolution* and with my own opinion that the British opposition thinkers had been moving in a republican direction.

24. For the engrained fear of republicanism in Anglo-American thought see Bailyn, pp. 281–285; Wood, pp. 53–70; and W. Paul Adams, "Republicanism in Political Rhetoric before 1776," *Political Science Quarterly*, 85 (1970), 397–421. I do not deny this fear, but think it has been overemphasized.

25. Wood, p. 10.

liament's decision to repeal the Stamp Act briefly bolstered hopes, as did contemporary English agitation for reform. Having backed away in face of the reaction to the Stamp Act, though, the British government renewed its effort to secure a colonial revenue. The Townshend Duties reaffirmed a parliamentary authority to tax the colonies. They also added to the powers and the numbers of the hated customs agents, who soon insisted on protection in the form of British troops. Meanwhile, the ministry continued its campaign against John Wilkes, who had become a hero in the colonies but was refused a seat in Parliament despite repeated victories in Middlesex elections. In England and America alike, events suggested an executive hostility to liberty, which neither Parliament nor the reformers could control. Increasing numbers of the colonists concluded that they could not rest with their original determination simply to defend the power of the purse, that they could not confide their liberties to any English friends. There were too many ways that Parliament could threaten their essential rights, too many indications that the ministry could not be stopped in its usurping course.

To growing numbers of the colonists, British actions in the decade after 1765 were ever harder to attribute to misunderstandings or mistakes. The sources of their tribulations, colonists were more and more inclined to think, lay in the very structure of the British state and in the character of their compatriots in England. England, they concluded—for how else could they understand her perseverance in such conduct—was an enslaved and rotten land, whose few remaining men of principle were helpless to affect affairs. Nor was this national debility a passing state. It was an irretrievable effect of a corrupting constitution.

The controversy that unfolded through the decade following the Stamp Act Crisis utterly destroyed the faith most patriots had had in the beneficence of Britain, not least because it undermined their former confidence in the system of mixed monarchy itself. For years the British opposition writers had been leveling a fundamental challenge at Englishmen who took their governmental equilibrium for granted, often in a manner that could test and modify received ideas. Criticizing modern governmental methods, the oppositionists had been increasingly inclined to emphasize that monarchies, by nature, were more susceptible to influence and corruption than nonhereditary commonwealths. From their original suspicions of the crown, they had drifted back toward Harrington's contention that the interests of hereditary orders are inherently opposed to the interest of the commons, which is liberty. The colonists, for whom the opposition writers offered a convincing explanation of the crisis, missed few implications of the opposition works.

Immersion in the opposition writings primed rebellious colonists for Thomas Paine's denunciation of the vaunted British constitution in the most influential pamphlet of the revolutionary years. Few readers followed *Common Sense* in its rejection of the principle of balanced government itself. That liberty depended on a proper mixture of the one, the many, and the few seemed, in the eighteenth century, to be the indisputable conclusion of all the best authorities in politics from Aristotle to De Lolme. But it had never been essential to the theory of a governmental balance that the one of a mixed government should be a king or that the few should hold their places by hereditary right. The theory was republican in origins, as every reader of the classics knew. And every patriot who was familiar with Harrington and his descendants was prepared for Paine's assertion that it was absurd to think that orders with hereditary differences of interest could ever work harmoniously in balance. Corruption and a hidden despotism were the necessary consequences of a constitution with hereditary parts.[26]

Recommended by the analysis of the condition of the English,

26. Philip S. Foner, ed., *The Complete Writings of Thomas Paine*, 2 vols. (New York: Citadel Press, 1945), I, 6–9 and below. *Common Sense* is generally recognized as a landmark in the American rejection of mixed monarchy, and M. J. C. Vile has argued that Paine reached this position through opposition to the cabinet system, *Constitutionalism and the Separation of Powers* (Oxford: Clarendon Press, 1967), p. 111. I only suggest that British opposition thought had long been moving toward the same conclusion.

Paine's republican conclusion was powerfully supported by the revolutionaries' reexamination of themselves, which necessarily accompanied attempts to understand the crisis they were passing through. In order to prepare and justify a unified response to British measures, the patriots were forced to define their own ideals. Again, their opposition understanding of events helped organize their thought. Guided to a clearer recognition of the dangers that confronted them, Americans could also reach a better understanding of the virtues that were threatened. Seeing what was wrong with England, they obtained new insights into what was right about themselves.[27]

Under pressure of the imperial disagreement, an image of America that had simmered through the years of British rule now bubbled to the top. The crisis speeded the identification of America as the special preserve of ancient Saxon virtues. Logically and historically, corruption was the obverse and the ruin of classical republican ideals. To decide that corruption was the fundamental source of America's ills was to realize that freedom, propertied independence, and civic virtue were the sources of its strengths.[28] But virtue could achieve its most complete expression only in a commonwealth. And freedom, as the opposition writers hinted, could be best secured in a republic.

27. This discussion of the transformation of the colonists' perceptions into an enthusiastic, republican faith was first suggested by Bailyn, pp. 138–143 and *passim*. It has since been amplified by Wood, chaps. 2–3, and I have depended on his explanation.

28. Perhaps nowhere was this realization more explicit than in Query XIX of Thomas Jefferson's *Notes on Virginia*, written in 1780 and 1781: "Those who labor in the earth are the chosen people of God, if ever He had a chosen people, whose breasts He has made His peculiar deposit for substantial and genuine virtue. . . . Corruption of morals in the mass of cultivators is a phenomenon of which no age nor nation has furnished an example. It is the mark set on those who, not looking up to heaven, to their own soil and industry, as does the husbandman, for their subsistence, depend for it on casualties and caprice of customers. Dependence begets subservience and venality, suffocates the germ of virtue, and prepares fit tools for the designs of ambition. . . . Generally speaking, the proportion which the aggregate of the other classes of citizens bears in any state to that of its husbandmen is the proportion of its unsound to its healthy parts and is a good enough barometer whereby to measure its degree of corruption. While we have land to labor, then, let us never wish to see our citizens occupied at a workbench or twirling a distaff. . . . The mobs of great cities add just so much to the support of pure government as sores to the strength of the human body."

By the time the news arrived from Lexington, if not before, most active patriots had passed the point at which they might have been content with restoration of the imperial relationships of 1763. Convinced that England was irrecoverably corrupt, the patriots had long since turned the critical apparatus of opposition ideology to a reconsideration of their own societies as well. Here, too, they found abundant symptoms of the cancer that originated overseas. There were symptoms of the illness in the luxury and spiritual declension that the clergymen perceived, in planters' debts, in the preemption of colonial offices by English party hacks.[29] It seemed that, having exhausted the possibilities for corruption at home, the English ministry was grasping now for every opportunity that could be found abroad. Its creatures filled colonial positions, barring local men, impoverishing the people, encouraging the spirit of subservience and dissipation that prepared a nation for despotic rule. Socially and morally, as well as politically, America was beginning to repeat the history of English decline. Separation from the source of the infection was the only way to safeguard a society that was not only precious to Americans, but possibly the final hope for liberty on earth. If independence meant a revolution, patriots were ready—even eager—for a revolution now. Republicanism no longer seemed an unavoidable necessity, to be embraced with dread, but an exhilarating opportunity through which Americans might reverse their national degeneration, achieve a full expression of their genius as a people, and make themselves a model for the rest of a benighted world.

III

Revolutionary republicanism was a creed for radical reform, touching and affecting institutions ranging from religion to primogeniture and slavery. The revolutionaries hoped that countless benefits would flow from their determination to adjust

29. The best account of the way corruption began to account for all manner of domestic ills is Wood, pp. 75–82, 107–118.

their attitudes and institutions to accord with new ideas. Most of all, of course, they hoped that the rejection of hereditary privilege would make it possible to form new governments that would be fully suited to the people's democratic character and to the preservation and perfection of their special way of life.[30]

The task seemed relatively easy and straightforward at the start. Years of revolutionary controversy had produced a definite and generally acceptable American ideal. What most Americans desired were balanced governments without hereditary parts and organized in such a manner as to block the openings for the corruption that had ruined the British state. Anyone familiar with the British opposition writers will recognize the source of many of the changes introduced into most revolutionary constitutions: annual elections guarded carefully from influence; equal legislative districts; property requirements for electors and for representatives; and stringent limitations on the patronage and powers of the new executives. Other changes can be traced to the commitment to equality and natural rights. The first new governments appeared at high tide of the early revolutionary spirit, when the people seemed to be displaying their capacity for democratic government by making sacrifices for the patriotic cause. Hostility to privilege united with a high opinion of the

30. The remainder of this chapter follows Wood, chaps. 5–13. Thus, its theme is the emergence of the Federal Constitution from a changing and developing consensus in revolutionary thought. Alternative interpretations, stressing changing fortunes of competing social interests, trace back to publication of Charles A. Beard's iconoclastic *An Economic Interpretation of the Constitution of the United States* (1935; rpt. New York: Macmillan, 1960), and to Merrill Jensen, *The Articles of Confederation: An Interpretation of the Social-Constitutional History of the American Revolution, 1774–1781* (Madison: University of Wisconsin Press, 1963), and *The New Nation: A History of the United States During the Confederation, 1781–1789* (New York: Vintage Books, 1965), works first published in 1940 and 1950. A neo-Beardian interpretation still has many advocates. Among the best is Jackson Turner Main. In *The Sovereign States, 1775–1783* (New York: New Viewpoints, 1973) and *Political Parties Before the Constitution* (Chapel Hill: University of North Carolina Press, 1974), the two most recent of several fine works, Main sees persistent conflict through the revolutionary years between the advocates of balanced government (or "Whigs") and populistic forces, who favored a more democratic structure. Revolutionary constitutions in the states were often, in his view, a product of a compromise between competing views. The Federal Constitution marked a triumph for the "Whigs."

people's virtue, with the influence of the opposition writers, and with fears derived from the colonial experience to strip executives of most of their traditional authority and place an overwhelming share of power in the lower houses of the revolutionary states.[31]

The revolutionary constitutions were created with deceptive speed, suggesting slighter changes than were actually involved. In fact, the revolutionaries had departed rather far from eighteenth-century constitutional ideas. Too far, more than a few of them concluded. Preoccupied with the abuses of executives, the framers of the revolutionary constitutions seemed to have encountered dangers at the opposite extreme. Most revolutionary thinkers were convinced that just and stable governments required a place for virtues foreign to the character of popular assemblies, virtues insufficiently provided for in most state constitutions. Fearing power, even critics were unwilling, for a time, to look to the executive for these. But the Revolution was not very old before the overwhelming power of the popular assemblies persuaded many men to wish for stronger upper houses than had been established in most states, bodies capable of checking the more volatile assemblies and imposing their superior stability and wisdom between the public good and the immediate enactment of the people's temporary will.[32]

31. This follows Wood in thinking that the repeated calls for a separation of powers in the first years of the revolution were essentially a demand for an end to executive influence upon and interference with the other branches of the government. For an opinion that the first state governments depended on a relatively "pure" theory of the separation of powers see M. J. C. Vile, *Constitutionalism and the Separation of Powers* (Oxford: Clarendon Press, 1967), chap. 4. William Clarence Webster, "Comparative Study of the State Constitutions of the American Revolution," American Academy of Political and Social Science *Annals*, 9 (1897), 380–420, is still a useful summary, although Webster takes the older position that the new constitutions were "little more than the pre-existing constitutions adapted to the changed circumstances of independence." For democratic sentiment see Elisha P. Douglas, *Rebels and Democrats: The Struggle for Equal Political Rights and Majority Rule During the American Revolution* (Chapel Hill: University of North Carolina Press, 1955).

32. Again, Jefferson's *Notes on Virginia* (Querry XIII) offers one of the best expressions of this desire: Under the present constitution of Virginia "the Senate is, by its constitution, too homogeneous with the House of Delegates. Being chosen by the same electors at the same time and out of the same subjects, the choice falls of course on men of the same description. The purpose of establishing different houses of legislature is to

The states' rejection of hereditary ranks, though seldom of bicameralism, eventually required a searching reexamination of the character of a second house. Weak governors and strong assemblies were the most immediate and clearest changes introduced by revolutionary thought. The most important and most difficult achievement, though, came as the critics of the revolutionary constitutions sought to reconcile an independent second branch of legislature with America's rejection of the old assumption that societies contain two types of men, each needing for their own protection the control of one branch of the government, each contributing a special virtue to the state.

While the desire for strong and independent upper houses had firm roots, it ran precisely counter to the democratic spirit of the Revolution, and it faced a crushing difficulty in societies where there was only one estate. A second house might be elected by the popular assembly, which would remove its members somewhat from the pressures of the people's will. But then the second house might be dependent on the first. Election by the people, on the other hand, would make the upper house a duplicate of the assembly, causing it to lack the different character required to make it check the lower house. Massachusetts tried to solve the problem by apportioning the upper house according to the wealth, not numbers, of the several districts—a solution with some precedent in Harrington's prescriptions. Several revolutionary states required that members of the upper house be men of greater property than was required for the assembly. Neither of these answers seemed entirely democratic. In face of the com-

---

introduce the influence of different interests or different principles. Thus in Great Britain it is said their constitution relies on the House of Commons for honesty and the Lords for wisdom, which would be a rational reliance if honesty were to be bought with money and if wisdom were hereditary. In some of the American states, the delegates and senators are so chosen that the first represent the persons and the second the property of the state. But with us, wealth and wisdom have equal chance for admission into both houses. We do not, therefore, derive from the separation of our legislature into two houses those benefits which a proper complication of principles are capable of producing and those which alone can compensate the evils which may be produced by their dissensions."

mitment to equality, the advocates of independent upper houses found it difficult to argue that Americans could locate any special group of men who were entitled by their special characteristics to a peculiar share of governmental power. A different solution, suggested by conservative opponents of Pennsylvania's very democratic constitution, proved to have more general appeal. The Pennsylvanians argued that a second house, in a republic, should be thought of simply as a check on the abuses of the first. Distinguishing the people from their representatives and calling for a double check on governmental power, they urged additional protection, not for any special group of men, but for the liberties of all.

Extending the conventional distrust of governmental power to the lower houses of assembly, the branches that had once been thought of as the very seats of liberty, conservatives in Pennsylvania anticipated a profound reorientation of ideas, which began to occur throughout America as different groups collected grievances against the revolutionary regimes. With the waning of the fervor that had carried them to independence, growing numbers of Americans regretted the enthusiasm that had led them to emasculate the parts of government least subject to the people's immediate control. Experience and opposition ideology had taught them to believe that threats to liberty would come from the executive, perhaps in collusion with a hereditary second house. They had guarded carefully against those dangers in the early constitutions. Now, many were afraid that they had tipped the balance much too far the other way. From Aristotle forward, advocates of balanced government had warned that popular republics could degenerate through excess of their virtues, bringing on a democratic despotism or collapsing into anarchy. More afraid of privilege and power, Americans had overlooked such warnings in the first years of the Revolution. Now, additional experience reminded them of ancient doubts about republican stability and classic warnings that a tyranny could issue from any form of government in which all power rested in a single set of hands.

In the 1780s, as in the years preceding independence, images of dissolution and corruption once more ordered many men's perceptions of events. Among established families in particular, a sense of social dislocation quickly gathered force. Suffering real hardships from the states' attempts to cope with the depression of the postwar years—hardships such as paper money, which could be interpreted as violations of their right to hold their property secure—established leaders often felt a deep revulsion for the new men who had found an opportunity to rise to powerful positions in the stress of revolution. According to received ideas, these men were demagogues who had been given an opportunity by populistic constitutions to lead the people into the injustices that were the characteristic products of unmixed democracy. It seemed to many that, under the new constitutions, liberty was rapidly becoming license and a leveling disdain for talent and distinction. Public virtue seemed in danger of completely disappearing in a wave of speculation and neglect of public goods. The laws had neither the stability nor character to encourage civic virtue. Instead, each individual sought private goods, each social group competed to control the overbearing lower houses and to use the powers of a poorly balanced government for selfish ends.[33]

The "better sort of people" were the loudest in their condemnations of the vices of the 1780s. What happened, though, cannot be represented as a victory for a reactionary class.[34] From the beginning of the quarrel with Great Britain, the strongest impulse of the revolutionary movement had been the colonists'

33. This analysis of the psychology of the Critical Period was first hinted at in Douglas Greybill Adair, "The Intellectual Origins of Jeffersonian Democracy: Republicanism, the Class Struggle, and the Virtuous Farmer" (Ph.D. thesis, Yale University, 1943). As improved by Wood, chap. 10, it is a major contribution to the understanding of Federalism.

34. It is the thesis of Jensen's *The New Nation* that conditions in the 1780s were not so desperate that a new constitution was, as Federalists said, the sole alternative to economic ruin and civil war. The objective weaknesses of the Confederation, Jensen argues, could have been corrected without a constitutional revolution. There is important truth in this observation, but it does not justify his depiction of the Federalists as conspiratorial counterrevolutionaries.

determination to preserve their liberties and way of life. The fundamental goal of the American Revolution had been a government of laws and not of men: freedom in the eighteenth-century sense of the security of every individual in his property and rights. From the beginning, nearly everyone agreed that liberty depended on consent, but few had ever thought that liberty could be secure in states in which the people or their most immediate representatives were given full control. Few had imagined that republican ideals entailed a democratic government in anything approaching modern usage of that phrase.

Behind the sense of crisis that developed during the Confederation years lay centuries of exploration of the strengths and weaknesses of balanced governments. In light of this long heritage, the troubles of these years did not seem inconveniences or temporary dislocations. They seemed mounting evidence of a degeneration that could only end in social dissolution and destruction of the nation's way of life. All literate Americans of the revolutionary generation were students of political disease. All had been educated to interpret the developments of the Confederation years as symptoms of a killing illness that could not be treated with expedients alone, an illness that endangered all their revolutionary hopes.

Between 1776 and 1787 the great majority of revolutionary leaders experienced a striking change of mind. Participating in the general reversal of opinion, Jefferson and Madison, along with those they would in time oppose, concluded that the popular assemblies had been granted such an overbearing share of power in the states that they, not the executives, not central government, now posed the greatest danger to republican ideals. Men from every station in society shared in the impression that the great American experiment was going wrong. Leaders from all sections of the country traced a growing battery of evils to a fundamental weakness in the basic structures of the revolutionary polities. The framers of the early revolutionary constitutions had produced an excess of democracy, and the debilitating influence of improper governments threatened to destroy the hopes for social, moral, and political improvement that defined the Revolution. Leaders set their minds, therefore, on a reform which might correct the first mistakes, restore the strength of government, and give the laws the character to lead the people back to the republican ideal. They sought a remedy for a disease that had become entirely national in scope, that threatened national character itself. They sought to save the Revolution through a constitutional reform.

Part II

THE QUARREL WITH FEDERALISM

When the newspapers tell us of the minions of power and of overgrown individuals in office and of other cant which seems to be copied from an English opposition print, what are we to think?

Gazette of the United States

CHAPTER 4

The Antifederal Connection

THE ratification of the Federal Constitution was the climax of developments that worked a major alteration in political and social thought. Yet it was years before this alteration was complete. Even when it was, preoccupations and beliefs much older than the Constitution still survived to influence men's perceptions and to shape a bitter disagreement over revolutionary goals. Indeed, the triumph of the Constitution in the midst of a ferocious party conflict is to be explained, in no small part, as consequence of the persistent influence of received ideas.

It is the thesis of this work that many of the central concepts of the eighteenth-century theory of the balanced constitution, along with expectations, fears, and values that derived from eighteenth-century British opposition thought, persisted in America long after 1789. They lived on not as fragmentary thoughts, but as a structured medium through which Americans continued to perceive the world and give expression to their hopes and discontents. Inherited ideas informed important aspects of the Antifederalist persuasion. Antifederalist predictions, in their turn, assured that some Americans—in Congress and without—would watch each step of the new government in anxious expectation that their liberty might be destroyed, anticipating that the danger would assume a quite specific form. As the policies of Washington's administration gradually took shape, too many governmental actions seemed to fall within the fearful pattern that had been predicted all along. As in the crisis that had led to independence, men began to see a carefully contrived conspiracy against their freedom. Discernment of this threat played an essential role in the development of systematic opposition to the new administration, helping to create a party that would call itself Republican and rest to a remarkable degree on a revival and Americanization of British opposition thought.

I

While it was years before most men could free themselves entirely from a set of mental habits that encouraged them to see the parts of the new government in older and more nearly classic terms, the Federal Constitution undeniably promoted and depended on a critically important transformation of ideas. New concepts had emerged as revolutionary thinkers justified American resistance to Great Britain and created revolutionary states. Sometimes dimly understood, these concepts nonetheless provided a new syntax for debates in the Constitutional Convention, and the Federalists explored them further in the effort to defend the framers' work. As the Constitution went into effect, a new American synthesis was beginning to emerge, a synthesis that rested on rejection of the ancient habit of associating the branches of a balanced government with a mixture of social estates.

With the dissociation of the concept of a governmental balance from the concept of an equilibrium between estates, the revolutionaries cut a crucial tie with their inheritance and moved decisively toward a distinctive governmental theory of their own. Decisive as it was, however, the rejection of this central tenet of the theory of mixed government did not invalidate the whole of the coherent universe of thought with which the concept of a social balance had been linked. A knowledge of the nature *and* the limits of the revolutionary transformation of ideas is indispensable for understanding what transpired.[1]

1. This chapter accepts the central argument of Gordon S. Wood, *The Creation of the American Republic, 1776–1787* (Chapel Hill: University of North Carolina Press, 1969), but it seeks to qualify Wood's assertion that adoption of the Constitution marked an end of classical politics in the United States.

The story of John Adams' misadventures is instructive at this point,[2] for Adams ranked among the greatest of the revolutionary heroes. No one had done more to bring on independence. No one had exerted stronger influence on the shaping of the revolutionary constitutions.[3] Once the constitutions had been written, though, Adams left for Europe, filling diplomatic posts where he was somewhat out of touch with new developments at home. With this misfortune, he combined vast scholarship, perverse integrity, and a decided lack of sensitivity to popular opinion. In consequence, when he determined to perform another service for his country, the product was a shelf of writings that would plague him to his death.[4]

Adams' service in the years around 1790 was to champion the cause of bicameralism and a strong executive against the heresy of single-chamber democracy, which was winning able advocates among the intellectuals in France. With many of his countrymen, Adams saw the developments of the Confederation years as evidence of a decline in that devotion to the common good which was the necessary core of sound republics. He feared that, in these circumstances, the advocates of unicameralism might find a willing audience, and he decided to employ his learning in defense of the bicameral systems adopted in most American constitutions. Thus far, he had a right to count on general applause, since simple democracy had few important friends in the United States.[5] Nevertheless, his defense of the American constitutions left many of his compatriots bewildered and outraged.

2. As Wood has also seen, Chap. 14.

3. Adams was the principal author of the Massachusetts constitution. In addition, his advice to George Wythe and Richard Henry Lee was probably the most important single source for the Virginia constitution, which became a prototype for several other states.

4. These were the three volumes of *A Defense of the Constitutions of Government of the United States of America*, published in 1787 and 1788, and the *Discourses on Davila: A Series of Papers on Political History*, which first appeared during 1790 as a series in the (Phil.) *Gazette of the United States*. They can be found in Charles Francis Adams, ed., *The Works of John Adams*, 10 vols. (Boston: Little & Brown, 1850–1856), IV–VI.

5. In fact, the first volume of the *Defense* appeared in America just before the Constitutional Convention, where it circulated among the delegates and initially received considerable praise. For example, see Rush to Richard Price, June 2, 1787, and

From the time in 1776 when he offered some "Thoughts on Government" for the consideration of Southern colleagues in the Continental Congress, John Adams had been a staunch and consistent advocate of balanced government. In the early days of revolutionary enthusiasm, he had been swept along with most of his contemporaries in the current of optimism generated by the spirited commitment to the patriotic cause and by the apparent fitness of a virtuous, united people for a revolutionary form of government. During the 1780s, though, his interpretation of American experience, like that of other Whigs, caused him to question the distinctive virtue of Americans, to reemphasize the universal conflict of the many and the few, and to insist more strongly on the necessity for a powerful executive to act as a balance between contending social forces. Against the proponents of simple democracy, he now advanced a learned, almost wholly classical defense of both the English and American alternatives, insisting that the principles behind the two were much the same.[6]

To Adams, the most important test for any government was its capacity to compel the formulation and execution of good and equal laws. No government in which the whole authority was given to a single legislative chamber could expect to pass this test.[7] The majority, while it was able, would oppress minorities.[8] More importantly, the majority would not prevail for long in any

---

Rush to Adams, July 2, 1788, in L. H. Butterfield, ed., *Letters of Benjamin Rush*, 2 vols., Memoirs of the American Philosophical Society, 30 (Princeton: Princeton University Press, 1951), I, 418, 468.

6. Adams' revision of his political theory as a result of his experiences and judgments during the 1780s is discussed in John R. Howe, Jr., *The Changing Political Thought of John Adams* (Princeton: Princeton University Press, 1966). I am not convinced, however, that Adams underwent a change in principle, as opposed to a change in spirit and emphasis, during these years. His earlier writings were also consistent with adherence to the theory of mixed government, and I am inclined to agree with Wood, chap. 14, that his contemporaries underwent a more radical change.

7. *Defense of the American Constitutions* in *Works*, IV, 406. Compare "Thoughts on Government" (1776), ibid., 194–195.

8. Unchecked, "the majority has eternally and without one exception usurped over the rights of the minority" (*Defense* in *Works*, VI, 10). See also *Discourses on Davila*, ibid., 252.

single-chamber state. However much we may insist on natural equality, native differences in fact distinguish men into the many and the few. If all the power of the state rests with a single legislative chamber, the government will come in time to aristocracy, since people naturally prefer the prominent as leaders.[9] The liberty of everyone can be secure only when the three great powers of government are placed in separate hands and the supreme, legislative power is divided between three branches founded on the three natural orders of the state.[10]

A plain republican in habits and desires, Adams never understood the abuse that greeted the publication of his views. Conscious of his own integrity, he felt betrayed by a people who had strayed from the principles of 1776, befuddled by the charge that it was he who had apostatized. In truth, his colleagues' minds had changed a good deal more than his. Principles had been transmuted so decisively—and yet so subtly—that the harder Adams tried to clarify his points, the more apparent it became that he was reasoning within a framework that his countrymen no longer shared. "Whenever I use the word 'republic' with approbation," he explained to his cousin, "I mean a government in which the people have . . . an essential share in the sovereignty."[11] Samuel Adams responded with a question: "Is not the *whole* sovereignty, my friend, essentially in the people" in a republic?[12] Not even Roger Sherman, whose suspicions of democracy were easily a match for Adams' own, could hold his silence when confronted with the diplomat's insistence on the presence of natural orders in American society, with its implicit

9. This argument was a distinguishing characteristic of Adams' thought. He believed that the tendency of deference to produce an aristocracy could only be prevented if the natural aristocracy were isolated in one branch of the legislature, where they could protect themselves and yet be subjected to the check of a democratic branch. See *Defense* in ibid., IV, 290–291.

10. *Defense*, ibid., IV, 579; V, 5–6. *Davila*, VI, 280.

11. Adams to Samuel Adams, October 18, 1790, *Works*, VI, 415.

12. Samuel Adams to John Adams, Nov. 25, 1790, in Harry Alonzo Cushing, ed., *The Writings of Samuel Adams*, 4 vols. (New York: Putnam, 1904–1908), IV, 344.

corollary that each order held or ought to hold a separate share of power.[13]

Adams was an eighteenth-century, classical republican, who saw no difference worth fighting for between a commonwealth and a mixed monarchy. His friends were living in a different mental world. "The English government," he still maintained, "is a republic."[14] A commonplace of British opposition thought, entirely comprehensible to every Whig two dozen years before, this statement was anathema to revolutionaries by the time the Federal Constitution went into effect. A literal conception of the people's sovereignty had given rise to an insistence on the value of a written constitution and to alterations of perspective that denied that any group except the people or their representatives could have a separate share of governmental power. From newer points of view, America's rejection of hereditary orders outweighed any superficial similarity between her governments and England's, and Adams' praise for English forms condemned him as a monarchist. His stubborn and continuing defense of eighteenth-century principles of government aroused suspicions that would follow him through all the rest of his career.[15]

The problem did not lie in Adams' antipopulistic sympathies. Most revolutionaries feared a single-chamber government. Most of the members of the Constitutional Convention entered on their work in the conviction that democracy had gotten out of hand in the United States and must be tempered by the institu-

13. See the exchange between Adams and Sherman in Adams' *Works*, VI, 429–431, 438.

14. Ibid., 429–431: "The monarchical and the aristocratical power in our constitution, it is true, are not hereditary, but this makes no difference in the nature of the power, in the balance, or in the name of the species of government."

15. The *Discourses on Davila*, aimed at the French Revolution, revealed Adams at his most reactionary and provided his opponents with credible support for charges that he favored the hereditary principle. In his comments on the danger of frequent elections and the need for an independent executive, he seemed to set criteria for the magistracy that could not be met through elections; and, discussing the aristocratic part of the government, he wrote that wisdom and integrity were more likely to be discovered by hereditary descent than by election. See *Works*, VI, 249, and Zoltan Haraszti, ed., "The 32nd Discourse on Davila," *William and Mary Quarterly*, 11 (1954), 90.

tion of a strong executive and independent upper house. Some members would have liked a closer imitation of the English constitution than they ultimately approved, though most were politic enough to keep such notions out of print. As the Convention went about its work, the processes of compromise and reconstruction rapidly outran most delegates' abilities to synthesize ideas and justify conclusions. Still, debates began and ended in the knowledge that America would not abide the hint of a return to hereditary forms. From first to last, all delegates agreed that they must frame a government that would derive in all its parts and powers from a democratic people.[16] Adams' failing was his inability to comprehend the changes in the theory of a balanced constitution that the concept of a democratic social order introduced.

The government created by the Constitutional Convention was without real precedent in Western thought. Wholly elective, neither national nor federal, it could not be fully understood or justified in Adams' older terms. To thinkers who had kept abreast of revolutionary changes, the people were no longer an abstraction, present at the origins of government and then embodied in a popular assembly. Represented in all parts of both the state and central governments, the people were a sovereign force who stood outside their governmental institutions, distributing a portion of their power to the several different parts, retaining yet another portion for themselves. Powers, not estates, were balanced in these governments. All their parts depended on a people who could not be differentiated into the many and the few. John Adams "made himself obnoxious" when he failed to see how thoroughly the landscape had been changed by these assumptions.[17]

Saying this, however, we should then go on to say that Adams' failing was less obvious than it appears with benefit of hindsight.

16. Max Farrand, ed., *The Records of the Federal Convention of 1787*, 4 vols. (1937; rpt. New Haven: Yale University Press, 1966).

17. Quotation from Gaillard Hunt, ed., *The Writings of James Madison*, 9 vols. (New York: Putnam, 1900–1910), V, 270.

The revolutionary transformation of ideas was both profound and subtle. It went forward slowly, sometimes almost imperceptibly, for more than twenty years, and few were able to adjust to all its implications at once. There was no sudden break with eighteenth-century tradition. Instead, there was a gradual transition attained by different individuals with different speeds—or not at all. Thinkers moved across a line that was so indistinct that, when they reached the other side, there was about as much that was continuous with their inheritance as not. For anyone whose mind was thoroughly conditioned to the old assumptions, the transformation might be difficult to grasp.

To illustrate, it may be useful to compare James Madison's defense of the new Constitution, as set forth in *The Federalist*, to classical-republican and eighteenth-century arguments in favor of mixed government.[18] Madison, the best political philosopher among the framers—perhaps the best America has ever reared—was one of those who were appalled by Adams' views. And yet the two men reasoned from a similar opinion of man's nature. Both of them believed that liberty, stability, and justice could only be assured by institutional arrangements that could guarantee protection for the rights of different social groups. Each sought a form of government that could resist the ravages of time.

With Adams and with all the classical and Renaissance proponents of mixed government, Madison assumed that any proper constitution must combine stability with liberty. The difficulty, he agreed, lay in the force of selfish interest, which made it certain that any group of men would seek its partial interests at other men's expense. The legislator's task, accordingly, was to divide the powers of the government in such a manner that no part of society could seize the state for partial ends. In contrast to proponents of mixed government, Madison did not believe that

18. Madison's *Federalist* numbers 47–51, along with number 10, were the most thorough contemporary justification of the structure of the new government. The best edition is *The Federalist*, ed. with intro. and notes by Jacob E. Cooke (Cleveland: World, 1961).

men fell naturally into a social order characterized by a duality between the many and the few. He pictured an American society comprised of a congeries of vertical and horizontal interest groups. Of these, however, the distinction between rich and poor, creditors and debtors, still seemed the most significant; and, in accordance with traditional ideas and with his own interpretation of American experience, Madison still feared that either of these pairs, if left unchecked, could prove a danger to the other's liberty. Unlike the older theorists, he neither wished nor thought it possible to distribute the powers of the state among conflicting social groups. Like them, however, he continued to believe that liberty depended on a governmental structure that could not be captured by a single set of men.[19]

If Adams never fully understood how radically the theory of the balanced constitution had been changed by Madison and others, this may have been because the most advanced of the new thinkers were themselves quite conscious of the limits of the transformation. These thinkers had decided that there was a fundamental difference between mixed monarchy and a republic. Still, they were determined to secure all of the benefits traditionally attributed to balanced states. They rejected the classical underpinnings of the theory of mixed government in the image of a society comprised of different estates, along with all its consequences for theories of representation and sovereignty. But they retained the largest portion of the superstructure of eighteenth-century constitutional ideas. They defended the new government in terms that could be difficult to distinguish from the old.

19. While he avoided the terms, there is abundant evidence that the distinction between the few and the many was still uppermost in Madison's mind. In fact, he still felt some attraction to the idea of founding one branch of a government on numbers, the other on property. See *Federalist* number 54, Cooke, p. 370, and Madison to Caleb Wallace, Aug. 23, 1785, along with Madison to John Brown, Oct., 1788, in *Writings*, II, 171–172; V, 284–288. Noting this, however, we can still insist that he was emancipated far enough from older ideas that the classical polarity was no longer paramount and transcendent. The famous argument of *Federalist* number 10 depends absolutely on the assumption that any polarization into two hostile groups will be impossible in the new Republic because of the diversity of interests.

"It is of great importance," Madison pronounced, "not only to guard the society against the oppression of its rulers, but to guard one part of society against the injustice of the other part. Different interests necessarily exist in different classes of citizens." Some governments protect the minority against the oppressions of the majority by providing for hereditary or self-appointed parts, "creating a will in the community independent of the majority." This proves "precarious security, because a power independent of the society may as well espouse the unjust views of the major as the rightful interests of the minor party, and may possibly be turned against both."[20] Large republics, fortunately, can accomplish the same purpose without encountering a similar risk. The size and social diversity of the United States render it unlikely that the government can be controlled by an oppressive majority.[21] To make it more unlikely still, the Constitution provides for staggered elections of officials who will be dependent in varying degrees on popular opinion, dividing the legislature into branches that will be "by different modes of election and different principles of action as little connected with each other as the nature of their common functions and their common dependence on the society will admit."[22] At the same time, the dependence of every part of the government on popular approval, the careful separation of powers, the elaborate checks and balances, and the residual powers of the states ensure a continuing identity of interests between the rulers and the ruled, preventing a degeneration of the government toward monarchy or aristocracy.[23] Both the equilibrium of the government and the quality of its decisions are secured by causing the different parts of the government to stand "on as different foundations as republican principles will well admit."[24] Madison and the other founders took a justifiable pride in their republican House of Representatives, which was to be elected on as democratic a basis as the most popular branches

20. *Federalist* number 51, Cooke, pp. 351–353.
21. *Federalist* number 10.
22. *Federalist* number 51, Cooke, p. 350.
23. *Federalist* numbers 47–51.
24. *Federalist* number 55, Cooke, p. 377.

of the state legislatures. On the other hand, a happy combination of compromise and purpose seemed to have assured a Senate that might contribute the virtues of wisdom and stability traditionally expected from an aristocratic branch of government, without resort to an undemocratic mode of selection.[25] Finally, the Convention had created in the Presidency a responsible executive whose independence and great powers might secure the benefits, without the dangers, of a monarchy.[26]

Making such revisions in accepted theory as were required by the assumption of a democratic social order and the concept of popular sovereignty, Madison was able, nonetheless, to invoke in defense of the new government nearly the whole of the vast and ancient body of arguments in support of a balanced constitution. Without disparaging his magnificent achievement, it is possible, moreover, to suggest that this accomplishment resulted from a singular ability to reduce to systematic theory an intent that he and his colleagues had kept more or less consciously in mind through all the compromises of the Constitutional Convention. The delegates at Philadelphia were accomplished and pragmatic politicians, trading separate interests and combining tested governmental techniques. But they were also theorists who sought to create a republican variety of balanced government.[27] Born under British rule, they knew by rote the virtues of mixed governments, and they were as much concerned as Adams to incorporate them in their plan. Reared in the Revolution on a diet of opposition writings, they were equally familiar with the dangers to which a balanced constitution would be exposed. Like Adams, they could not escape an inherited conviction that the equilibrium of balanced constitutions is a delicate and fragile thing. Like him, they sought to guard against political decay.

25. *Federalist* numbers 62–63 are Madison's fullest discussion of the Senate.
26. Hamilton defended the executive in *Federalist* numbers 67–77.
27. Although Wood's is the best introduction to the theory of the Constitution, he is not alone in the attempt to reemphasize the theoretical preoccupations of the Convention. See also Paul Eidelberg, *The Philosophy of the American Constitution: A Reinterpretation of the Intentions of the Founding Fathers* (New York: Free Press, 1968).

In modern politics, an accusation that a measure violates a proper separation of the parts of government may fall on muffled ears. The charge retains conventional authority, yet it wholly fails to summon up the range and depth of fears that it suggested to the generation of the founders. Every literate American of the revolutionary generation was familiar with traditional ideas about the degeneration of balanced governments. Remarkably little of the customary language about corruption failed to apply to the new American system. Even for Madison, the parts of the new government were still associated with the traditional combination of democratic, aristocratic, and monarchical virtues. Liberty was still taken to depend on their continued equipoise. Men were still selfish, power still ambitious, one part of government still likely to encroach on the proper province of another. Americans still feared the simple species of government—aristocracy, monarchy, or democracy—and they still associated tyranny with the gradual accumulation of the powers of a government in a single set of hands.

At Philadelphia, the men who framed the Constitution sought assiduously to apply the conclusions of English and American thought and experience to the task of protecting their plan of government from the historical cycle of degeneration. Little time was needed to dispose of the possibility of corruption on the British model, for this was all-but-universally accepted as a threat. The Virginia Resolutions, introduced at the beginning of debates, provided for the ineligibility of representatives and senators for other state or federal offices, and, despite the demurs of Nathaniel Gorham, James Wilson, and Alexander Hamilton, an exclusion of placemen was never in doubt. Controversy centered on the wording, as the delegates attempted to hit upon a balance that would prevent corruption without unduly restricting the eligibility of qualified men to office.[28]

28. The fullest debate on this subject occurred on June 22 and 23, but Farrand's index, *Records*, IV, 111, allows a student to trace its development through the Convention. The final wording reflected a desire to prevent, not only executive influence, but also the proliferation of needless offices by the legislature in order to serve its members'

Of course, the exercise of executive influence on members of the legislature was only one of the ways—although the most notorious—in which the independence of the branches of the government could be undermined, its balance ultimately destroyed. Accordingly, the prohibition of the use of patronage was only one of many safeguards that the delegates wrote into the plan. The two essential, guiding principles of the Constitutional Convention—the principles within whose bounds the compromises were arranged—were the independence of the several branches of the government, or separation of powers, and the continuation of the equipoise between them, which was the purpose of the system of checks and balances. The evidence of the delegates' concern to provide against any deviation from the original equilibrium of the proposed government is so entirely overwhelming that a very few examples should suffice to make the point. The compromises on the manner of electing the President and Senate succeeded, in part, because the delegates were seeking a means of removing the various parts of the legislature in differing degrees from popular opinion, yet hesitated to violate the separation of powers by giving the elections to the lower house. The question of an executive veto on legislation provoked extensive examination of the proper equipoise between the branches. Powers were distributed among the parts of government with careful attention to the maxim of separation of powers, and the delegates tried conscientiously to award each branch sufficient agency in the exercise of the others' functions to assure it the means to protect its own share of the balance—sufficient agency, no more.

In the end, the Federalists were satisfied with the promised stability of the new constitution. During the ratification contest, they often stressed the elaborate safeguards against degeneration.

---

interests: "No Senator or Representative shall, during the time for which he was elected, be appointed to any civil office under the authority of the United States which shall have been created, or the emoluments whereof shall have been increased, during such time; and no person holding any office under the United States shall be a member of either House during his continuance in office" (Article I, section 6, clause 2).

Their opponents, however, were not content. Fearing that the Constitution would prove all too readily susceptible to the corruption that the framers tried so hard to bar, the Antifederalists followed a train of thought that would retain a potent influence for another twenty years.

II

Of major American political movements, Antifederalism is not the easiest to understand. Through the agency of the Confederation Congress, the Constitutional Convention laid before the people a plan for thorough reorganization of the federal government. Different individuals opposed the scheme for contradictory reasons.[29] A bewildering variety of economic, sectional, and personal considerations all affected men's positions. It is also puzzling to reflect that, on its face, the ratification controversy was a struggle between contending social interests, calling forth an intensity of rhetoric seldom equalled in American disputes.[30] Yet opposition to the Constitution disappeared almost as quickly as it rose.

There is no quick solution to the puzzle. For present purposes,

29. Thus, while most Antifederalists objected to replacing the existing league of states with a government that would act directly on the people, James Monroe condemned the Constitution for preserving in the Senate the representation of individual states which had been the central defect of the Confederation. See "Observations on the Constitution," in Stanislaus Murray Hamilton, ed., *The Writings of James Monroe*, 9 vols. (New York: Putnam, 1900–1910), I, appendix 1, especially pp. 333–339. Both Northerners and Southerners argued that the opposite section would be unduly favored by the Constitution, and Antifederalists could not decide whether the majority or the minority would be most endangered. The complexity of Antifederalism has made it possible for historians to arrive at and convincingly defend nearly opposite opinions of the Antifederalist position on democratic government. See Jackson Turner Main, *The Antifederalists: Critics of the Constitution, 1781–1788* (Chicago: Quadrangle Books, 1964), and Cecelia M. Kenyon, "Men of Little Faith: The Anti-Federalists on the Nature of Representative Government," *William and Mary Quarterly*, 12 (1955), 3–46. For a full, chronological account see Robert Allen Rutland, *The Ordeal of the Constitution: The Antifederalists and the Ratification Struggle of 1787–1788* (Norman: University of Oklahoma Press, 1966).

30. Building partly on recognition of the strength of Main's evidence of class conflict in the ratification contest, Wood shows that both sides often pictured the controversy as a struggle between the "better sort" and another group, identified either as the mass of the people or the licentious part of them. See *Creation of the American Republic*, chap. 12, especially pp. 483–499.

however, most of the pieces can be set aside. Without attempting to explore the many other motives that affected every man, we can insist that the specifically announced objections to the structure of the novel plan of government assumed a more coherent pattern than has commonly been seen. The Antifederal response to the new Constitution was heavily conditioned by the heritage of British thought—more heavily, indeed, than was the thought of their opponents. Understanding this we may obtain a new perspective on the party controversy of the years to come.

From the viewpoint of its ideology alone, the rapid demise of Antifederalism no longer seems the hardest problem to resolve. Violent as was the language of the ratification debate, real as was the contest of competing social groups, controversy still was channeled into relatively narrow bounds. While each side charged the other with antirepublican motives, there was, in fact, no serious divergence in fundamental political philosophy. Both sides were liberal, both republican. They agreed that the genius of the people was democratic, and they were equally committed by their public principles to abide by the verdict of the nation. To do so was all the easier for the losers because their objections to the Constitution never reached as far as the underlying principles of governmental structure around which the Convention had ordered its plan. Few Antifederalists denied that an American national government should include a bicameral legislature within a system of balanced and separated powers. Antifederalist objections focused first on the question whether America ought to have a national government, and then on the question whether the one proposed promised sufficient safeguards for republican liberty.[31]

Aside from objections to the absence of a bill of rights, the most persistent Antifederalist criticism of the Constitution was an argument that America was incapable of supporting a

31. A sound opinion of Antifederalist ideas can be formulated from the writings of its leading advocates and from the excellent sampling of less important pieces collected in Cecelia M. Kenyon, ed., *The Antifederalists* (Indianapolis: Bobbs-Merrill, 1966).

genuinely republican government of national extent.[32] During the eighteenth century, particularly through the influence of Montesquieu, republicanism had come to be identified as a species of government best suited to small states. Historical examples of successful republics, notably Venice, Switzerland, and Holland, seemed to conform to this precept, and political logic lent it powerful support. The image of a republic, in this age, was most tellingly conveyed by the word "virtue," which suggested a powerful, communitarian sense of the common good, an individual readiness to sacrifice selfish interest for the interest of the whole. This spirit was naturally associated with small and homogeneous communities, while the principles of strength and stability, which appeared particularly requisite in larger states, were commonly associated with monarchy and aristocracy.

In 1787, America's sense of national identity was rudimentary at best. Economic and social differences between a democratic North and an aristocratic South, an agricultural West and a commercial East, were banalities of conversation. Federalists recognized these differences without undue concern. James Madison found them a source of comfort. But Antifederalists insisted that it was impossible to unite this great and diverse people under one government without oppression of some of its social interests and frequent appeals to military force.[33]

No matter how insistently the Federalists proclaimed that the proposed government was federal rather than entirely national, no matter how carefully they enumerated the residual powers of the people and the states, they were never able to refute this objection. Part of the difficulty lay in the transitional state of the

---

32. On this point see section 2 of Kenyon's introduction to *The Antifederalists*, pp. xxxix-xlvii, and Wood, pp. 499–506.

33. A few good examples, in addition to those below, are *The Writings of Monroe*, I, 314–320; Adams to R. H. Lee, Dec. 3, 1787, *Papers of Samuel Adams*, IV, 324–325; and "Philadelphiensis," in *The Antifederalists*, pp. 69–87. The old fear of standing armies and rule by military force played a significant part in Antifederalist arguments. The Federalists, of course, had a resounding rebuttal: a confederation had *no* way to enforce its decisions except military force. See Hamilton's *Federalist* number 8, Cooke, pp. 24–28.

theory of sovereignty, which led opponents to approach the problem of federalism from different points and along nonconvergent lines. The Antifederalists clung to the classical theory of sovereignty, which denied the possibility of two sovereign authorities in the same state—the infamous monster *imperium in imperio*. They were convinced that, sooner or later, the federal authority would swallow the states, leaving the people to suffer the tyranny of a consolidated government. More clearly grasping the newer concept of popular sovereignty, the Federalists were less inclined to see a paradox in the idea of two parallel authorities exercising different powers on the same sovereign people. But conflicting concepts of sovereignty were not the only reason why opponents often missed each other's point. The difference over sovereignty was thoroughly entangled in a wider theoretical divergence that saw the two sides argue generally from different matrixes of thought.

Antifederalists were generally inclined to picture a more profound, if not a broader, division of interests in American society than some of their opponents did. Indeed, this conception of a profound division of interests was a fundamental reason for their fear of a national republic. The Antifederalists believed that a national legislature small enough to provide a rational government would prove incompatible with a free and adequate representation of all the American people. As their best-remembered spokesman put it, "A full and equal representation is that which possesses the same interests, feelings, opinions, and views the people themselves would were they all assembled." But this would be the case only if they were represented by "men from among themselves and genuinely like themselves."[34] True interest representation was admittedly impractical, since it would swell a legislature into a mob. Yet it was patently impossible for

34. "Letters from the Federal Farmer," in Forrest McDonald, ed., *Empire and Nation* (Englewood Cliffs, N.J.: Prentice-Hall, 1962), pp. 98, 146. With nearly every other twentieth-century historian, McDonald attributes these letters to Richard Henry Lee. Recently, however, Gordon Wood has demonstrated good cause to doubt the attribution. See "The Authorship of the *Letters from the Federal Farmer*," *William and Mary Quarterly*, 31 (1974), 299–308.

any one man accurately to reflect and adequately to represent all the trades, interests, and religions of Delaware—as the Constitution would provide—or for any ten to stand in place of all the planters, mechanics, and small farmers of Virginia.

The difficulty, as the Antifederalists saw it, was not so much the diversity of America's socio-economic groups as the probability that none of the common people at all would win a seat in the federal legislature. Unless the lower house of the legislature was expanded to an unmanageable size—an alternative they also rejected—the vast electorates would invariably choose their representatives from among the socially prominent. In electoral districts spreading over several counties and including twenty or thirty thousand souls, no mechanic or small farmer could hope to compete with the natural aristocracy of planters, lawyers, and merchants. For all their populism, the Antifederalists rivaled John Adams in their fear that the people's natural deference to the rich and the well-born would result in an elective aristocracy.[35] Federalists, who inclined to the newer, agency theory of representation, took pride in the democratic House of Representatives and saw in the large numbers of the electorate a guarantee against the rotten boroughs and electoral corruption prevalent in England.[36] Antifederalists, who held to the concept of actual representation, saw in the small numbers of the lower house a fertile field for influence and bribery and only "the shadow" of democratic representation.[37]

35. For some excellent and geographically scattered expressions of the fear of deference and a small representation see, in addition to the "Federal Farmer," George Bryan ("Centinel"), "John DeWitt," and Melancton Smith in *The Antifederalists*, pp. 1–25, 108, 382–389.

36. For example, Hamilton's speech in the New York Convention, Harold C. Syrett and Jacob E. Cooke, eds., *The Papers of Alexander Hamilton* (New York: Columbia University Press, 1961–), V, 54–55, and Madison's speech in the Virginia Convention, *Writings*, V, 158–159.

37. The phrase was George Mason's, but the belief was widely shared. And the fears of a small representation and corruption went hand in hand. Thus, the "Federal Farmer" said that the proposed constitution would make it "extremely difficult to secure the people against the fatal effects of corruption. . . . Where there is a small representation a sufficient number to carry any measure may with ease be influenced by bribes, offices, and civilities" (McDonald, p. 109). See also pp. 146, 149–150, 171.

Moreover, many of the sharpest critics of the Constitution still associated the people with the lower house of legislature, still identified the lower house as the particular preserve of the many in a government. The Federalists were not themselves emancipated totally from this heritage of the theory of mixed government. With their newer concept of representation, however, the Federalists were less inclined than their opponents to insist on a House of Representatives that would be filled with common people. In the Constitutional Convention, Wilson, Madison, and others persistently denied that any single branch of the new legislature could be identified with democracy. And day by day, in the short period of the ratification contest, the Federalists' insistence on a newer theory took on added clarity and force. They were compelled to insist on the democratic character and origins of all the parts of the proposed government, for the Antifederalists insisted on approaching it as a mixed government of fairly classic mold.[38]

In their effort to defeat the ratification of the Constitution, the Antifederalists called upon every variety of local prejudice, every sort of fear. Giving pattern to their blasts, however, was a more substantial line of criticism followed with remarkable consistency by Antifederalists from Maine to Georgia. This criticism was suggested by the superficial similarity of the new plan of government to the mixed government of England and by traditional modes of criticism of the English form. Confronted with the Constitution, Antifederalists looked first at the "democratic" part of the new government. They concluded that the small, unrepresentative lower house would be a poor reflection of the people. Worse, it seemed entirely likely that the more aristocratic and monarchical branches would entirely overbalance the democratic

38. Only by recognizing the extent to which they were still thinking in terms of mixed government is it possible to see how Antifederalists such as Elbridge Gerry, who made some of the strongest attacks on democracy in the Constitutional Convention, could seemingly reverse themselves so radically as to attack the finished plan as undemocratic. It was perfectly consistent to abhor simple democracy and yet to insist on a genuinely democratic branch in a balanced government.

part. The smaller, more prestigious, more distant Senate and the powerful, single executive, linked as they were in the exercise of so many important functions, would combine to overbear the assembly and reduce the only branch which flowed immediately from the people to a helpless sham. The balance of the Constitution was tilted from the start, and the cooperation of President and Senate required by its numerous violations of a separation of powers, together with remaining opportunities for executive influence on the representatives, assured the eventual destruction of its democratic aspects. One writer called the Constitution "a many-headed monster of such motley mixture that its enemies cannot trace a feature of democratic or republican extract, nor have its friends the courage to denominate [it] a monarchy, an aristocracy, or an oligarchy."[39] Another reasoned that "this government will commence in a moderate aristocracy; it is at present impossible to foresee whether it will, in its operation, produce a monarchy or a corrupt, oppressive aristocracy; it will most probably vibrate some years between the two and then terminate in the one or the other."[40]

The Antifederalists, in sum, insisted that the Constitutional Convention had concocted an improper mixture: a balanced government without a truly democratic part. Moreover, the framers, in their violations of a proper separation of the parts of government, had introduced the killing poison of corruption into the very structure of the plan. Flawed in the beginning, the Constitution must grow worse with time. It would inevitably degenerate in the direction of the simple forms of government that had been given undue portions of the power.

39. "Observations on the New Constitution and on the Federal and State Conventions," in Paul Leicester Ford, ed., *Pamphlets on the Constitution of the United States* (Brooklyn: n.p., 1888), p. 8. Ford attributed this pamphlet to Elbridge Gerry. It was probably the work of Mercy Otis Warren. See Charles Warren, "Elbridge Gerry, James Warren, Mercy Warren, and the Ratification of the Federal Constitution in Massachusetts," Massachusetts Historical Society *Proceedings*, 64 (1932), 143–164.

40. George Mason, "Objections to the Proposed Federal Constitution," in *The Antifederalists*, p. 195.

But was this, after all, exactly what the framers wanted? As they analyzed its weaknesses, the Antifederalists began to wonder if the inclination of the Constitution toward monarchy or aristocracy was wholly accidental. Visions of conspiracy, we should remember, were endemic in the revolutionary years. In the context of traditional ideas, social and political events were seldom thought of as having causes apart from conscious purpose, and the purposes of any group organized to have an impact on government were automatically thought of as malignant. Suggested by prevailing modes of criticism of the English form of government, Antifederalist suspicions directed them to find, as English writers always found, a villain of the piece.

The Federalists, moreover, fairly asked for a conspiratorial analysis of their motives. Suspicions had been thoroughly aroused before their opponents ever saw the product of the gathering at Philadelphia, and subsequent events confirmed the early fears. The members of the Constitutional Convention debated in strict secrecy, exceeded the authority their states had given them, and produced a document shocking in the degree of change that it proposed. Then, in support of a plan of government suspiciously similar to the old, British form, they went to the people with an unshakeable opposition to prior amendments or the calling of a second convention, an offensive haste in pushing the process of ratification, and tactics of questionable legality in some of the states. When these actions were added to the undisguised antipopulism of some of the Federalist leaders, their opponents had all the evidence they needed for charges that the self-styled "better sort" had secretly launched an aristocratic conspiracy against American liberty.

The Antifederalists very generally identified the Constitution as a halfway step in a conspiracy by the aristocratic part of the American people to revive the tyranny of mixed monarchy or to introduce the horrors of aristocracy and despotism to the United States. Unable to have their way at a single stroke, the argument contended, the few had planned in secret and were forcing upon the people by means of scare tactics and illegal actions a plan of government deliberately contrived to steal their liberty.[41] Constitutional violations of a separation of powers and the improper balance between the parts of the new government, with their incentives to an inappropriate cooperation between the branches, would in time assure the withering away of its slight republican aspects. At that day, the favored few, whose immediate objects were the lucrative offices of the new government, would be free to assume the hereditary titles to which they aspired, and the American commons would be reduced to the miserable level of European "slaves."[42]

III

Despite their apocalyptic warnings against the new Constitution, most of its opponents determined to make the best of the nation's decision to ratify the plan. A few sulked in their states for a time. Some continued to discuss the possibility of forcing radical amendments. Once ratification was a fact, however, most Antifederalists found themselves on different mental terrain. The classical-republican foundations of American constitutional thought taught that a constitution, once established, changed only for the worse. The accepted task for friends of liberty was neither counterrevolution nor reform. It was to guard against social and political degeneration, to force a strict adherence to the original principles of a government, to see that things became no worse. The revolutionary generation inhabited a mental universe that contained no familiar ways of thinking about progressive constitutional improvement, that encouraged men to think that constitutional change, like water, always flowed downhill. Partly

41. For a particularly clever attack along this line see "Montezuma," ibid., pp. 61–67.

42. Perhaps because of their long experience with group-conscious constitutional warfare and because of the roughshod tactics of Federalists there, the Pennsylvania Antifederalists collected in Kenyon were especially prone to charges of conspiracy. One of the best short examples of the accusation is the "Address . . . of the Minority of the Convention . . . of Pennsylvania," ibid., pp. 27–60. But the charge was ubiquitous. For other good examples see McDonald, p. 135; Ford, pp. 5–6; and Luther Martin in Kenyon, pp. 169–171.

for this reason, the Antifederalists did not persist as an organized movement determined to overthrow the government they had opposed.[43] Nor, in my opinion, were they rapidly transformed into Jeffersonian Republicans bent on resisting the new order in a subtler fashion. Attempts to demonstrate a continuity of personnel between the Antifederalists and the first Republicans ultimately come to ground on two impassable bars: the paucity of evidence about the political affiliations of men who were not leaders of opinion, and the generalization-defying exceptions among the men who were. Of the best known Antifederalists, some acquired a notoriety during the 1790s as trimmers between the parties. Several others became Federalists. Of the great Republican leaders, not one had stood in the front ranks of Antifederalism.[44] For the most part, historians now agree that the Constitution's victory introduced new issues and led to a realignment that made the distinctions of the ratification contest obsolete.[45]

43. For a fuller and more systematic discussion of the origins of constitutional literalism see Lance Banning, "Republican Ideology and the Triumph of the Constitution, 1789–1793," *William and Mary Quarterly*, 31 (1974), 167–188.

44. Among leading Antifederalists, Gerry became an Adams Federalist in the 1790s and, eventually, a Republican Vice President. Randolph, who supported ratification after refusing to sign the Constitution, preserved his reputation for trimming through most of the 1790s. Lee died before party alignments had solidified, although he lived long enough to help lead the "high-flyers" during the organization of the new government. Patrick Henry, Samuel Chase, and Luther Martin all became Federalists in time. Madison, of course, had led the movement for a new Constitution. Of the other Republican leaders, Gallatin and Monroe had been Antifederalists, although the former was unknown at the time and Monroe's Antifederalism was always moderate and intellectually distinctive. Jefferson at first disliked several features of the plan, but declared himself on balance in favor of it, insisting that he was much less an Antifederalist than a Federalist.

45. The relationship between the parties of the 1790s and the parties of the ratification contest is very much a matter of debate. Two of the best arguments for a continuity of personnel are Alfred F. Young, *The Democratic Republicans of New York: The Origins, 1763–1797* (Chapel Hill: University of North Carolina Press, 1967), and Norman K. Risjord, "The Evolution of Political Parties in Virginia, 1782–1800," *Journal of American History*, 60 (1974), 961–984. On the other side, see Joseph Charles, *The Origins of the American Party System: Three Essays* (Chapel Hill: University of North Carolina Press, 1956), Noble E. Cunningham, Jr., *The Jeffersonian Republicans: The Formation of Party Organization, 1789–1801* (Chapel Hill: University of North Carolina Press, 1957), and Paul Goodman, *The Democratic-Republicans of Massachusetts: Politics in a Young Republic* (Cambridge, Mass.: Harvard University Press, 1964). I agree with those who conclude that ratification introduced a new situation, a

Still, there remains one sense in which the origins of Jeffersonian Republicanism were undeniably Antifederalist. The extreme suspicions generated in the ratification controversy did not abruptly disappear in 1789. Distrust of Federalist motives, doubts about the structure and stability of the new form of government, and fearful expectations for the future—all following from some of the strongest currents in Anglo-American political thought—had been planted deeply in individual minds. These doubts survived to guide the conduct of some members of the First Federal Congress. They were the seeds from which persistent opposition to the new administration eventually grew.

Only in a limited degree was the meeting of the First Congress really a fresh start. The members assembled in New York to complete an unfinished plan for a government that would, in their opinion, settle the fate of liberty, not only in America, but in the world. Part of a generation enchanted with origins and the making of history, these legislators were convinced that the slightest error in the foundations they were completing could have enormous consequences in the space of ten or a hundred years. And yet the Constitutional Convention had left it up to them to create executive departments, establish a federal judiciary, provide for steady revenues, and grapple with the nearly crushing problem of the revolutionary debt. Some of the members had opposed the Constitution, distrusted the intentions of their Federalist colleagues, and intended to watch the completion of the plan with conscientious suspicion. All the members worked in full awareness that amendments must be drafted and every forward step taken with the greatest care if the doubts and fears of large numbers of the people were to be put to rest. Each member acted in the light of personal experience, state and sectional considerations, and other motives no historian could hope to trace. Each acted also, though, on the basis of his share in the

---

new set of issues, and a significant realignment of political groups, although I also believe that Young and Risjord have shown that Antifederalists overwhelmingly became Republicans. The Federalists of 1787 divided more sharply after ratification and produced leaders for both parties, although a majority of those who voted for the Constitution probably became Federalists in the 1790s.

collective wisdom and accumulated nonsense of eighteenth-century thought.

The Federalists in the first session of Congress, ably led by James Madison, meant to complete the strong central government outlined in the Constitution.[46] For years their fears had concentrated on the overbearing power of the lower houses in the states and on the states' supremacy within the federal system. Behind these evils, they detected an abiding popular affection for the people's closest representatives and local governments. Experiences of the last ten years had demonstrated beyond doubt that dangers to American liberty proceded overwhelmingly from the forces of localism and an overbearing democracy. The framers of the Constitution had adopted every conceivable device to protect the people from their rulers. The present task was to resist the tendency for the people's democratic sentiments to emasculate the national government or to confide all its authority to the House of Representatives.[47]

At every step in their efforts to secure the independence of the executive from legislative domination, however, and to defend the sphere of federal authority against encroachments by the states, the Federalists aroused a vocal opposition. Led in the House by Elbridge Gerry of Massachusetts, John Page of Virginia, and James Jackson of Georgia, represented in the Senate by Pennsylvania's William Maclay, this opposition was not a congressional party, united over a broad range of issues, so much as an identifiable band of men who tended to draw together on

46. A good general account of the first session of Congress is John C. Miller, *The Federalist Era, 1789–1801* (New York: Harper & Row, 1960), chaps. 1–2.

47. This is well-known Hamiltonian reasoning, as in *Federalist* number 17. It is less well known that, for a time at least, all the great Republican leaders also expected threats to the stability of the new government to come from this direction. Discussing the tendency of power to encroach on liberty, Madison told Jefferson, "I must own that I see no tendency in our governments to danger on that side" (*Writings*, V, 273–274). See also "Observations on the Constitution," in *Writings of Monroe*, I, 327, and Jefferson to Madison, March 15, 1789, in Julian P. Boyd, ed., *The Papers of Thomas Jefferson* (Princeton: Princeton University Press, 1950–), XIV, 661: "The executive in our government is not the sole, it is scarcely the principal object of my jealousy. The tyranny of the legislatures is the most formidable at present and will be for long years. That of the executive will come in its time, but it will be at a remote period."

questions of basic constitutional importance to challenge the conclusions of Madison and other Federal leaders. Whether or not they genuinely accepted Antifederalist warnings of a conspiracy against liberty, these members plainly acted on a conviction that, with ratification of the Constitution, America had reached or even passed the point at which federal power and checks on democracy were still compatible with republican liberty. In contrast to the Federalists, they feared a further concentration of authority in the less democratic branches of the federal government, and they meant to check this recent trend by defending the sphere of state authority and the powers of the House of Representatives. They brought with them to New York the Antifederalist fears of monarchy, aristocracy, and corruption. These they kept alive and passed in strident form to the foes of Hamiltonian finance.[48]

One of the first decisions to confront the new Congress touched on all the fears and expectations gathered in the ratification contest. This was the question whether the Houses of Congress should respond to Washington's inaugural message and, if so, in what style they should address the President. One group of men, strongest in the Senate, where they were led by John Adams and Richard Henry Lee, urged a princely title for the

48. Historians are mostly agreed that the Federal Congress was free of persistent parties until after the appearance of the Hamiltonian Program. In this they confirm the contemporary opinion of Fisher Ames, whose letters to his Boston friend, George Richards Minot, are as good a record of the first House as Maclay's famous *Journal* is of the first Senate. Ames continually complained about the House's slowness and attention to trivia, but he was impressed from the first with the quality of his colleagues and their freedom from faction. "There is less party spirit, less of the acrimony of pride when disappointed of success, less personality, less intrigue, cabal, management, or cunning than I ever saw in a public assembly." Repeatedly, however, Ames singled out for criticism this group of "violent republicans," these "new lights in politics who would not make the law but the people king, who would have a government all checks, who are more solicitous to . . . expiate upon some high-sounding principle of republicanism than to protect property, cement the union, and perpetuate liberty." The Virginians in particular, he complained, "see evils in embryo, are terrified with possibilities, and are eager to establish rights and to explain principles to such a degree that you would think them enthusiasts and triflers." He remained willing to credit the group with good intentions, but his patience was tried by "those who modestly assume the rank of champions of liberty." See Seth Ames, ed., *Works of Fisher Ames*, 2 vols. (Boston: Little, Brown, 1854), I, 31–71.

President, perhaps His Highness or His High Mightiness.[49] They were reasoning from the credible assumption that a high tone in the federal government would be necessary to inspire affection, pride, and a requisite awe in a particularistic people. Fortunately for the country, colleagues in the House refused to take the matter quite so seriously. As it was, the issue was not resolved before it provoked the most extreme suspicions.

Since debates in the upper house were held in private during the first years of the new government, it is impossible to recover the complete story of the controversy over titles in the Senate, where the issue started, where it occupied the major portion of the members' time between April 13 and May 14, and where a majority was in favor of a high style of address. But the reactions of the House and the people were recorded in the contemporary press. To some men, it is clear, the desire for high-sounding titles seemed a clear confirmation of Antifederalist fears. In the House, as Fisher Ames recalled, "not a soul said a word *for* titles. But the zeal of these folks could not have risen higher in case of contradiction."[50] Josiah Parker and George Clymer opposed titles as inconsistent with democracy, Thomas Tucker warned that the people would see in titles a tendency to revive the government they had rejected in the Revolution, while Aedanus Burke and John Page went so far as to caution the House that titles were in fact first steps toward monarchy and aristocracy.[51] In the event, the moderating influence of Madison and other friends of strong government in the House prevailed over the "high-flyers" in the Senate, and Washington was not cursed with a princely prefix. But the debate over the tone of the new government raged on in the press and among the people for months and years to come.

49. I think it significant that Lee should have led this group. It suggests, again, that many Antifederalists were at heart attached to older principles of mixed government, much as Adams was. Some of the considerations involved in the argument over protocol are discussed in James H. Hutson, "John Adams' Title Campaign," *New England Quarterly*, 41 (1968), 30–39.

50. *Works*, I, 36.

51. The debate can be found in Joseph Gales, comp., *The Debates and Proceedings in the Congress of the United States*, 42 vols. (Washington, D.C.: Gales & Seaton, 1834–1856), I, 332–337. This compilation is conventionally cited as *Annals of Congress*.

In itself, the battle over forms of address seems more amusing than important, as some contemporaries saw. In retrospect, however, it had considerable importance both as the opening chorus of a long public lament over the "manners" of the new government and as the first of several issues during the first session of Congress to stir half-hidden fears that contemporaries of every persuasion had as a heritage of old opposition and recent Antifederalist thought. These fears were an inescapable inheritance of every American of the revolutionary age, and it was not necessary for a man to have been an Antifederalist for them to have an effect. On the contrary, in at least two cases their effect was most striking in men of Federalist persuasion.

William Maclay, for example, was a Pennsylvania Federalist at the beginning of 1789, though an irascible democrat who came to the first Senate with a mind molded in a classic opposition pattern.[52] From his first days in the Senate, Maclay opposed any attempt to move beyond the strict words of the Constitution. He arrived in New York with a fear of monarchy, he saw every "high-toned" measure as a move in that direction, and he worried continually about executive influence. Early in the session he began to divide his colleagues into "courtiers," who favored high-toned measures and curried executive favor, and independents, among whose numbers he proudly (and somewhat masochistically) ranked himself.[53] The controversy over titles led Maclay to reflect that while some of the revolutionaries had wanted to abolish all the panoply of hereditary forms, others had only wanted to transfer the crown to America, where they could enjoy its gifts.[54] By July, he had identified a "court party," with Adams at its head, who were working for executive power, high-toned government, and a consolidation of the states. He already suspected that this group was using corrupt means to

52. Mark his early aversion to Lee as a "notorious Antifederalist," in Edgar S. Maclay, ed., *The Journal of William Maclay: United States Senator from Pennsylvania, 1789–1791* (New York: Albert & Charles Boni, 1927), p. 6.

53. Ibid. Maclay took inordinate pride in his crochety independence, yet he was also markedly sensitive to any imagined slight from those in power.

54. Ibid., pp. 9–12.

secure votes.[55] For some time he tried to fathom Washington's position in the drama, finally deciding that "the greatest man in the world" was a passive instrument of a plot. Using the tested tools of executive influence and bribery, "the creatures that surround him would place a crown on his head that they may have the handling of its jewels."[56]

No one, to my knowledge, moved as rapidly as Maclay from an early concern over the desire for a high-toned government to a thoroughgoing condemnation of a conspiracy to corrupt the infant state. But the controversy over titles touched off fears of a similar nature in a number of minds. It is remarkable, for example, how quickly Benjamin Rush, the revolutionary physician, shifted from the staunchest Federalism to an intense concern with governmental and national degeneration. For years Rush had been a leader of the conservative opponents of Pennsylvania's radical, revolutionary constitution. He attended the Pennsylvania ratifying convention, wrote in support of the Constitution, opposed a bill of rights as unnecessary, and insisted that extreme democracy posed the greatest threat to American liberty.[57] By June 1789, however, his worries fell decisively on the other side:

The citizens of Pennsylvania are truly republican and will not readily concur in a government which has begun so soon to ape the corruption of the British Court, conveyed to it through the impure channel of the

55. Ibid., pp. 106–114. Note that Maclay identified "republican" with "independent" (or "country?") and opposed this group to a "court" or "monarchical" party. It was ironic that Maclay and many others should have put Adams at the head of a court party, even though he asked for it. For Adams had been one of several Americans to predict that "we shall very soon have parties formed—a court and a country party—and these parties will have names given them. One party . . . will support the President and his measures and ministers, the other will oppose them." In any such struggle, Adams' sympathies lay with the country. See Adams to Roger Sherman, June 20, 1789, in *Works*, VI, 434–435.

56. *Journal*, pp. 119–120. "For some time past . . . I could see how the watches went, but I did not know before the way they were wound up." Now it is apparent they are wound by executive influence on the members of Congress. And influence "is neither more nor less than corruption" whether it comes through "court favor, loans, jobs, lottery tickets, contracts, offices" or bribes. "Walpole was a villain. What, then, must be the man that follows his footsteps?"

57. See especially his letter to David Ramsay of March or April, 1788, which he circulated widely at the time as a statement of his position. *Letters*, I, 453–455.

city of New York. . . . There is more *known*, *said*, and *felt* upon this
subject than is proper to be communicated or than will be believed
while Congress is perfumed with British incense in New York.

Why should we accelerate the progress of our government towards
monarchy? Every part of the conduct of the Americans tends to it.[58]

In light of recent Antifederalist warnings, the attempt to secure a title for the President seemed significant in itself. It acquired additional significance, however, as it gradually came to
seem a part of an undemocratic, even antidemocratic, pattern of
high government salaries, extravagant entertainments, and
"courtly" Presidential levees. By the last half of 1789, the correspondence columns of newspapers such as the Boston *Independent Chronicle*, which had supported the Constitution and
avoided criticism of the new government during the first half of
the year, included increasing numbers of letters warning against
the dangerous drift of affairs and often suggesting the presence of
a plot behind it.[59] To growing numbers scattered through the
country, the desire of the high-flyers to set a courtly tone for the
government indicated a distressing trend in federal affairs.

Back in the House, not long after the debate on titles, the
representatives embarked on the task of creating the executive
departments authorized by the Constitution. Arguments on this
issue are especially interesting to follow because they plainly
revealed the members' uncertainty about the nature of the new
system, as well as their inherited expectations about the system's
future. At issue first was the question of who should have the
authority to remove undesirable executive officials. Both sides in
this disagreement were chiefly concerned to assure a responsible
executive, but they differed significantly on the question of
means. Madison and his supporters argued that vesting the removal power in the President alone would protect the separation
of powers while ensuring that the whole executive, through its
head, could be held responsible for its conduct. Advocates for

58. To John Adams, June 4, 1789, ibid., pp. 513–514.
59. See particularly the pieces signed, "A.," August 6, 1789; "A Real Republican,"
August 13, 1789; and "Junius," October 8, 1789.

Senate concurrence in the exercise of the removal power usually supported their case by appealing to the language of the Constitution on the appointment of executive officers, but Theodorick Bland hinted at the sources of their thought when he insisted that only a concurrent exercise of the removal power could ensure that officers would be responsible to the legislature, not wholly dependent on a President with monarchical powers of changing ministries.[60]

As the argument developed, the crux of the controversy became clear, and it was remarkably reminiscent of the ratification debate on the nature of the new government. At every stage Madison and his fellow advocates of a strong government insisted that clear responsibility and a proper separation of powers required a concentration of executive authority. They believed that the new system demanded a dismissal of outmoded fears in favor of new ideas and the "advantages arising from energy, system, and responsibility." Like the Antifederalists, however, Madison's opponents were unable to clear their minds of British precedents or to dismiss the maxims of opposition thought. They could not clearly distinguish a President from a king, and they retained a potent fear of an irresponsible ministry.

Nowhere were these fears more prominent than in the debate over organization of a Treasury Department, the traditional seat of British prime ministers.[61] Elbridge Gerry stood alone in questioning the wisdom of conferring the Treasury on a single head, but he evidently touched important fears when he warned against the danger of creating a ministry along British lines. Powerful, single offices of the type his colleagues envisioned, Gerry predicted, would erect around the President a set of men able to govern in his name. "An oligarchy will be confirmed upon the ruins of the democracy."[62]

60. *Annals of Congress*, I, 387–399.
61. Ibid., pp. 400–412.
62. Ibid., pp. 400–404. It was in large part this fear of a ministry which had led Antifederalists such as Mason and Clinton to desire an executive council. See Kenyon, especially p. 304.

Gerry lost his bid for a triple-headed Department of the Treasury, but found considerable support for his fears. James Jackson of Georgia, perhaps the most fervid democrat in the First Congress, advanced a similar warning against the rise of a ministry and its attendant corruptions. When the House reached the point of creating a Secretary of State, he pleaded again for the members to assert some control:

Are we then to have all the officers the mere creatures of the President? This thirst of power will introduce a Treasury bench into the House, and we shall have ministers obtrude upon us to govern and direct the measures of the legislature and to support the influence of their master. . . . I suppose these circumstances must take place because they have taken place in other countries. The executive power falls to the ground in England if it cannot be supported by the Parliament; therefore, a high game of corruption is played.[63]

Fears of a ministry and of the rise of ministerial influence were plainly present in a sizable group of representatives. Federalists might object, not for the first time or the last, that English experience was irrelevant to the American government. Fisher Ames might mock the cassandras, writing that "the champions of liberty drew their swords, talked blank verse about treasury influence, a ministry," and so on.[64] In the case of the Treasury, nevertheless, the old fears had a lasting effect on the organization of the new government. Of all the cabinet members, only the Secretary of the Treasury was specifically charged to report directly to the Congress, and he alone was denied the right to approach the Congress on his own initiative. The considerations behind these provisions were explicit. John Page objected to permitting the Treasury an initiative in approaching Congress because it would "create an undue influence within these walls . . . thus laying a foundation for an aristocracy or a detestable monarchy." Gerry warned that, once established, powerful ministers would be distinguished by insignia, "court favor," and

63. Ibid., p. 506.
64. *Works*, I, 56.

patronage. And Samuel Livermore cautioned against threatening the independence of the branches of the government and establishing "tenets subversive of the liberties of my country."[65]

There is a danger, to be sure, of exaggerating the size and importance of this Whiggish opposition in the first session of Congress or of suggesting that all their speeches were consistently or constantly along these lines. These members were an inconstant and small minority, outargued and outvoted by the Madisonian Federalists on nearly every point. They were generally ignored in the press. They were significant, not for what they accomplished, but for the way they expressed their oppositon to Federalist plans, for what they revealed about a set of expectations present among an important part of the people as the new government went into effect, and for what their words suggested about a powerful inclination present in the minds of men who had been Federalists and Antifederalists alike. A sizable group of Congressmen came to New York in what is best described as a "Country" frame of mind. On issues that seemed likely to affect the constitutional relationship of rulers and ruled or the balance between the parts of the new government—titles, salaries, a bill of rights, the structure of the executive, and the popular instruction of representatives—they drew together to warn against a likely degeneration of the new government. They anticipated this degeneration. They expected it to follow a familiar pattern cut out overseas.

In the passage from England to America, the language about degeneration had undergone some changes, as we might expect. But the rhetoric of eighteenth-century British oppositionists was perfectly recognizable in its new dress. Libertarians in the First Congress, like Antifederalists before them, warned against aristocracy and monarchy, rather than despotism. By 1789, however, tyranny and hereditary government were interchangeable terms in most American minds. Democracy had introduced a whole new range of worries for American thinkers, yet American

65. *Annals of Congress*, I, 616–632.

attacks on titles and on courtly Presidential levees are easily related to traditional concerns with a depravity of manners that could spread from the government throughout the nation. Most importantly, perhaps, the old and always-central fear of a degeneration of the governmental balance through encroachment by its executive part, with all of its attendant ideas about influence and corruption, remained unchanged, although Americans were vague as yet about the forms this threat would take.

With each new issue, nonetheless, the rhetoric of the "Country" Congressmen became more strident, more conspiratorial. In direct proportion to the success of Madison and his friends in completing their plan for a strong government and reconciling most of the nation to the new federal system, there grew an undercurrent of alarm. As yet, the alarm was concentrated among a small band in the House and Senate, but it was stirring in the press and in individual minds across the country. The fuse was laid. And Alexander Hamilton was ready with the match.

CHAPTER 5

The Rise of Opposition

FOR more than fifty years after the onset of the quarrel that led to independence, a single problem served as fulcrum for much of American political thought. In origin or in consequence, nearly every important question for political decision touched upon the larger issue of the maintenance of liberty in a popular state. Sooner or later, debate turned upon this subject, and the participants were likely to reason from one of two related patterns of concern that every literate American had as a heritage of eighteenth-century thought. From classical and British exponents of the theory of balanced government, Americans had learned that liberty was often endangered by its own excess. From addenda to the theory by English Whigs and oppositionists, Americans had inherited, as well, a rather different concern with the corruption of free governments by ministerial influence and the drive for power of their executive parts. These patterns of concern were threads in a single fabric. Both were commonly present in most American minds. At different times, however, one thread or the other permitted a more compelling explanation of political and social events.

Between 1765 and 1776 an ideology derived from the concerns of English oppositionists dominated American thought. It justified colonial resistance, helped define a national character, and contributed fundamentally to American constitutional ideas. Later, as the circumstances of the Confederation period reminded men of different dangers, attention turned to older fears of the destruction of free states by popular license and anarchy. Ratification of the Constitution marked a temporary predominance of classical fears of an excess of liberty, but concern about corrupting influence and governmental power persisted in the Antifederal critique. Establishment of a new government did not immediately alter these concerns.

Ideologically, the Federalists of the 1790s held to the dominant opinion of 1789 that republican government in America was most endangered by popular license, selfishness, and localism. Events of the decade were easily construed as additional confirmation of this idea. Their opponents, on the other hand, soon turned to a modified version of eighteenth-century opposition ideology for an understanding of their discontents. Years of revolutionary exhortations had induced in many Americans of the early 1790s a hypersensitive preoccupation with the incursions of power on liberty. Close familiarity with the maxims that had shaped the Revolution and suffused Antifederalist attacks on the new Constitution had instructed men in the subtlest signs of conspiratorial purpose, the earliest indications of constitutional decay. More than a few Americans expected constitutional degeneration, and they thought they knew the warning signals of decline. These ideological circumstances help explain the exaggerated fear of a "high-toned" government with which some men watched the inauguration of the new republic. They also help explain the hysterical fears and fantastic predictions that greeted the program of Hamiltonian finance. By the end of 1789, variations on old opposition fears had begun to appear in private correspondence, legislative speeches, and the public press. In the controversy over Hamiltonian finance, these worries spread throughout the country and coalesced into a systematic condemnation of Federalist government and its impact on republican life.

I

Aggravated by the campaign for a high-toned government, by the Federalists' social style, and by the success of the friends of a strong executive in the previous session, democratic fears of aristocracy and Antifederalist suspicions of a design to subvert republican government were rising in pitch as the members assembled in New York for the second session of Congress. It is hard to imagine how, by deliberate intent, Alexander Hamilton's economic program for the new republic could have been better calculated to exacerbate these fears. His plans for the funding of the revolutionary debt, federal assumption of state obligations, creation of a national bank, and governmental encouragement of American manufactures were not only a catalyst for sectional confrontation. They seemed an excellent confirmation of persistent Antifederalist suspicions of an engulfing federal power. More than that, they inevitably brought to mind the entire system of eighteenth-century English governmental finance, with all the consequences that entailed for minds shaped by British opposition thought. Coming in conjunction with the high style of the new government, the antipopulistic pronouncements of some of its supporters, and measures such as an excise tax and a professional army, the Hamiltonian program might as well have been designed to awaken specific expectations about the course and nature of governmental decay that were never very far beneath the surface of revolutionary minds.

As the full scope of the Federalist program for the young republic gradually became apparent in the years after 1789, growing numbers of Americans concluded that the infant nation was developing, within a few brief years, the whole extent and reach of the social and governmental corruption that had crept into English life in the course of the eighteenth century, destroying English freedom. To William Maclay and increasingly to others—old Federalists and Antifederalists alike—it came to seem that Hamilton was an American Robert Walpole, a prime minister who was deliberately creating a corrupted following in the legislature, a ministerial cohort that would subvert the popular will and destroy representative government. Calling itself "Republican," a persistent opposition to Hamilton and the Federalist program had begun to spread from the capital throughout the country by the end of 1792. In its formation, growth, and program, this party was dependent to an important and unrecognized degree on an Americanization of eighteenth-century opposition thought.

Of course, neither the full scope of the Hamiltonian program nor the ultimate response of its opponents was apparent all at once. In Hamilton's mind, however, funding, assumption, a national bank, and government encouragement of native manufactures were inseparable parts of a carefully reasoned plan for establishing the economic future and the political character of the new republic. No part of this program was simply a pragmatic response to a specific problem. Each was an integral part of a great vision of the American future. Little that Hamilton did during his years in office was done apart from his calculation of the present and future place of America in the world. Hamilton's lifelong quest was for glory, and the most productive years of his search for lasting fame were guided by his desire to prepare his infant nation for a future as a great imperial power. To his mind, this end required the avoidance for the present of any confrontation with British power, while America constructed a strong central government and bases for a national strength that could rival Britain's own. Hamilton's ideal was a great republic, and his model for greatness was Britain. He realized that Britain's strength rested on commerce, manufacturing, a sound currency, and the world's best system of public finance. He meant to make America a match.[1]

In earlier years, Hamilton had wielded the rhetoric of British oppositions with the best of his revolutionary compatriots.[2] He

1. My interpretation of Hamilton is most heavily influenced by Gerald Stourzh, *Alexander Hamilton and the Idea of Republican Government* (Stanford: Stanford University Press, 1970), the best analysis to date of Hamilton's thought and a very worthwhile study of the political thought of his entire generation. Also useful for their analysis of the close relationship between Hamilton's domestic and foreign policies are relevant sections of Jerald A. Combs, *The Jay Treaty: Political Battleground of the Founding Fathers* (Berkeley: University of California Press, 1970), although Combs's assessment of Hamilton's motives should be approached with care.

2. "A Full Vindication of the Measures of the Congress," in Harold C. Syrett and Jacob E. Cooke, eds., *The Papers of Alexander Hamilton* (New York: Columbia University Press, 1960–), I, 45–78.

had shared the concern with an apparent decline of republican virtue that had distressed most of his contemporaries during Confederation times.[3] But Hamilton may also have been influenced more than most Americans by a different current in British thought, one that has received little attention from historians of the new nation.

During the newspaper warfare of the 1730s and 1740s in England, literary champions of Walpole's ministry evolved a novel rejoinder to the attacks of Bolingbroke and others on ministerial influence. Rather than reject the opposition charges out of hand, they admitted them in part and went on to argue that a certain degree of influence had become indispensable to the stability of the balanced constitution. This "Court" argument—as it may be called in contrast to its "Country" counterpart—never attained the systematic scope or popularity of its opposite, nor is it possible to follow a school of "Court" writers from the Age of Walpole into the period of American independence. By the end of the eighteenth century, nevertheless, "Court" ideas were a familiar part of British constitutional thought. Employing Harringtonian precepts in a way that admitted the reality of a feudal past and justified the governmental techniques of contemporary England, "Court" thinkers offered a reasoned alternative to opposition versions of the history of English liberty.

As J. G. A. Pocock has pointed out, the stance of the "Country" opposition in the eighteenth century was that of a radical right, urging a return to an ancient, balanced constitution that had been steadily undermined since the Glorious Revolution by the rise of ministerial influence and government by money.[4] In response to this style of attack, Walpole's defenders criticized the

3. "Publius," in ibid., 562–582. This venomous attack on Samuel Chase, who had taken advantage of his office in the Continental Congress to obtain information that he used for the personal profit of himself and his friends, is most useful for an understanding of Hamilton's values.
4. "Machiavelli, Harrington, and English Political Ideologies in the Eighteenth Century," *William and Mary Quarterly*, 22 (1965), 572. Pages 571–580 of this article provide the best short introduction to Court and Country historiography.

opposition's belief in the antiquity of the Commons, pointing correctly to the feudal character of English government as late as the Tudor period and marking the Revolution of 1689 as the earliest point from which they could discern an uninterrupted predominance of the Commons. Defenders of a Whig ministry thus seized on a Tory version of history in an attempt to identify Walpole with liberty and the principles of 1689, while condemning his opponents as renegades. This version of history permitted them to see an uninterrupted growth of liberty over the past forty years and to present the rise of ministerial government as a defense of the free constitution.[5]

When Walpole's critics demanded greater independence for the branches of government, his supporters replied that the absolute separation of powers that their opponents seemed to want would completely incapacitate a government of three quite different heads. Some amount of interdependency, they insisted, was necessary to assure enough cooperation to make decision possible.[6] From their view of history, moreover, greater independence of the parts of government and increased restraints on the crown would only compound constitutional troubles. Beginning with a Harringtonian account of the rise of the commons in the reign of Henry VII, "Court" writers argued that only after the Restoration had the commons' control of the balance of property become complete. The Glorious Revolution fixed the balance in the commons, and, since that time, their share of the property and the accompanying political power had constantly grown. Neither the property of the nobility nor the revenues of the crown had kept pace with the growth of popular wealth. As a result, the real power of the realm had come to rest so overwhelmingly in the hands of the House of Commons that only the agency that the Crown and the Lords had acquired in that body

5. Isaac Kramnick, "Augustan Politics and English Historiography: The Debate on the English Past, 1730–1735," *History and Theory*, 6 (1967), 33–56.

6. It may be worth suggesting here that Montesquieu's formulation of his theory of checks and balances may have required an appreciation of both sides of the Court-Country debate he witnessed while in England. Only the Country contribution has been recognized.

through the action of influence preserved England from simple democracy. From the "Court" point of view, assaults on "corruption" were, in present circumstances, attacks on balanced government itself.[7]

"Court" writers had slight impact in America. Compared with the extensive body of opposition literature, "Court" writings were a journalistic flash of the 1730s and 1740s whose greatest influence in England itself awaited the years after 1800 and the opposition to the movement for parliamentary reform.[8] Yet parts of the extensive body of "Court" arguments were adopted by leading political writers, becoming a significant, if minor, part of constitutional thought.

Among these writers, David Hume could command a place on any political bookshelf, and one of Hume's most popular essays was a succinct presentation of "Court" ideas. Writing "Of the Independence of Parliament," Hume argued that the real power of England's mixed government was so distributed that the Commons could at any time usurp the whole of government. The King's legislative veto had become an empty form, his powers as executive had come to be dependent on the Commons' grant of supplies. The Lords were a support to the executive, but lacked the strength to stand alone. By right, therefore, England ought to be dependent on a majority in the Commons. Only one thing prevented this result: "The Crown has so many offices at its disposal that, when assisted by the honest and disinterested part of the House, it will always command the resolution of the whole, so far, at least, as to preserve the ancient constitution from

7. The fullest account of these ideas in the newspapers of the 1730s is in Isaac Kramnick, *Bolingbroke and His Circle* (Cambridge: Harvard University Press, 1968), chap. 5. My summary depends primarily on two of the best known "Court" treatises of the 1740s: [John Perceval, 2nd Earl of Egmont], *Faction Detected by the Evidence of Facts*, 2d ed. (London: J. Roberts, 1743) and Samuel Squire, *An Historical Essay upon the Balance of Civil Power in England* (London: M. Cooper, 1748).

8. For the later history of "Court" ideas and their place in the writings of Paley and Hume, see Corinne Comstock Weston, *English Constitutional Theory and the House of Lords, 1556–1832* (New York: Columbia University Press, 1965), pp. 130–132, 137–141. Using the Court idea that the mixture of the one, the few, and the many was now effectively located within the Commons, opponents of parliamentary reform could argue that it might destroy balanced government.

danger." Some degree of "corruption," in other words, was necessary to preserve the balanced constitution.[9]

From the rebuttals of opposition writers or from Hume's popular essays, American political thinkers were familiar with the defense of ministerial influence. In view of this familiarity—and recalling the widespread Federalist fear that the lower house might overbalance the new government in democratic America—we are obliged to ask what role, if any, "Court" ideas may have played in the party contest of the 1790s. Was Hamilton's economic program deliberately intended to create an executive influence in the legislature, as Republicans would come to charge? Were the Federalists ever tempted to make a "Court" response to the Republicans' "Country" challenge?

One of these questions can be answered with a fair amount of confidence. A careful search of Federalist writings, both public and private, fails to uncover any systematic use of "Court" ideas in replies to Republican attacks on corruption. Throughout the 1790s, Federalists responded to Republican accusations by denying the existence of any improper influence of the executive on the legislature, by denying, in fact, that corruption on the English model was even possible among legislators genuinely responsible to a broad electorate.[10] It may be that the derivation of American revolutionary thought from the opposition side of English politics made any admission or defense of executive influence not only suicidal, but to a large degree unthinkable.

The question of a possible influence of "Court" ideas on Federalist motives is not, however, quite so easily dismissed.

9. Charles W. Hendel, ed., *David Hume's Political Essays* (Indianapolis: Bobbs-Merrill, 1953), pp. 68–71. While defending influence, Court writers traditionally insisted that it would never be so powerful as absolutely to control the Commons. See Squire, p. xv: influence poses no danger "unless we suppose that the majority of both Houses of Parliament, that 500 gentlemen of the first quality . . . should suffer themselves to be reduced into a conspiracy . . . to deliver up themselves, their wives and children, their relatives and friends, bound hand and foot, into the king's power."

10. As John Howe has pointed out in "Republican Thought and the Political Violence of the 1790s," *American Quarterly*, 19 (1967), 147–165, Federalists also countered charges of corruption with attacks on malicious, demagogic subversives, which were not unlike the Walpolian response to Bolingbroke.

Indeed, a subtle connection seems entirely likely. During his years in the Continental Army, Hamilton had developed an interest in political economy, and he was particularly influenced by the works of David Hume.[11] Hume impressed him not only with his advocacy of protectionism and his dictum that men will be governed by their passions, but also with his presentation of "Court" ideas. Years later, in the Constitutional Convention, Nathaniel Gorham moved to strike from the Virginia Plan the clause excluding placemen from the legislature, suggesting that placeholders might have preserved the "due influence of the government" in Britain. Hamilton joined in the debate, remarking that the passions of men must be interested in serving their country. He agreed with Gorham that it would be impossible to judge the effect of such an exclusion in Britain: "It was known that one of the ablest politicians (Mr. Hume) had pronounced all that influence on the side of the Crown which went under the name of corruption an essential part of the weight which maintained the equilibrium of the constitution."[12]

There can be no doubt that Hamilton took the English financial system as a model for his economic program or that he was familiar with "Court" ideas. Recalling the force of English historical example to men of his generation, remembering the way in which that history was understood, we have sufficient reason to suspect that Hamilton may have taken the situation of America in 1789 to be very like the situation of England one hundred years before. He may, accordingly, have designed his financial system to affect political ends similar to those that history attributed to the ministers of William III.[13] Certainly, Hamilton came

11. Hume's influence on Hamilton is a central theme for Stourzh. See also John C. Miller, *Alexander Hamilton: Portrait in Paradox* (New York: Harper, 1959), pp. 46–48. For Hume's likely influence on some of Madison's most important ideas, see Douglas Adair, "That Politics May be Reduced to a Science: David Hume, James Madison, and the Tenth Federalist," *Huntington Library Quarterly*, 20 (1957), 343–360.

12. Max Farrand, ed., *The Records of the Federal Convention of 1787*, 4 vols., rev. ed. (New Haven: Yale University Press, 1966), I, 375–376.

13. Some of Hamilton's opponents clearly saw a parallel between the two periods and the two programs, as will be shown below. Hamilton's own papers for the period

to the Treasury with his concerns still focused on the conflict of localism and nationalism. He had no idea that the battle with Antifederalism was already won, and it seems plausible to think that he may have compared Antifederalism to the English Jacobitism and near-Jacobitism of the period from 1689 to 1715. He believed that, in order to avoid a localistic counterblow against the Constitution, the new government would have to act quickly to spread its everyday impact and visibility throughout the nation and to attach men's selfish interests to its success.[14] Confronted with a similar situation, historical tradition said, the architects of the British financial system had devised a striking model of success.

Since the early eighteenth century and the writings of Charles Davenant, the British financial structure of funded debt and chartered bank had commonly been understood as a powerful instrument for attaching men of wealth to a government's success. Hamilton was one of several Americans, early in the Confederation years, who seems to have reflected on this character of a public debt and considered the use of wartime obligations for nationalist ends. As early as 1782, he was working with Robert Morris and others to unite the army and the civilian creditors into an irresistible force for pressuring the country into a grant of broader taxing powers to the Congress.[15] From that time forward, he hoped that all the creditors could be made to look to the

---

immediately preceding the *Report on Public Credit* and for the months of its passage through Congress (vols. V-VI of his *Papers*) reveal almost nothing about his general objectives and intent. Surviving correspondence is almost entirely concerned with technical aspects of the program.

14. Hamilton's best expression of this idea may be his *Federalist* number 27.

15. E. James Ferguson, "The Nationalists of 1781–1783 and the Economic Interpretation of the Constitution," *Journal of American History*, 61 (1969), 241–261, explores the movement for constitutional reform in this period, argues that the Federalist program of the 1790s was essentially completed at this time, and stresses the organic relationship of constitutional and economic reform in the minds of the men around Morris. Ferguson also points out that it was widely accepted at the time that the English financial system had lent stability to a new regime. See also Ferguson's *The Power of the Purse: A History of American Public Finance, 1776–1790* (Chapel Hill: University of North Carolina Press, 1961), part 2 of which explores the movement in greater detail.

federal government for satisfaction of their claims.[16] In Congress in 1783, he spoke repeatedly in favor of a congressional power to appoint collectors of the proposed impost and to provide for civilian creditors as well as the army, embarrassing his cause by admitting his hope that the public creditors would pressure their several states and that the proposed federal officeholders would have a selfish interest in advancing federal power. If Congress would adopt a plan for relieving both the army and the civilian creditors, he explained to General Washington, "the personal influence of some, the connections of others, and a sense of justice to the army . . . might form a mass of influence in each state in favor of the measures of the Congress."[17]

Hamilton's ideas were little changed at the time of his famous reports to the new Congress, and he made no attempt to conceal the nationalist ends of his economic measures. The *Report on Public Credit* relied primarily on arguments from justice, public morality, and sound policy, but Hamilton also admitted a political intent:

If all the public creditors receive their dues from one source . . . their interests will be the same. And having the same interests, they will unite in support of the fiscal arrangements of the government. [If state and federal obligations are provided for separately,] there will be distinct interests, drawing different ways. That union and concert of views among the creditors, which in every government is of great importance to their security and to that of public credit, will not only not exist, but will be likely to give place to jealousy and opposition.[18]

Preparing some "Notes on the Advantages of a National Bank" at President Washington's request, Hamilton advanced a similar justification for that institution:

An attentive consideration of the tendency of an institution immediately connected with the national government, which will interweave itself into the monied interest of every state, which will by its notes insinuate itself into every branch of industry and will affect the interests of all classes of the community, ought to produce strong prepossessions in its

16. Miller, p. 92.
17. *Hamilton Papers*, III, 246–247, 293.
18. Ibid., VI, 80–81.

favor in all who consider the firm establishment of the national government as necessary to the safety and happiness of the country and who ... believe that it stands in need of additional props.[19]

On the issue of assumption of state debts, Hamilton was both anticipated and followed in these arguments. As early as November 7, 1789, for example, a newspaper correspondent remarked that "a public debt is a band of union and interests a powerful and opulent class of citizens to support the government under which it is contracted."[20] On April 24, 1790, another writer put the point in even stronger terms: "A national debt attaches many citizens to the government who, by their numbers, wealth, and influence, contribute more perhaps to its preservation than a body of soldiers."[21] Writing his father in a vocabulary suggestive of the English roots of these ideas, Oliver Wolcott, Auditor of the Treasury, defended assumption in a similar vein:

I can consider a funding system as important in no other respect than as an engine of government. The only question is what that engine shall be. The influence of a clergy, nobility, and armies are and ought to be out of the question in this country, but unless some active principle of the human mind can be interested in support of the government, no civil establishments can be found which will not appear like useless and expensive pageants.[22]

Statements such as these are subject to misunderstanding. Not even to one another, it should be said at once, did Federalists admit that the presence of public creditors in Congress constituted an executive influence in that body similar to the one

19. Ibid., VIII, 223.
20. Reprinted in the Philadelphia *Gazette of the United States* from the Hartford *American Mercury*. See also the earlier statement of this idea by Robert Morris, quoted in Ferguson, *Power of the Purse*, pp. 123–124.
21. "The Tablet," *Gazette of the United States*. Compare the same column, April 17, 1790.
22. George Gibbs, ed., *Memoirs of the Administrations of Washington and John Adams, Edited from the Papers of Oliver Wolcott, Secretary of the Treasury*, 2 vols. (New York: by subscription, 1846), I, 43. Back from the senior Wolcott, Governor of Connecticut, came a letter strongly agreeing that "there certainly cannot exist any other cement" of union than assumption and fearing that its failure would mean the overthrow of the national government (ibid., p. 45).

created in England by the presence of placemen in Parliament—the charge, I hope to show, that was the centerpiece of early Republican indictments of their program. No Federalist ever suggested that the power of the lower house should be offset by the creation of an executive influence there. "Court" ideas, in brief, cannot be shown to have influenced the Federalists in the same sense that it can be shown that the Republicans were influenced by English "Country" thought. Less directly though—through the influence of Hume, through the rebuttals of opposition writers, and most especially through the prevailing interpretation of eighteenth-century English history—their subtle influence may have had an important effect.

It has long been a conviction of scholars who have concerned themselves with Hamilton's political thought that he was peculiarly guided by an assumption that men are dominated by self-interest and have to be governed accordingly.[23] For commendable objects or ill, it is often said, Hamilton designed a program deliberately calculated to serve the interests of monied men in order to enlist their support for the government. Understood in light of the preceding century of English political conflicts and the interchange of "Court" and "Country" ideas, this interpretation gains new clarity and force. The greatest care is necessary, though, in order to avoid a statement of the argument that swallows the Republican indictment.

Hamilton differed from his contemporaries only in degree in his assessment of the importance of self-interest in politics, and his conviction of its importance did not narrow his conception of the public good.[24] Throughout his career as Secretary of the Treasury, Hamilton's overriding ends were strong public credit,

23. The conviction is about as ubiquitous among scholars sympathetic to Hamilton as among those hostile to him. See the sampling of eminent opinion in Jacob E. Cooke, ed., *Alexander Hamilton: A Profile* (New York: Hill & Wang, 1967). Stourzh, who is more interested in what Hamilton had in common with his generation, is a useful corrective.

24. Indeed, in so far as Hamilton conceded that, for a few men like himself, disinterested public service and the quest for fame might override self-interest, he made a concession to virtue that Jefferson did not. It was Jefferson, not Hamilton, who said his party would become "wolves" when placed in power.

efficient administration, and a firm federal union. In part because of his understanding of English history and "Court" ideas, he and a few others of similar mind were able to see the enormous burden of revolutionary debt as a great instrument for nation-building, a tool for binding an important class of citizens to the nationalist cause. But Hamilton did not design his program for the benefit of monied men. Nor did he seek to draw the monied classes to his personal support. The monied classes profited, without a doubt, but that was incidental to his purpose. He never meant for monied men to use the government. He intended the reverse.[25]

Significantly, Federalist arguments that seem to derive from the "Court" side of English thought, expressing a hope that holders of the public debt would be influenced by their economic interests to support the government, appeared almost exclusively in the years before the Constitutional Convention and in the debate over federal assumption of state debts. They suggest a purpose quite different from the one imagined by the Republican opposition or by those historians who have read them as support for the idea of a capitalist conspiracy or for Hamilton's desire to serve the plutocratic interests. Read carefully, the arguments have an unmistakably defensive tone. Even when the financial program is identified as an "engine of government," what is envisioned is less an ongoing agency of an administrative purpose than a protective barrier against the incursions of localism. Assumption of the state debts had several purposes, but it origi-

25. The contrary opinion has recently been well stated in Combs's *The Jay Treaty*, pp. 35–37. Stressing Hamilton's distrust of the common people and his statement that only a few choice spirits might rise above selfish interest, Combs argues that Hamilton's object "was to concentrate the powers of government" in the hands of the rich and well-born in order to "create . . . an aristocracy dedicated to the proper national interest." Combs suggests that Hamilton may have hoped that a permanent influence in government and great wealth would raise these men above corruption and give them true nobility. This interpretation is riddled with inconsistencies. If the creditors were the rich and well-born whom Hamilton admired, it would have been unnecessary to bribe them to the right. Additional wealth would not have made them better men, nor was wealth alone enough to produce the kind of aristocrat of whom he (and the whole classical tradition) spoke. Hamilton did not believe that monied men were less corrupt than the rest, but he did believe that they could be used.

nated most clearly in the Federalists' desire to defend the national government against the centrifugal tendencies that all of them feared. Its "leading objects," in its author's mind, "were an accession of strength to the national government and an assurance of order and vigor in the national finances."[26]

The Hamiltonian program was conceived in the days before there was a party conflict. It was aimed against the old American evil of localism. Its author was a man incapable of partial, sectional, or narrowly personal ends, who sought nothing less than to be the classical legislator of a great American state.[27] He was villified by his opponents, not because his program really intended to benefit one group at other groups' expense, but because his vision of a great republic—a commercial, manufacturing country dependent on public credit, British investment, and a sound system of public finance—necessarily threatened their contrasting ideal of a virtuous American state.[28]

26. Hamilton to Edward Carrington, May 26, 1792, in *Hamilton Papers*, XI, 428.

27. Stourzh is astute in leading off his study with a quotation from Hamilton's attack on Samuel Chase, mentioned in note 3 above. There is no better source for an understanding of what Hamilton sought for himself or of what the economic program was *not* intended to achieve. Hamilton considered Chase to be one of a "tribe" of avaricious extortioners who had demonstrated that "notwithstanding our youth and inexperience as a nation, we begin to emulate the most veteran and accomplished states in the arts of corruption." He believed that "when a man appointed to be the guardian of the state . . . descends to the dishonest artifices of a mercantile projector and sacrifices his conscience and his trust to pecuniary motives, there is no strain of abhorrence of which the human mind is capable, nor punishment the vengeance of the people can inflict, which may not be applied to him with justice." Hamilton would have been pleased to have us apply to his conduct as an officer the standard he applied to Chase: "The station of a member of Congress is the most illustrious and important of any I am able to conceive. He is to be regarded not only as a legislator but as the founder of an empire. . . . To form useful alliances abroad, to establish a wise government at home, to improve the internal resources and finances of the nation would be the generous objects of his care. He would not allow his attention to be diverted from these to intrigue for personal connections, to confirm his own influence. . . . Anxious for the permanent power and prosperity of the state, he would labor to perpetuate the union and harmony of the several parts. He would not meanly court a temporary importance by patronizing the narrow views of local interests."

28. It should be evident by now that I accept the abundant evidence of James M. Banner, *To the Hartford Convention: The Federalists and the Origins of Party Politics in Massachusetts, 1789–1815* (New York: Knopf, 1970), and Linda K. Kerber, *Federalists in Dissent: Imagery and Ideology in Jeffersonian America* (Ithaca, N.Y.: Cornell University Press, 1970), that the Federalists were, in their way, as loyal as Republicans to the republican revolution. My primary quarrel with Richard Buel, Jr.,

II

Because each part of his program was integral to the whole, Hamilton took pains in the *Report on Public Credit* to anticipate objections to his plan and to answer counterproposals already circulating in the country, giving particular attention to proposals for discriminating between original creditors and present holders of the debt. Unless the debt could be funded at its full face value to its present holders, the certificates of indebtedness would fail to serve the country as foundation for a circulating currency, a need further planned for in Hamilton's scheme for a national bank.[29] Failure to fund at full value would jeopardize future demands for credit, breach the public's faith with its creditors, and erect a poor foundation for the public and private morality of the new state.[30] Failure to assume the state debts would make nonsense of plans for a consistent, national economic program, while encouraging the centrifugal forces that already seemed full strong enough. Nevertheless, Congress quickly divided the Secretary's proposals into the separate questions of funding and assumption, and debate soon centered on the subject of discrimination. The ensuing controversy threatened a quick end to the constitutional experiment.

From the first, considerations derived from revolutionary ideology had a place among the objections to Hamilton's plan, though not the leading part. The *Report on Public Credit* having established the terms, early debate on Hamilton's proposals was relatively narrow and overwhelmingly concerned with questions of public morality and justice. Full payment of the principal and interest of the foreign debt was never at issue, and few questioned the need to pay the domestic debt at par, since both were clearly necessary to establish public credit.[31] But sectional feelings gen-

---

Securing the Revolution: Ideology in American Politics, 1789–1815 (Ithaca: Cornell University Press, 1972), a book which has much to commend it, is its failure to accept this evidence.

29. *Hamilton Papers*, VI, 70–71, 76–77.

30. Ibid., pp. 78–81.

31. The best discussion of the intricacies of Hamiltonian funding is Ferguson, *Power of the Purse*, pp. 292–297, 329–330.

erated by the concentration of the debt in Northern and Eastern hands, along with agrarian hostility toward financial speculation, engendered intense controversy over the question to whom the domestic debt should be paid.[32] James Jackson, John Page, Thomas Tucker, Thomas Scott, and others in the House were soon demanding that some distinction should be made between original holders of the debt and present holders who had purchased their certificates for fractions of face value. To Hamilton's surprise, James Madison, his longtime comrade and the most influential member of the House, entered the debate on the side of these radicals of the first session, and battle was joined between Hamilton's proposal and Madison's project of paying present holders the highest value the certificates had reached on private markets, returning the difference between that and the par value to the original holder.[33]

On one side, William Smith, Theodore Sedgwick, Elias Boudinot, and Fisher Ames urged full payment to the present holders along lines sketched out in Hamilton's *Report*. They argued that any scheme for discrimination would amount to a unilateral breach of contract with the creditors, a violation of public morality as unworkable as it would be unjust. In defense of the creditors, they joined with Hamilton in pointing out that men who had purchased depreciated certificates in the years before 1789 had rendered a valuable service to impoverished original holders at considerable risk to themselves. On the other side, friends of a discrimination emphasized the plight of widows and warriors who had sacrificed for the patriotic cause. Forced by a defaulting government to surrender their certificates in order to survive, they now were being asked to mortgage their futures to the speculators who had taken advantage of their distress. A

32. The appearance of Hamilton's report fueled a speculative mania in which monied men close to the seat of government, some Congressmen included, rushed for the further reaches of the country to buy state certificates at their deflated market value. This spectacle infuriated men who were already sympathetic to the original holders, and it was roundly denounced in Congress.

33. Debate on funding, which occupied the House for much of February, 1790, is in *Annals of Congress*, I, 1180–1224, 1234–1239, 1248–1322; II, 1324–1354.

Madisonian discrimination, its supporters thought, would satisfy the demands of public credit by discharging the debt in full, and it would better serve the cause of republican morality and justice.

Economic interest and sectional advantage plainly lay beneath these arguments over public morality. So, however, did other considerations that have received less historiographical attention. It is noteworthy that the debate on funding was opened by James Jackson, a radical of the first session and conspicuous foe of the speculative rage, in a speech that favored heavy, direct taxes on the present generation over the permanent and growing burdens imposed on posterity by a funded debt. Jackson doubted "whether a permanent funded debt is beneficial or not to any country." He believed that every state that had adopted a funding system—Florence, Genoa, Venice, Spain, France, and especially England—had grown weaker as a result. A funding system, he explained, settles upon future generations "a burthen which they can neither bear nor relieve themselves from," making it inevitable that the taxes of "the honest, hard-working part of the community will promote the ease and luxury of men of wealth."[34]

Resuming the argument on the following day, the Georgia Congressman let slip another worry that should not be overlooked:

We learn from Blackstone that the reason for establishing a national debt [in England] was in order to support a system of foreign politics and to establish the new succession at the Revolution; because it was deemed expedient to create a new interest, called the moneyed interest, in favor of the Prince of Orange, in opposition to the landed interest. . . . I hope there is no such reason existing here.[35]

Jackson and John Page of Virginia were not alone in questioning the propriety in a republic of any plan that would enrich a few at the expense of the many.[36] The funding program, from the

34. Ibid., I, 1180–1182.
35. Ibid., I, 1214.
36. Compare "Equity," in the Boston *Independent Chronicle*, Jan. 14, 1790, and Rush to Madison in L. H. Butterfield, ed., *Letters of Benjamin Rush*, 2 vols., Memoirs of the American Philosophical Society, 30 (Princeton: Princeton University Press, 1951), I, 539.

first, stirred memories of English experience and neo-Harringtonian fears of a shift in the balance of property, which might eventually undermine the social structure that supported a republican state. These fears would become much more explicit as the opposition grew.

Meanwhile, discrimination failed to carry by a large majority, and attention turned to the question of assumption of state debts. On this issue, the representatives divided primarily according to the interests of their several states. Both sides also recognized, however, that assumption, which could only be supported by internal taxation, was a crucial question for the relationship of state and federal authority.[37] Sherman, Ames, Sedgwick, and other advocates of the assumption argued that the state debts had been acquired in the common defense and that assumption would equalize burdens and benefits in an efficient manner, while lending strength to the union.[38] Opponents, led by Madison, Jackson, and Page, protested the increased taxation assumption would require, the sectional inequities that would result, and the reduction in the power of the states.[39]

The debate on assumption stretched from late in February into July, rivaled in its grip on Congressional interest only by the issue of the future location of the national capital, which was occasioning behind-scenes maneuvers intimately connected by

37. The Hamiltonians wanted assumption partly *because* it would require an excise tax and a consequent extension of federal authority. Both sides in the ratification contest had realized that the spheres of state and federal authority would be determined in practice by the staking out of revenue resources. Monroe's relatively calm and lucid Antifederalism particularly emphasized this point. See Monroe to Jefferson in Stanislaus Murray Hamilton, ed., *The Writings of James Monroe* (New York: Putnam, 1898), I, 211–212.

38. Even Elbridge Gerry, who had worried conspicuously about executive influence in the first session of Congress, was not bashful about using the argument concerning the self-interest of the creditors. But he, too, approached the subject defensively, reasoning that rejection of assumption would "establish two contending parties, the continental creditors and the state creditors. The latter will oppose every measure of the general government which they suppose is intended, in prejudice of themselves, to promote the interest of the former" (*Annals of Congress*, II, 1373). See also the similar arguments of Ames, Sedgwick, and Boudinot, ibid., pp. 1386, 1419, 1654.

39. Debate on assumption is in ibid., pp. 1355–1470, 1531–1579, 1642–1674, and 1744–1753.

sectional interest to the question of assumption. Assumption failed originally in the House, and persistent efforts by its proponents could not revive it. Sectional hostilities rose to dangerous highs. With Madison and his allies immovably opposed and advocates of the measure threatening to wreck the financial program if it did not pass, serious talk of a dissolution of the union appeared on both sides. In this atmosphere Thomas Jefferson, who had recently assumed his duties as Secretary of State, arranged the famous dinner at which Madison and Hamilton agreed to trade the passage of assumption for a future location of the capital on the Potomac. The sense of crisis that moved the leaders also prompted negotiations in both Houses of Congress. Alterations in the assumption bill and shifts of individual positions permitted both measures to go through.[40] The crisis over, Congress adjourned with signs of relief.

The bargains struck to carry the assumption were indicative of the nature of divisions during the second session of Congress. Confrontations on matters of local and sectional concern were ultimately resolved by the determination of both sides to preserve the union. The issues that divided men had not been cast, in general, in highly ideological terms. Both sides had been willing to charge their disagreements to honorable differences of view. All of Fisher Ames's letters during the second session dealt with the passage of funding and assumption through the Congress. Interestingly, he was less concerned with factionalism than he had been the year before. His spleen, which was considerable,

40. In a recent article, Jacob E. Cooke seems to have discredited the universally accepted opinion that the bargain between Hamilton and Madison assured the passage of the assumption and residence bills. Cooke argues that, while a bargain did take place, it was never consumated. Instead, the measures passed separately as a result of negotiations and compromises on their own merits. Pennsylvania and Virginia had arranged a residence bargain before the dinner took place, while compromises concerning interest rates and adjustments in amounts to be assumed were more important than the location of the capital in changing votes on assumption. See "The Compromise of 1790," *William and Mary Quarterly*, 27 (1970), 523–545. See also Cooke's defense of his argument against the challenge of Kenneth R. Bowling, "Dinner at Jefferson's," ibid., 28 (1971), 629–648. Still, Cooke probably implies a disjunction of the two issues more complete than his evidence will support. The complicated maneuvers on these issues may never be entirely understood.

was reserved this year primarily for Pennsylvanians, whose maneuvers to locate the capital at Philadelphia he blamed for the impass over assumption.[41] Similarly, Oliver Wolcott admitted the difficulty of reaching a fair settlement on these issues and stressed the honest motives of opponents, although he did condemn their tendency to "indulge their minds in fanciful theories of republican liberty."[42] On the other side, Benjamin Rush may have expressed the concern of a small minority when he warned that funding and assumption "will in seven years introduce among us all the corruptions of the British funding system," but William Maclay was two years ahead of his fellows in interpreting the whole second session of Congress as a contest pitting Hamilton and his following of self-interested speculators and "courtiers" against the more disinterested part of Congress.[43]

Outside Congress, too, passions were relatively cool. Most newspapers carried articles on both sides of the debate on Hamilton's proposals. Arguments on the issues differed little from those in the House, with real heat generated only in denunciations of preying speculators. Contributors to the Boston *Independent Chronicle* or to Thomas Greenleaf's New York *Journal*, both of which would one day lead the opposition, seemed less angry than they had the year before, calling just as loudly as the proadministration *Gazette of the United States* for action—any action—on the debt. Criticism of the national government concentrated on the expense and dangers of a dawdling Congress.

The first effects of funding and assumption, then, were not substantially different from earlier stirrings over titles or Presidential receptions. Once again, the issues at hand jogged inherited fears for the security of liberty. Neither side, as yet, spoke predominantly in those terms, though it is also clear that neither could escape an association of specific problems with the most

41. Seth Ames, ed., *Works of Fisher Ames*, 2 vols. (Boston: Little, Brown, 1854), I, 75–78.

42. George Gibbs, ed., *Memoirs of the Administrations of Washington and John Adams* (New York: by subscription, 1846), I, 47.

43. *Letters of Rush*, I, 543; Edgar S. Maclay, ed., *The Journal of William Maclay* (New York: Albert & Charles Boni, 1927), pp. 230, 321, 330.

basic ideological concerns. Fears were still diffuse and poorly rationalized for all but a tiny few. But the personal and sectional hostilities left in the wake of Hamilton's *Report* had opened channels for their flow. Completion of the economic program during the next session of Congress would speed a polarization of sentiment at the capital and in the country at large, encouraging a further rationalization of the differences between the sides.

III

The last session of the first and longest Congress, which met in New York between December 6, 1790, and March 3, 1791, saw the completion of Hamilton's financial program with the creation of a national bank and the adoption of an excise tax on luxuries such as wines, spirits, coffee, and tea. Divisions in Congress again followed lines of sectional and economic interest, since the bank appealed primarily to the commercial East while the excise threatened genuine hardship to the whiskey-selling agrarians of western Pennsylvania and Virginia. But the tone of accusations with which opponents faced each other now began to rise.

A form of tax traditionally odious to men of an English political background, the excise provoked in Congress and in the press the loudest warnings to date against the incursions of power on liberty. Typical in tone and content of the essays and petitions that were beginning to circulate in the press were these excerpts from a single issue of a Philadelphia daily:

Your liberties are in danger—a blow is this moment aimed at them which, if not diverted by timely remonstrances, will cast you into a state of abject slavery.

[The excise establishes] principles dangerous to liberty and subversive of domestic peace and comfort by trampling under foot the barrier of private possessions and annihilating at one blow that once pleasing doctrine that every man's house is his castle.[44]

Congressional rhetoric was less flamboyant, but feelings were

44. From a paragraph signed "A Watchman" and a petition circulating in Philadelphia, *Dunlap's American Daily Advertiser*, January 14, 1791.

hardly less intense. Madison was one of several who preferred an excise to direct (and even more inflammatory) taxes on landed property, and the bill was easily passed. Yet Jackson, Livermore, Gerry, and others revealed some of their deepest fears in an attempt to amend the measure to guard against the possibility of interference by the revenue officers in the freedom of elections.[45] Friends of the unamended bill were equally quick to attack proposals derived from irrelevant British precedent.

Still, the opposition to a national bank derived from the same British traditions. Not surprisingly, William Maclay immediately identified the bank as "an aristocratic engine" and "a machine for the mischievous purposes of bad ministers."[46] In Pennsylvania, hostility toward banking reached back a decade to the furor over the Bank of North America.[47] Agrarian prejudice and democratic hostility to special privilege were themselves sufficient to assure an opposition to the bank. But criticism of the institution had strong roots as well in a long English tradition of opposition to the nature, power, and influence of privileged corporations. To anticipate once more, Jeffersonian agrarianism was rationalized, in larger degree than has been realized, in terms of a Harringtonian concern for the preservation of a democratic and agrarian balance of property. In Congress as well as in the administration, debate on establishment of a national bank concentrated on issues of constitutionality, but inherited fears of the influence of privileged corporations and the further aggrandizement of financial at the expense of agrarian interests occasionally peeked through, as when Madison himself objected to "the great and extensive influence that incorporated societies had on public affairs in Europe. They are powerful machines which have always

45. Debate on this amendment is in *Annals of Congress*, II, 1924–1927.
46. *Journal*, p. 345.
47. See the fine short discussion in Eric Foner, *Tom Paine and Revolutionary America* (New York: Oxford University Press, 1976), pp. 192–197, which suggests a well developed condemnation of the dangers of concentrations of men of wealth by western Constitutionalists such as William Findlay, John Smilie, and Robert Whitehall. See also Gordon S. Wood, *The Creation of the American Republic, 1776–1787* (Chapel Hill: University of North Carolina Press, 1969), pp. 401–402.

been found competent to effect objects on principles in a great measure independent of the people."[48]

IV

Americans who paused for bearings in the spring of 1791 could be pleased with the success of a federal experiment that most of them had undertaken with considerable trepidation. The Constitution was by then a working instrument of government, accepted on all sides as a starting point for further debates. The nation's finances were at last in order, its economic future bright. There had been no lack of controversy during the three sessions of the First Congress, but everyone had anticipated serious differences between geographical sections and interest groups. These seemed to have been weathered rather well.[49] Divisions in the Congress had been sectional and periodic, rather than factional and formed. Alignments had not persisted over the whole range of issues at hand, and loyalty to the union had triumphed over partial ends.[50] The public temper was generally benign. In all the country not a single newspaper, as yet, had adopted a genuinely partisan stance.

48. *Annals of Congress*, II, 2009. Debate on the bank is on pages 1940–2012.

49. Indeed, passions seemed a little cooler at the close of the First Congress than they had been since the summer of 1789. The radical suspicions generated in the ratification contest and voiced in the controversies of 1789 had receded in the press. And, looking back over the third session, Ames reflected that "this session has passed with unusually good temper. The last was a dreadful one" (*Works*, I, 96).

50. On the nature of alignments in the First Congress see Noble E. Cunningham, Jr., *The Jeffersonian Republicans: The Formation of Party Organization, 1789–1801* (Chapel Hill: University of North Carolina Press, 1957), pp. 4, 7. This is the premier study of the development of Republican Party organization, and I have depended on it throughout this work. More sophisticated quantitative analyses of voting blocs in the first Congress are Mary P. Ryan, "Party Formation in the United States Congress, 1789 to 1796: A Quantitative Analysis," *William and Mary Quarterly*, 28 (1971), 523–542, and H. James Henderson, "Quantitative Approaches to Party Formation in the United States Congress," ibid., 30 (1973), 307–324. These scholars conclude that the Third Congress probably marks the transformation of sectional voting blocs into a two-bloc system that cohered over a broad range of issues. The most extensive information on voting patterns in the Congresses of the 1790s is Rudolph M. Bell, *Party and Faction in American Politics: The House of Representatives, 1789–1801* (Westport, Conn.: Greenwood Press, 1973). This information, however, is organized by what seems to me an unacceptable thesis.

Yet warnings of a different temperament were beginning to appear. In December 1790, the Virginia Legislature had put on record an explicit rationalization of the fears that had occasionally surfaced during the congressional debates on funding, assumption, the excise, and the bank. Your memorialists, they wrote,

discern a striking resemblance between this system and that which was introduced into England at the Revolution—a system which has perpetuated upon that nation an enormous debt and has, moreover, insinuated into the hands of the executive an unbounded influence which, pervading every branch of the government, bears down all opposition and daily threatens the destruction of every thing that appertains to English liberty. . . .

To erect and concentrate and perpetuate a large monied interest is a measure which . . . must, in the course of human events, produce one or other of two evils: the prostration of agriculture at the feet of commerce or a change in the present form of federal government fatal to the existence of American liberty.[51]

Virginia's remonstrance against funding and assumption provoked Hamilton to his earliest surviving denunciation of opposition to his plans.[52]

During the last months of 1790, in conjunction with the non-partisan elections for the Second Congress, criticisms of the financial program had become noticeably more numerous in the press. While these were seldom as carefully ideological as the remonstrance of the Virginia Legislature, they often hinted at their origins in the same connected set of worries about corruption of the government, a change in the distribution of property, and popular loss of the classical republican virtues. An extraordinary and widely known "advertisement" that appeared in the

51. *American State Papers: Finance*, 1, 90–91. The Virginia leadership was almost unanimously opposed to assumption. The remonstrance was the work of a committee consiting of Patrick Henry, Henry Lee, and Francis Corbin, two of whom had been Federalists in 1788 and all of whom would be Federalists before 1800. Henry was probably the primary author. Harry Ammon, "The Formation of the Republican Party in Virginia, 1789–1796," *Journal of Southern History*, 19 (1953), 291.

52. *Hamilton Papers*, VII, 149–150. Hamilton naturally saw the remonstrance and concurrent attempts by state legislatures to instruct their senators as stirrings of disunionism.

Boston *Independent Chronicle* on August 12, 1790, was typical in its hostility toward financial manipulation, its identification of the monied interest as a cohesive group, and its hint of a governmental conspiracy against the public:

Wanted

A number of Stock-Jobbers, Speculators, and Negotiators for the purpose of aiding and assisting certain members of the Robin-Hood Society [that is, Congress] in accomplishing their foreign contracts. As this fraternity are about to receive the reward of their seven-months' services, many of them wish to dispose of their exhorbitant wages in such a manner as will augment their property twofold during recess. As they began their speculations during session, they mean to continue them for the short time they adjourn to attend to their reelection; when this is accomplished it is expected they will return to Philadelphia and there spend the remainder of the year in promoting their own interest to the impoverishing of their constituents.[53]

More indicative of the concerns that had influenced the Virginians were occasional contributions to the New York *Journal*. "Is there a party marshalled" by the Treasury, one writer asked. Could Hamilton have in view "a political increase of salaries and multiplication of offices to give a ministerial strength to party and political energy to a confederation which must destroy the states or be destroyed?" "It has been declared by the ministerial cohort that assumption was necessary to the general system of revenue." In fact, assumption was wanted "to provide for the interest and to secure to the standard of the general government a mercenary corps of adventurers."[54] The desire for public good and reputation had given way, another correspondent argued, to avarice for a "place, post, or pension." A "system of influence and corruption" was "diffusing its horrid, baneful influence" through the federal government.[55]

At the turn of the year, as we have seen, the proposal of an

53. It is interesting to wonder whether we might be able to make an imagistic connection between this "Robin-Hood Society" and the Walpolian "Robinarchy" that Bolingbroke condemned.

54. "M," New York *Journal*, July 2, 1790.

55. "A Republican," reprinted from the Boston *Gazette*, New York *Journal*, Sept. 7, 1790.

excise tax had been the occasion for another rise in the frequency and pitch of criticisms of the financial program. This rising criticism was reflected in the staunchly Federalist *Gazette of the United States*, whose editor had been content, till now, with simple celebration of the new government. In February 1791, the proadministration sheet opened an attack on critics. Still motivated primarily by fear of disunionism, editor John Fenno repeatedly warned his readers against "the insinuations of men who are prone to predict evil and impose censure," pointing out that "prejudices and suspicions for which there is no real foundation" could undermine confidence in the government.[56] Exactly a year before, the *Gazette* had printed a purported letter from London that defined the sort of suspicion Fenno had increasingly in mind:

The greatest danger to be apprehended in your public affairs is a jealousy between the different branches of government. I could perceive by the debates that the representatives were not free from a suspicion that the executive officers would establish too powerful an influence. . . . A temper of suspicion indulged by individuals against public characters or by one branch of the government against the other will impede public business and be attended with no useful consequences.

Until the spring of 1791, these suspicions were no more than a suggestive undercurrent in the stream of political life. The *Independent Chronicle* had opened the year with a moderate number of essays criticizing the funding system for its complexity and injustice to original creditors, but well into the spring (and despite passage in the meantime of the excise and the national bank) controversy on national issues rarely appeared. Among men in positions of authority, harsh indictments of opponents' motives were equally hard to find. Interpretations such as Maclay's, though certainly suggestive of the origins and directions of concerns, were the product of a fringe. The public mood began

56. "The Tablet," Feb. 2, 1791. Fenno, like Hamilton, had been especially quick to denounce Virginia's remonstrance and was currently attacking attempts by Pennsylvania and North Carolina legislators to instruct their senators.

to change between the adjournment of the First Congress and the meeting of the next.

This change was partly in the minds of national leaders. Having acted as congressional leader of the Federalist forces in the first session of Congress, Madison moved to the head of the opposition to funding and assumption. His surviving correspondence is somewhat uncommunicative of his reasons, but it does reveal an emphasis in private as well as in public on the injustice that the measures did to the original creditors and to his state. There is no evidence that, at this time, the great congressional leader saw a deeper danger in the Treasury plan. Madison declined to vote for the assumption, but, after it had passed, he wrote his father that the measure had carried by a small majority out of fear of the consequences of its failure. He recommended acquiescence, pointing out that the original provisions of the bill had been adjusted so that "in a pecuniary light, the assumption is no longer of much consequence to Virginia."[57]

During these same months, Thomas Jefferson, who had not assumed his post at State until April 1790, was at least as sanguine as his younger friend about the course and future of the government. Relationships within the administration were cordial at the time, and Jefferson seems to have considered the assumption as a problem in reconciling local interests, a problem scarcely worth the tensions and delay that it produced. He thought the measure sectionally unjust, but he accepted compromise as necessary for the sake of public credit and the union.[58]

If we are to understand the gradual development of the Republican Party and its thought, we must bear in mind the good faith and good hopes with which the two Virginians entered the new government. In the beginning both were nearer Federalists than not. Their first objections to administration policy were specific

57. Gaillard Hunt, ed., *The Writings of James Madison* (New York: Putnam, 1900–1910), VI, 19.

58. Julian P. Boyd, ed., *The Papers of Thomas Jefferson* (Princeton: Princeton University Press, 1950–), XVI, 493, 536–538, 540–541, 601.

and unashamedly sectional, not overtly ideological, not yet condemnatory of Federalist government as a whole. Similarly, during the third session of Congress, it was not so much the National Bank as the arguments advanced in its defense to which they raised objections. Already troubled by what seemed to them a sectional bias in the federal laws, they saw in Hamilton's broad construction of constitutional powers another blow at the barriers against an indefinite expansion of federal authority and the power of a northern majority to oppress contrasting interests. Only after the completion of Hamilton's economic program did Jefferson and Madison turn explicitly and systematically to the charges of conspiracy and corruption that others had occasionally suggested in Congress and the press.

Soon after the dissolution of the First Congress, in May and June of 1791, Jefferson and Madison, who had long since developed the closest and most effective political partnership in American history, left together for a tour of upper New York, Vermont, and Connecticut. The trip was meant to be a holiday, a chance to see the country before the government left New York, but it is an indication of rising tempers in the country that many of Hamilton's supporters saw it as a political excursion undertaken to establish links with New York's Antifederalists and to stir up discontent.[59] The tour did give the Virginians an opportunity to meet some local leaders. More importantly, perhaps, it gave them time to talk with one another about their growing dissatisfaction with the course of the federal government and the complacency of the public mood.

By this time, the Virginians' discontent was moving to a different plane, and the public mood was undergoing a decisive change. For some months, as Jefferson had argued with the Secretary of the Treasury about the nation's foreign policy and listened to the conversations over dinner tables in New York, his

---

59. Cunningham, pp. 11–12; Adriene Koch, *Jefferson and Madison: The Great Collaboration* (New York: Oxford University Press, 1950), pp. 115–116; and Dumas Malone, *Jefferson and the Rights of Man*, Vol. II of *Jefferson and His Time* (Boston: Little, Brown, 1951), pp. 359–363.

queries to his correspondents about the public mood had revealed his own uneasiness.[60] Earlier in May, he and Madison had initiated the negotiations that would bring Philip Freneau to Philadelphia to establish a national newspaper to counterbalance the uncritical praise of the Federalists in the *Gazette of the United States*. They left on their trip, moreover, in the midst of a public furor that Jefferson had accidentally helped to raise.

The Rights of Man, Thomas Paine's defense of Lockian contractualism, republican government, and written constitutions against the challenge of Edmund Burke's *Reflections on the Revolution in France*, appeared in London in February 1791. John Beckley, clerk of the House of Representatives and soon to be an organizer of popular discontent, lent a copy of Paine's book to Madison, who gave it to Jefferson in turn. At Beckley's request, Jefferson sent the work along with a note of explanation and approval. In this circuitous fashion, it eventually arrived at the establishment of an American printer, an enterprising fellow who published it in May with a foreword taken from Jefferson's note: "I am extremely pleased to find . . . that something is at length to be publicly said against the political heresies which have sprung up among us. I have no doubt our citizens will rally a second time to the standard of Common Sense."[61] Issuing from Jefferson's general disgust with the tendency of thought in Federalist social circles and specifically directed against the writings of John Adams, these words were quickly printed far and wide. Jefferson genuinely regretted their publication, but they were remarkably successful in altering the public mood. They also put the Secretary of State at the head of rising discontent.

Twentieth-century readers may sympathize with Oliver Wolcott, who dismissed the explosion following Jefferson's note as a

60. Merrill D. Peterson, *Thomas Jefferson and the New Nation* (New York: Oxford University Press, 1970), is particularly instructive on the relationship between Jefferson's ideas about commercial policy and his more general philosophy, as well as on the debates within the administration early in 1791 that produced tensions between the two great secretaries. I have reserved a fuller discussion of foreign policy considerations for chapter 8.

61. Cunningham, pp. 9–11; Malone, p. 357.

controversy over "whether Tom Paine or Edmund Burke are the greatest fools."[62] With the appearance of the newspaper series signed "Publicola," John Quincy Adams' rejoinder to Jefferson and Paine, the heated argument turned increasingly on the question whether the English had a constitution or not. To contemporary Americans, however, more was at issue than the proper definition of a constitution. Writing about European governments, "Publicola," who was universally mistaken for the senior Adams, seemed to consider aristocracy a trivial imperfection in an English constitution that was generally quite sound. The House of Lords and the monarchy nearly disappeared from "Publicola's" discussion of the English government, for, like his father, John Quincy Adams was essentially concerned to advocate a set of institutional arrangements that would guarantee a people's liberty against a preference for empty declarations that could sacrifice real liberty for speculative definitions. On these grounds, "Publicola" preferred the English constitution to the new one of the French. Like his father, he identified the principles of the English Constitution with those of the American, because both were predicated on a governmental balance. Circumstances found him defending a hereditary, unwritten constitution against more "enlightened" French ideals. Like his father, he was mistaken for an advocate of mixed monarchy.[63]

In the years before the execution of Louis XVI, Americans were overwhelmingly disposed to see events in France as the beginning of a universal revolution inspired by the American example and promising the benefits of liberty, republicanism, and written constitutions to all mankind. The Adamses were students of the classic theorists of balanced government, more impressed with structural arrangements than with symbols. French neglect of the lessons of history and of the essential principles of Anglo-American constitutionalism seemed evident to

62. Gibbs, I, 69.

63. The letters of Publicola first appeared in the Boston *Centinel* between June 8 and July 27, 1791. They are reprinted in Worthington Chauncey Ford, ed., *The Writings of John Quincy Adams* (New York: Macmillan, 1913), I, 65–110.

them, and they tried repeatedly to get their countrymen to recognize those facts. Instead, their effort to temper the enthusiasm for things French made them apostates and counter-revolutionaries in the public mind. For years John Adams was an appealing target for all the suspicions of conspiracy endemic in American political life.

The reaction to "Publicola" was immediate and loud. Newspapers throughout the country were flooded during the summer of 1791 with pieces of every length attacking the series that everyone supposed came from the pen of the Vice President himself. Excerpts from a few of the longer replies indicate their general tone. "Agricola" considered it natural to find an enemy of freedom in a British monarchist like Burke, but he was astonished that "the unquestionable rights of man and the principles of liberty and free government should find an enemy in the lists of those who have ranked high as American patriots." He was sure that "Publicola's" purpose could not be to defend the rejected British government. It must be "to encourage and support the idea of a change of the government of these states from a republican to an aristocratical system."[64] Similarly, "A Republican," in Boston, branded the letters part of a wider attempt "to recommend the British constitution to the citizens of these states as a model for their imitation."[65]

Reminding everyone of the *Discourses on Davila*, in which the senior Adams had come close to advocating the hereditary principle, the letters of "Publicola" became another occasion for public definition of the differences between American and British forms. Once again, the critics demonstrated that for most Americans the abolition of hereditary privilege and the adoption of a written constitution by popular consent heavily outweighed any structural similarity that might remain between American and

64. "Agricola," no. 1. This three-part series made its appearance in Dunlap's *American Daily Advertiser* on June 5, 1791. It was reprinted in Boston by the *Independent Chronicle*.

65. *Independent Chronicle*, June 30, July 7, and following. Compare *American Daily Advertiser*, Sept. 5, 1791, and New York *Journal*, Sept. 3, 1791.

British institutions, more particularly because the spread of corruption through the British system was seen to vitiate any genuine balance there.[66] Rather than promoting a reexamination of admiration for the French, the Adamses' praise of the British constitution succeeded only in reviving the old charges of aristocracy and counterrevolution. Criticism of the French experiments was considered a criticism of American ideals.

The appearance of the letters of "Publicola" was thus an important occasion in the development of an ideology of opposition to Federalism. From the revival of the old suspicions of Federalist motives, it was a short step to a more general consideration of conspiracy and corruption in American affairs. Two long series that made their appearance together in the Boston *Independent Chronicle* of August 25, 1791, were early examples of the crucial reconsideration of the direction of the American polity that began to occur in the midst of the attack on Adams. "The Ploughman" concerned himself primarily with the principles of John Adams, devoting his essays to a defense of representative government and a consideration of the democratic social structure that made mixed government unnecessary in America. The attack on Adams as an advocate of the British constitution, which played a minor part in "The Ploughman's" pieces, moved to the front in the letters of "The Watchman" and became the starting point for a criticism, not only of "political heresies," but of the general course of American affairs.

Our government is professedly republican. . . . Whatever . . . tends to destroy the influence of [the people] and throw it into the hands of the few, the rich, or the well-born is . . . contrary to the spirit of our government. Wherever great property is, there generally is influence. Whatever therefore tends . . . to vest in a few so great a quantity as to make the distribution vastly and extravagantly unequal must in a de-

66. Besides "A Republican" see "Sketch of the British Constitution" in *American Daily Advertiser*, July 13, 1791. Paine had replied to Burke: "A mixed government is an imperfect everything, cementing and soldering the discordant parts together by corruption to act as a whole. . . . The parts cover each other till responsibility is lost, and the corruption which moves the machine contrives at the same time its own escape" ("The Rights of Man" in Philip S. Foner, ed., *The Complete Writings of Thomas Paine* (New York: Citadel Press, 1945), I, 339).

gree weaken the force and spirit of this government. Whatever measures draw towards the administration such an attachment, or give to them such a degree of influence, as that all their acts and doings shall be tacitly admitted as good and salutary . . . are highly dangerous to the continuance of our Constitution. . . .

The great danger to be apprehended at present to our government is that the democratical part, that is the people, will lose their due and proper influence in the government. The sources of this danger are various: . . . the influence made and increasingly in favor of the executive, the monarchical part, by the multiplicity of officers; . . . the vast accumulation of property occasioned by the funding system, etc. in the hands of those who have been called the natural aristocracy.[67]

By the end of summer 1791, the political mood of the country had undergone a radical change. Criticisms of the specific measures of the Federalist administration were much more numerous in the press and they were increasingly joined by more generalized attacks along lines laid down by the remonstrance of the Virginia Legislature and the letters of "The Watchman." A Philadelphia correspondent, for example, urged his readers to turn their concerns from the writings of "Publicola" to the dangers of the funded debt, "the parent of idleness, extravagance, national poverty, unnatural inequality among citizens, or wars, corrupt influence, aristocracy, tyranny, and slavery."[68] A committee of the western counties of Pennsylvania appealed to neighboring counties in Virginia, Kentucky, and its own state for support in opposing, not just the excise, but the funding system as a whole, "a system which has taken away all republican equal-

---

67. "The Watchman," no. 2, *Independent Chronicle*, Sept. 8, 1791. "The Ploughman" contributed 15 numbers between Aug. 25, 1791 and Jan. 19, 1792, "The Watchman" 6 numbers between Aug. 25 and Oct. 20, 1791. The third number of an earlier series, occasioned by the *Discourses on Davila*, had anticipated "The Watchman" in several respects, but it appeared in quieter times and failed to take hold. After an attack on the hereditary parts of the British constitution, "The Political Scrutator," attacked "the constant tendency of this government to enrich the opulent and impoverish the poor. . . . If the genius of the federal government is aristocratic, the compensation, salaries, and pensions which have been so freely granted have a direct tendency to increase this disposition. . . . They are to be accounted for upon that destructive system of 'influence' which has corrupted the government of Britain to its root and will infallibly operate the same evil in this country" (*Chronicle*, Sept. 9, 1790).

68. Philadelphia *General Advertiser*, July 20, 1791.

ity in fortune, weakened industry, shaken morality, introduced corruption, and laid the foundation of the dissolution of the government itself."[69] Even Madison, who had finally succeeded in his negotiations with Freneau, was privately revealing similar concerns, imagining that "the stock-jobbers will become the pretorian band of the government, at once its tools and its tyrants, bribed by its largesses and overawing it by clamors and combinations."[70] By this time, the *Gazette of the United States* was in full cry against the critics of the government, and others were joining in the chase.[71] Early in 1792, a rejoinder to the critics by one of Fenno's correspondents made clear the direction of the opposition's attacks: "When the newspapers tell us of the minions of power and of overgrown individuals in office and of other cant which seems to be copied from an English opposition print, what are we to think?"[72]

69. Ibid., Sept. 30, 1791; also printed the same day in the *American Daily Advertiser*.

70. To Jefferson, Aug. 8, 1791, in *Writings of Madison*, VI, 58–59; see also p. 55. The unseemly scramble for shares in the Bank of the U.S. provoked this outburst.

71. "Can it possibly be considered as a criterion of patriotism to excite jealousies and suggest suspicions respecting the general government? Can those men be friends to the peace, the happiness, the prosperity, or freedom of their country whose whole merit as political characters arises from their secret and open cabals against this government and the present administration?" (*American Daily Advertiser*, Aug. 29, 1791). Dunlap was a staunch democrat and foe of "Publicola," but this was apparently the editor's own position. His paper remained open to both sides.

72. "Civis," *Gazette of the United States*, Jan. 7, 1792.

CHAPTER 6

Party

MEETING in Philadelphia in the wake of the furor over "Publicola" and just a week before the first issue of the *National Gazette*, the Second Congress differed markedly from the First. While half its members remained essentially unaligned, the other half sided consistently either with James Madison or against him.[1] This was the first session of Congress to call forth considerable contemporary comment on congressional parties. Fisher Ames, for example, told one of his correspondents that the causes he had explained in a former letter had given rise to "a regular, well-disciplined opposition party." "We have," he estimated, "near twenty *Antis*, dragons watching the tree of liberty and who consider every strong measure and almost every ordinary one as an attempt to rob the tree of its fair fruit."[2] Similarly,

1. Noble E. Cunningham, Jr., *The Jeffersonian Republicans* (Chapel Hill: University of North Carolina Press, 1957), pp. 22–23 and appendices. Two-thirds of the time on major issues, Madison could count on the Virginia, North Carolina, and Georgia delegates, half the Maryland delegates, Tredwell of New York, and Findley of Pennsylvania. Most of the New England delegates opposed Madison with equal consistency, while representatives from the middle states were generally unaligned. I am not convinced that the more sophisticated quantitative methods of roll-call analysis mentioned in chapter 5 note 50, provide a better understanding of the rise of parties, primarily because the existence of a "party," unlike the presence of a voting bloc, is very much a matter of contemporary perceptions. For this reason, it does seem to matter most which representatives aligned themselves with Madison on major issues.

2. To G. R. Minot, May 3, 1792, in Seth Ames, ed., *Works of Fisher Ames*, 2 vols. (Boston: Little, Brown, 1854), I, 118–119, 114–115. See also Wolcott to Michael J. Stone, June 9, 1792, in George Gibbs, ed., *Memoirs of the Administrations of Washington and John Adams* (New York: by subscription, 1846), I, 80. The earlier letter referred to by Ames (Nov. 30, 1791, *Works*, I, 101–106) should be read by every

on the other side, Thomas Jefferson presented Washington with an opinion of Alexander Hamilton and his supporters that may remind the reader of the earlier strictures of William Maclay. When the President expressed a fear that Jefferson's plans for an early retirement would give rise to public discontent, Jefferson took advantage of the opening to voice his opinion that the "single source" of public discontent was the Treasury. His colleague there had contrived a system that flooded the states with paper money, encouraged men to abandon useful pursuits in favor of speculative gambling, and "introduced its poison into the government itself." Having voted for the funding program in order to promote their own pecuniary interests, some congressmen had ever since "lent all the energy of their talents and instrumentality of their offices to the establishment and enlargement of this system."[3] Before the end of 1792, a set of fears and expectations that had prompted objections to administration plans since the first days of the government had come together in an integrated whole. This systematic ideology was both a product and a cause of the emergence of the first political party of the modern sort.

I

In the first session of the Second Congress, the most important issue of a theoretical nature concerned the proper ratio of representatives to population and the proper apportionment of representatives among the states. Occasioned by the Census, the question of apportionment was frankly contested in terms of state and

student of the development of the first party system. It is a long and serious attempt on Ames's part to alert Massachusetts to the presence of a subterranean discontent, founded on deep socio-economic differences, which had given rise to a consistent Southern opposition based on principles he considered irreconcilable with sound government and ultimately Antifederalist.

3. "Anas," in Paul Leicester Ford, ed., *The Works of Thomas Jefferson*, 12 vols. (New York: Putnam, 1904), I, 192–198. This followed an earlier conversation in which Jefferson had urged Washington to put the post office under jurisdiction of the State Department, partly because "the Department of the Treasury possessed already such an influence as to swallow the whole executive power."

sectional interests, but the problem of the proper ratio of representatives to population touched on fundamental questions of governmental theory. Advocates of a larger number of representatives, who were already beginning to see themselves in the classic role of a legislative minority who nevertheless represented a majority of the people, urged the necessity of a fuller representation of all the interests among the people and stressed the superiority of a larger representation in resisting legislative corruption. Their opponents insisted on the superior convenience, lesser expense, and greater stability of smaller numbers, while stubbornly maintaining that the smaller numbers could effectively represent all views. In this debate and in scattered arguments throughout the session on a further assumption of state debts, the minority's concern with influence and corruption was fully aired.

The fieriest dragon of the session, William Branch Giles of Virginia, took the lead among the Madisonian minority in advancing a systematic account of the rapid degeneration of the infant government. All representative governments, he said, display a natural tendency to degenerate from republicanism to monarchy, primarily because of the unequal distribution of wealth among their citizens. The abundant resources of America naturally favor inequality, and the federal government's handling of the public debt had given inequality another boost by gathering scattered debts into a minority of hands and greatly increasing their value. This policy enlisted, in opposition to the agricultural and republican interests of the country, "a great monied interest . . . who, having embarked their fortunes with the government, would go all lengths with its administration whether right or wrong." The government gave rise to this interest with a funding plan that placed the management of the debt as far as possible from the reach of future legislatures. Giles

saw systems introduced to carve out of the common rights of one part of the community privileges, monopolies, exclusive rights, etc. for the benefit of another with no other view . . . but to create nurseries of immediate dependents upon the government whose interest will always stimulate them to support its measures however iniquitous and tyrannical.

A fuller representation, acting to combat the influence of this monied interest in the Congress, could decide whether America "would preserve the simplicity, chastity, and purity of her native . . . republicanism . . . or whether she will . . . prostitute herself to the venal and borrowed artifices and corruptions of a stale and pampered monarchy."[4]

Giles's speeches on a fuller representation were the earliest congressional attempt to delineate a systematic justification for formed opposition to the Federalist program. They seized the only intellectual grounds for such an opposition that had proven tenable in Anglo-American politics. With remarkably little revision of the premises relating to the methods of subverting legislative independence, Giles was able to invoke the traditional rhetoric of eighteenth-century oppositions to charge the Federalist administration with a deliberate attempt to undermine the constitutional structure that guaranteed liberty and democracy. With little change, the whole apocalyptic ideology seemed to apply. This revisionary use of English opposition ideology had periodically been anticipated since 1789, in other congressional speeches, in newspapers, and in private correspondence, but Giles's speeches constituted the strongest and most systematic indictment of the administration to date. As such, they drew an appropriate response from congressional Federalists and from the Secretary of the Treasury himself. Yet Giles's speeches were a moderate expression of ideological developments beginning to occur in the country at large, and they were not the strongest reason why Hamilton decided to quit his policy of silence and confront his opponents direct.

Hamilton must long have been concerned with the rising op-

4. *Annals of Congress*, Second Congress, pp. 546–548. Earlier debate on the question, including a comparison by Giles of methods of corruption in Britain and America, occurred on Nov. 14 and 15, 1791, and can be found on pp. 178–191.

position to his economic program and must have discussed its development with his friends. Still, his surviving papers for 1791 and much of 1792 fail to contain any comments on partisan politics. Not until after the adjournment of the first session of the Second Congress do we have direct evidence of his feelings and views. Then, as an early step in a campaign that was to culminate in a full-blown newspaper war, Hamilton composed a long letter to Edward Carrington, a Virginia Federalist and Continental Army friend to whom he looked for Southern help. This letter was one of the most important documents of the developing party struggle.[5]

Unbosoming himself to Carrington, Hamilton confessed that he had accepted his office at the Treasury only in full confidence of Madison's general support. Madison's opposition to the funding program had surprised him, but he had remained reluctant to accept reports that Madison's conduct originated from anything other than disinterested and honest motives.

It was not 'til the last session that I became unequivocally convinced of the following truth—That Mr. Madison, cooperating with Mr. Jefferson, is at the head of a faction decidedly hostile to me and my administration and actuated by views in my judgment subversive of the principles of good government and dangerous to the union, peace, and happiness of the country.[6]

Jefferson was an unrestrained enemy and had proven it by bringing Philip Freneau to Philadelphia to publish a newspaper "devoted to the subversion of me and [my] measures . . . [and] generally unfriendly to the government of the U. States." Madison's private conduct had been less objectionable,[7] but his uniform public opposition showed him to be an enemy as well. Though

5. It was dated May 26, 1792. Harold C. Syrett and Jacob E. Cooke, eds., *The Papers of Alexander Hamilton* (New York: Columbia University Press, 1960–), XI, 426–445.

6. The reference to "me and my administration" is one of many indications that Hamilton indeed saw himself as a prime minister.

7. Hamilton in fact misjudged his men. Madison, an old college roommate of the revolutionary poet, had done more than Jefferson to bring Freneau to Philadelphia.

quiet during the last session of Congress, he was still "the promp-
ter of Mr. Giles and others who were the open instruments of
opposition."

Condemning his opponents' ambitions, Jefferson's questionable attachment to the Constitution, Madison's changeableness,
and the friends' "womanish" opinions in foreign affairs, Hamilton
charged the opposition leaders with a willingness to destroy the
government itself in order to destroy his administration. He
tended to find the root of their conduct in ambition, but he
admitted the possibility that they might by now believe their
own propaganda, their "bugbear of a faction in government unfriendly to liberty." In any case, he was determined to treat them
as irreconcilable foes.

While we may question Hamilton's interpretation of his opponents' motives, he was certainly correct, in general, in his information about their conduct and views. Jefferson was recording in
his "Anas" evidence of Hamilton's preference for a British constitution,[8] and he had already expressed to Washington his conviction that Hamilton's ambition and the economic program
were subversive of the government. Madison, not content with
his recognized role as prime mover of the congressional opposition to Federalist policy, had begun to take an anonymous part in
the newspaper opposition as well.[9] More than the other irrita-
tions, it was this public attack on his policies, carried forward by

8. The best known would eventually find its way into the preface to the "Anas."
Jefferson recalled a dinner in April 1791 at which John Adams had remarked that the
British constitution, purged of its corruption, would be the most perfect on earth.
"Hamilton paused and said, 'purge it of its corruption and . . . it would become an
impracticable government; as it stands at present, with all its supposed defects, it is the
most perfect government which ever existed.'" "Hamilton," Jefferson concluded, "was
not only a monarchist, but for a monarchy bottomed on corruption" (*Works*, I, 167–
183).

9. Madison's anonymous contributions to the *National Gazette* through the end of
1792 are reprinted in Gaillard Hunt, ed., *The Writings of James Madison* (New York:
Putnam, 1900– 1910), VI, 67– 123. In the early months of the paper's history, while
Freneau was pretending objectivity, Madison's contributions were largely of a theoretical nature. They became gradually more anti-Federalist and ended in thundering attacks on Hamiltonian policy: "The Union: Who Are Its Real Friends," printed on April
2, 1792; "A Candid State of Parties," printed on Sept. 26; and "Who Are the Best
Keepers of the People's Liberty," on Dec. 20.

Madison and others in the *National Gazette*, that provoked Hamilton's countermeasures. In his letter to Carrington, the Secretary had said that Jefferson censured the funding program "on principles which, if they should become general, could not but end in the subversion of the system." Through the agency of Freneau's newspaper, they threatened to do exactly that.

II

The first issue of the semiweekly *National Gazette* appeared in Philadelphia on October 31, 1791, not long before the publication of Hamilton's *Report on Manufactures*. For a few months, Freneau, who had been encouraged to undertake the venture partly by a place as translator in Jefferson's Department of State, tried to build his circulation and establish a national reputation by maintaining a nonpartisan stance.[10] After the turn of the year, his mask began to slip. In several anonymous essays, Madison sought to lay a groundwork for later attacks on the Federalist program.[11] In an essay on "Parties," he tacitly charged the Federalists with encouraging the growth of artificial party distinctions by promoting inequalities of wealth. Any neo-Harringtonian would have recognized the danger to republican society and government that such a development involved.[12] In another essay, he proposed the replacement of Montesquieu's

10. The best history of the *National Gazette* may be chapter 8 of Lewis Leary, *That Rascal Freneau: A Study in Literary Failure* (New Brunswick, N.J.: Rutgers University Press, 1941).

11. The subtleties of the relationship between Madison, Jefferson, and Freneau may never be completely clear. Leary, p. 244, probably underestimates their connection in his attempt to stress Freneau's autonomy, though I would agree that Jefferson did not control or even try to control the *National Gazette*. Madison probably continued to work more closely with the editor than Jefferson did. Still, it is probably true, as Madison told Edmund Randolph (*Writings*, VI, 117–118), that, in coaxing Freneau to come to Philadelphia by offering him a minor place in the State Department, he and Jefferson were simply encouraging a wider dissemination of views similar to their own. Freneau remained largely independent as an editor, and his radicalism eventually outran the party leaders'. Yet the leaders did take the initiative with the editor, used their combined influence in an attempt to assure his success, and worked with others in the orchestration of some of the paper's campaigns. Until Freneau decided to drown with Citizen Genet, the *National Gazette* was a Republican party sheet.

12. *National Gazette*, Jan. 23, 1792; also in *Writings of Madison*, VI, 86.

categorization of governments into those depending on fear, honor, or virtue by one that would recognize their dependence on force, public interest, or corruption. Describing a government proceeding from corruption, Madison plainly meant his readers to keep the Federalists in mind. This was a government

substituting the motive of private interest in place of public duty, converting its pecuniary dispensations into bounties to favorites or bribes to opponents, accomodating its measures to the avidity of a part of the nation instead of the benefit of the whole, in a word enlisting an army of interested partisans whose tongues, whose pens, whose intrigues, and whose active combinations, by supplying the terror of the sword, may support a real domination of the few under an apparent liberty of the many.[13]

Along with Madison's essays, after the beginning of 1792, Freneau also reprinted from Dunlap's *American Daily Advertiser* a less subtle attack on the administration. "Caius" accused Hamilton personally of creating a system that threatened to "overwhelm and destroy . . . every free and valuable principle of our government." Having loosed a flock of preying harpies by means of his funding system, Hamilton had gone on to produce the assumption, enlarging the debt and assuring its perpetuation. The national bank was the consummation of his scheme, marking "the union of the government itself with the new-created monied interests" and permitting placemen, in the guise of bank directors, to sit in Congress. Hamilton's proposals for manufactures would be a final touch, creating other monopolies as dangerous as the bank for encouraging "inequality, corruption, and oppression." Taken together, these measures threatened the complete subordination of the agircultural interests to the monied interests and the introduction to America of "all the weaknesses, vices, and deformities of the decayed and expiring constitution of Britain."[14]

13. "Spirit of Government," ibid., Feb. 20, 1792; *Writings*, VI, 93–95.
14. With the exception of the last, from number 3, all the quotations are from the first of "Caius's" four letters, reprinted in the *National Gazette* on Jan. 1, 1792. "Caius" advanced his thesis in the first letter and went on to elaborate particular points in three additional numbers. Number 2, reprinted on Jan. 26, discussed funded debts as con-

By April 1792, a month before Hamilton's letter to Carrington, the *National Gazette's* original mask of objectivity was
completely gone. March 15 had seen the first letter of "Brutus,"
attacking along the front opened by "Caius."[15] "Brutus" too accused the administration of perverting the government to serve
the few by means of an economic program that attached the
monied interests to the Treasury Department and threatened to
make the poorer classes tributary to their combined power.[16] To
these charges of perversion of the government, moreover,
"Brutus" added a broader concern with the tendency of speculative habits to discourage industrious pursuits, to increase inequalities of wealth, and to undermine the character of the
people.[17] With adoption of the plan for manufactures, "Brutus"
feared, the enemies of state governments would see

a consolidated, energetic government supported by public creditors,
speculators, members of these several companies, and others receiving
bounties and exemptions rising upon the ruins of our free republics;
they will also see the people . . . ruled by . . . an alliance . . . between the

---

stantly expanding sources of corruption. Number 3 argued that Bank directors sitting
in Congress were a new variety of placemen and attacked privileged corporations.
Number 4 returned to the tendency of a funded debt to continue to expand.

15. It is not usually possible to establish the direct influence of one anonymous
newspaper series on another, but the great similarity between their arguments certainly
suggests that "Brutus" had at least read "Caius," if he was not in fact the same man.
Both writers, it might also be remarked, were joining in the growing trend in the
antiadministration press toward the revival of pseudonyms suggestive of the Whig-
historical, opposition, and ultimately classical roots of their ideas.

16. In this and in the third of his six letters on "The Funding System," "Brutus"
expanded on "Caius's" charges by adding public stockholders to the list of new placemen in Congress. Pointing out that the value of the debt depended on the Treasury's
ability to enforce taxation on the body of the people, "Brutus" charged that congressional stockholders had to be "the uniform and active partisans of fiscal arrangements
and new assumptions of power" (*National Gazette*, March 19, 1792).

17. Concern for a democratic balance of property and for the moral fiber of the
people had earlier been expressed by any number of people. See "A Farmer," *National
Gazette*, March 1, 1792, and particularly "Anti-Monopolist," in the Philadelphia *General Advertiser*, Jan. 23 and 24, 1792. Provoked, like "Caius," by the *Report on Manufactures*, the latter writer presented the funding system and the proposal of privileged
corporations, both of which he took to favor a closely associated few at the expense of
the many, as evidence that "our political bark seems to be gently sailing down that
current leading from freedom to slavery which that of every other nation has gone
before it."

government and these wealthy public creditors and companies of its own creating, cemented by reciprocal advantages—these receiving favors from the government and the government in return their united support in all its abuses. . . . These are not visionary fears but apprehensions justified by [the experience of] other countries, particularly England, from whence all these schemes are imported.[18]

Elaborating his thesis in additional letters, "Brutus" stretched his contributions into the early part of April. When he was finished, the argument was taken up by "Sidney," who set his extended criticism of the excise in the context of concern with the corruption of the government and the people.[19] The two of them were strongly reinforced by other contributors, including Madison and Freneau himself.[20] Freneau, in fact, seized every issue and occasion to further the cause of the rising "Republican interest." He joined in the campaign to replace Vice President Adams with Governor Clinton of New York. He encouraged the growth of the Democratic-Republican Societies, which were beginning to organize popular suspicions of the Federalist government.[21] Above all, he continued to attack the corrupting effects of the Hamiltonian financial program.

III

By midsummer of 1792, contributors to Freneau's gazette had developed a systematic ideology of opposition to the Federalist administration. In the establishment of the national bank and in Hamilton's *Report on Manufactures*, critics had found the needles they required to sew together the assorted fears and suspicions present from the earliest days of the new government and as old as Shaftesbury's opposition to the ministers of Charles II. Identifying congressmen who acted as directors of the national bank

18. "Brutus," no. 3, *National Gazette*, March 22, 1792.
19. "On the Secretary's Report on the Excise," eight numbers, ibid., April 23 to May 24, 1792. The first and last numbers are most important for the general context of "Sidney's" thought.
20. Both Madison, in "The Union," and Freneau attributed the establishment of a system of corruption to a desire for hereditary government.
21. Eugene Perry Link, *Democratic-Republican Societies, 1790–1800* (New York: Columbia University Press, 1942).

or held certificates of public debt with an older kind of place-man—for they seemed equally dependent on the government—"Caius" and "Brutus," like Jefferson or Giles, were able to announce the discovery of a system in Hamilton's measures closely akin to the methods British ministers had used to create an executive influence in the legislature. That done, they had only to follow the well-known model of English opposition thought to weave together the criticism of legislative corruption with democratic hostility to special privilege, agrarian distaste for speculative gains, and a neo-Harringtonian concern for a certain equality of wealth—all of which derived, in any case, from the same connected matrix of ideas. Once the parallel was drawn between America and England, a few charged phrases were enough to summon up the powerful old visions of freedom in decay. And these were easily combined, in turn, with the fears of counter-revolution started by the Antifederalists and aggravated by the comments and writings of Federalists such as Hamilton and Adams. The product, many times over, was a criticism that might take the form of Freneau's own satire, "Rules for Changing a Limited Republican Government into an Unlimited Hereditary One," which recommended every Federalist measure from the use of pompous styles of address through funding to creation of a professional army. A helpful model, of course, was England.[22]

Other newspapers soon fell in with this systematic line of attack.[23] A few, as we have seen, had anticipated its directions, for the component ideas were the common stock of the revolutionary age. The *National Gazette*, however, was certainly the primary

22. Two numbers, *National Gazette*, July 4 and 7, 1792. Freneau was no laggard at spotting conspiratorial purpose—at one point he suggested that popular resistance to the funding program would be a good excuse for introduction of a standing army—or at turning a good sentence: "Money will be put under the direction of government and the government will be put under the direction of money."
23. Some of the better examples are "Brutus," New York *Journal*, Jan. 21, 1792; "Plan for a Nobility in the United States," reprinted from the *American Daily Advertiser* in the *Independent Chronicle*, May 10, 1792; "A Correspondent," *Independent Chronicle*, April 19, 1792; and "Job Squarators," ibid., May 17, 1792. All these writers refer specifically to Federalist imitation of British precedents for corruption.

source of the development and national dissemination of a neo-opposition ideology. And there is every reason to suspect that here, as in much else, it served as organ of a more or less concerted effort by the leaders of the developing Republican party. Hamilton thus struck close to center when he opened his counterattack on his tormentors with a shot at the improper connection between Jefferson and Freneau: "The editor of the *National Gazette* receives a salary from government. *Quere*—Whether this salary is paid him for *translations* or for *publications* the design of which is to vilify those to whom the voice of the people has committed the administration of public affairs."[24]

In two more notes signed "T. L." and in a series of longer essays signed "An American," all of them printed in the *Gazette of the United States* in July and August 1792, Hamilton pushed forward a campaign against his opponents.[25] He identified Jefferson, the employer and director of Freneau, as the head of an opposition to the administration and a determined foe of the government itself, calling on him to resign his office if he could not support the administration. Jefferson's friends, led by Madison and Monroe, jumped to the defense, while Freneau proved eminently capable of his own.[26] The *National Gazette* and its Federalist rival, which was in fact as closely tied to Hamilton as the other sheet was to the opposition, were soon involved in a bitter feud over the relative independence of their editors, and the controversy started by the charges of "T. L." soon rippled out through other papers from the capital into New England and the South. By summer's end, every section of the country was involved in the spectacle of newspaper warfare between the cabinet ministers. Everywhere, there was a growing pressure to take sides. The threat of rapid polarization of the public must have been a major consideration in Washington's decision to intervene.

24. "T. L.," *Gazette of the United States*, July 25, 1792.
25. These are all available in *Hamilton Papers*, vol. XII.
26. Philip M. Marsh, ed., *Monroe's Defense of Jefferson and Freneau against Hamilton* (Oxford, Ohio: privately printed.)

In the middle of August, in similar letters to the two principals, he appealed for tolerance and an end to the public dispute. Their replies made clear the fundamental sources of the quarrel.

While Hamilton admitted his agency in the public disagreement and indicated his willingness to help repair the breach, he felt he could not immediately withdraw. His quarrel, he explained, was not with Jefferson as an individual, but with a "formed party" which meant to destroy the funding system and so subvert the federal government.[27] A fuller explanation was unnecessary at the time. At Mount Vernon in July, Washington had become concerned with antiadministration sentiment in Virginia, and he had written an earlier letter to Hamilton in which he summarized opposition arguments as communicated to him by Jefferson and asked for Hamilton's response.[28] The Secretary had answered every specific objection to his conduct and had replied as well to the more general charges of corruption and subversion of the government. In this letter as in his public essays, Hamilton appealed to his known propriety as sufficient defense of his motives, denied that ownership of the public debt or stock in the national bank could create an improper interest, and turned his opponents' denunciations of a "corrupt squadron" back upon themselves. Throughout the decade, Hamilton would treat the charge of monarchical conspiracy as absurd, and he would insist, as he did in this letter, that dangers to the American republic would not come from the Cato's who defended the administration, but from the Catilines and Caesars who sought to arouse popular prejudice against it.[29]

27. *Hamilton Papers*, XII, 347–349.
28. Ibid., pp. 129–133.
29. Ibid., pp. 229–258. Beginning with Jefferson and continuing to the present, too much has been made of Hamilton's professed admiration for Caesar. Hamilton did yearn for military glory, and he admired Caesar's military accomplishments. In the 1790s, however, Hamilton, with many others, usually referred to Caesar as a prototype of demagogic politician, who used his popularity to destroy the Roman Republic. For a recent comment on misunderstanding of the image of Caesar in Hamilton's thought see Thomas P. Govan, "Alexander Hamilton and Julius Caesar," *William and Mary Quarterly*, 32 (1975), 475–480.

Jefferson, too, expressed regret over his involvement in a public controversy, but he denied that he had encouraged Freneau to come to Philadelphia in order to oppose Hamilton's administration, that he had ever contributed personally to the newspaper dispute, or that he—unlike some others—had ever tried to influence the legislature.[30] He freely admitted that he had opposed the economic program in private and again offered a justification of his views. Hamilton's program

flowed from principles adverse to liberty and was calculated to undermine and demolish the republic by creating an influence of his department over the members of the legislature. . . . to draw all the powers of government into the hands of the general legislature, to establish means for corrupting a sufficient corps in that legislature to . . . preponderate . . . , and to have that corps under the command of the Secretary of the Treasury for the purpose of subverting step by step the principles of the Constitution, which he has so often declared to be a thing of nothing which must be changed.[31]

This was neither the first nor the last time that Jefferson tried to convince the President that the danger to the republic was real

30. Except on the occasion of the assumption. Whether the dinner-table bargain was consummated or not, Jefferson believed it had been responsible for passage of assumption. He later identified his role in it as perhaps the worst mistake of his career, complaining that Hamilton had duped him at a time when, newly arrived in New York, he was ignorant of the context of affairs. Several historians have faulted Jefferson for disingenuousness on this point, remarking that he had a sound understanding of the crisis and indicated no compunctions at the time. But Jefferson's complaint should be seen in the context of his later conviction that funding and assumption were first steps in a design for subverting the republic, which Hamilton had conceived in the Confederation Period and managed to make him an unwitting party to.

31. *Writings of Jefferson*, VII, 136–149, especially pp. 138–139. The later explanation of Hamilton's design in the preface to the "Anas," which is emphasized in the introduction to this work, repeats the charges advanced in this letter of 1792. Hamilton's object, Jefferson recalled, had been to "create a machine for the corruption of the legislature." Congressmen enriched by the financial program became a "phalanx of the Treasury" committed to Hamilton's support, giving the Secretary effective control of the whole government. "Nothing like a majority in Congress yielded to this corruption. Far from it. But a division . . . had already taken place in the honest part of that body between the parties styled republican and federal. The latter being monarchists in principle adhered to Hamilton of course, as their leader in principle, and this mercenary phalanx added to them ensured him always a majority in both houses."

and profound, and, on these matters, he spoke increasingly as a party man presenting party views.[32]

Washington's intervention in the public quarrel had a chastening effect, but neither Hamilton nor his opponents were ready to recede. Actually, Hamilton's attack reached its crescendo in September with the simultaneous publication of his "Catallus" papers in the *Gazette of the United States* and several pseudonymous exchanges with Jefferson's defenders in the *National Gazette*.[33] Freneau soon decided to let other newspapers carry the brunt of the dispute, but it continued with slight abatement until the end of the year. Only in December, pressed by other business and confronted with Monroe's knowledge of his affair with Maria Reynolds, did Hamilton decide to desist.

A host in himself, Hamilton managed throughout the controversy to remain on the offensive. Under his prodding, the exchanges centered more and more on questions of Jefferson's attitude toward the Constitution and his conduct and morality while governor of Virginia and ambassador to France.[34] These were brilliant tactics, but Hamilton's attack was probably a strategic mistake. It pitted his own prestige against that of a greater revolutionary hero in a public contest he might have expected to lose. By challenging his opponents' motives, it also forced them to develop the very arguments he feared.[35] Through

32. Any number of passages could be cited from his works, but see particularly his summaries of conversations with Washington in July and October ("Anas," ibid., I, 227–231, 233–237) and his letter of May 23, which Washington had used for the outline of objections he sent to Hamilton. Merrill D. Peterson, *Thomas Jefferson and the New Nation* (New York: Oxford University Press, 1970), p. 463, notes that March 1792 marks the first occasions on which Jefferson began to speak of "we" and "they" in correspondence.

33. The newspaper exchange can be followed easily and almost in full in *Hamilton Papers*, vols. XII-XIII.

34. There is room to wonder whether Hamilton deliberately avoided a more direct confrontation on the issue of the economic program. He prepared but never published a full defense. See "The Vindication," *Hamilton Papers*, XI, 461 ff.

35. Neither was it a good idea, obviously, to start an argument about attitudes toward the Constitution.

the summer and fall of 1792, the newspapers were filled with the opposition's attempt to define its character and justify its role. In conjunction with the direct exchanges with Hamilton and the concurrent election campaign, these writings brought an enormous accession of strength to the "Republican interest." They had an important part in the transformation of a congressional opposition into a great national party.[36]

All sorts of considerations, economic, sectional, or personal, clearly influenced men to link themselves with the rising Republican party, and it is difficult to estimate their relative importance. But ideas were also a bond. Relatively few Americans took an active part in politics during the 1790s. Those who did were usually well educated, still somewhat deferential, and extremely well informed.[37] If they could not afford a newspaper themselves, they usually had access to a tavern that subscribed to several prints.[38] With their printings of debates in Congress, public proclamations, and the like, these papers kept their readers easily as well informed as citizens today, and with their many essays on political affairs, they made it easier for readers to perceive the issues on a fundamental plane.

It can be shown quite clearly that the growth of a cohesive

36. For the election of 1792, an important stage in party development, see Cunningham, pp. 29–32 and chap. 2. The battle, in many parts of the country, was clearly one between supporters and opponents of Treasury policy.

37. An attempt to bring more rigor to our understanding of the nature of politics in the early national years—not wholly successful, but useful in some respects—is Ronald P. Formisano, "Deferential-Participant Politics: The Early Republic's Political Culture, 1789–1840," *American Political Science Review*, 68 (1974), 473–487. It is often estimated that perhaps a quarter of those eligible participated in state elections in the early 1790s. And the only eligibles were free, white, adult males who paid a tax at least.

38. Though it does not, in my judgment, present a useful analysis of Republican thought, Donald H. Stewart, *The Opposition Press of the Federalist Period* (Albany: State University of New York Press, 1969), contains a wealth of useful information about the newspapers of these years. See pp. 16 ff. for circulation figures and estimates that nearly everyone who could vote had access to papers. A circulation figure of 2000 copies was good for an influential paper, but several times that many people probably read an issue and countless others were exposed to the most important essays by way of reprints in other sheets.

opposition party closely paralleled the development of a systematic and constitutionally fundamental justification of its existence and intent. By the end of 1792, Republican leaders were agreed on the nature of their discontent. In the pages of the *National Gazette*, in other newspapers, in speeches and public meetings, and in countless unrecorded conversations, they had defined themselves to one another, and they had attracted hundreds of ordinary citizens to their support. The arguments by which they accomplished this were designed for general, not sectional, appeal. As any student of the eighteenth-century heritage must see, they were not essentially new, but a revision of the English opposition ideology that was at the roots of American revolutionary thought. They were, in fact, so thoroughly familiar to the literate proportion of the people that, without a fully systematic explication, they were comprehended and assented to in every corner of the land.

Writer after writer, in the last half of 1792, hammered home the opposition themes, less often in long and careful argumentation than in a few phrases loaded with the apocalyptic connotations made familiar by a century of Anglo-American concern for the future of free government in the world. The old division of Federalist and Antifederalist, they said, must give way to one between the friends of the republic and a clique who would betray it. The latter, they explained, had concocted in the economic program a new, but equally insidious, system of corruption. This system was designed, at once, to undermine the balance of the federal republic and to prepare the way for its replacement by a different kind of state. With the aid of its dependents in the legislature, the executive controlled two branches of the government and threatened to destroy all opposition to its plans. Meanwhile, vices spread by the corrupting influence and example of speculative habits and the monied creatures of administration, whose swollen wealth endangered the foundations of a free society, prepared the country for the transformation to hereditary government, which authors of the system plainly had in mind.[39]

39. The *National Gazette*, in pieces such as Madison's "A Candid State of Parties" (Sept. 26), "Paradox" (Oct. 13), and "Mirabeau" (Dec. 12), continued to be the primary source of systematic presentation of the neo-opposition view, although long pieces in the same tradition of argument continued to appear occasionally in other papers as well. For example see "The Crisis," eleven numbers, *Independent Chronicle*, Sept. 6, 1792 to April 26, 1793. Brief but clear attempts to conjure up the imagery of neo-opposition thought—from catchwords to short paragraphs that appeared alone or in the midst of longer pieces—were legion. Reference might be made to a few striking examples from the *National Gazette*: a correspondent in the paper of Aug. 11; "Cato" on Aug. 18; a different "Brutus" on Sept. 1; "Monitor" on Oct. 13; and unsigned paragraphs on Oct. 10 and Dec. 8—something in nearly every issue. And Federalists clearly recognized the English sources of these attacks, repeatedly condemning them as irrelevent in American circumstances. For some additional examples see *Gazette of the United States*, Feb. 18, April 11, and May 2, 1792.

CHAPTER 7

On Domestic Grounds

On February 1, 1793, eleven days after the execution of Louis XVI, the revolutionary French Republic declared war on Great Britain. Soon the activities of the Republic's ambassador, Edmund Genet, were leading topics of controversy in the American press. Foreign policy assumed a growing importance in American political debate, pulling into the arena men whom domestic issues had never touched. A time was coming when American parties would be identified as "French" or "English" and the singing of foreign songs could touch off fighting in the streets. In the popularization of the political contest and in the transformation of congressional groupings into great national parties, historians agree, nothing equalled the influence of the French Revolution and the foreign war. For some time to come, however, the quarrel over Hamiltonian finance retained its leading place in the American debate. And the explosive impact of events in Europe can be fully understood only in the light of preexisting quarrels over liberty at home.

I

News of the execution of the king and the beginning of the war with Britain—the events that generated the first serious divergence of American opinions about the Revolution in France—arrived in the United States not long after the adjournment of the second session of the Second Congress. Sitting between November 5, 1792, and March 2, 1793, during the later months of the newspaper war between Hamilton and the Jeffersonians, this session of Congress was a ferocious party battleground.[1] The Republican minority believed they had secured a majority of seats in the succeeding Congress during the recent congressional elections, and they meant to postpone important business until then. The most advantageous manner of accomplishing this end was to open an offensive against the Federalist system along the lines suggested by supporters in the press.

Early in the session, a motion to reduce the size of the army gave Republicans an opportunity to display their familiarity with traditional denunciations of the dangers of a standing army.[2] Then they moved into an effort to prevent department heads from appearing in the House to present or defend executive programs. Opponents of this very minimal sort of influence failed by five votes to forbid reference of legislative plans to executive officers, but they did succeed in preventing occasional appearances of department heads to explain their measures and in preventing reference of a plan for a sinking fund to the Secretary of the Treasury. Next, they moved to achieve the logical goal of their public ideology. The high point of the session was an attempt to force Alexander Hamilton to resign.[3]

1. Noble E. Cunningham, Jr., *The Jeffersonian Republicans* (Chapel Hill: University of North Carolina Press, 1957), pp. 50–51. Ames remarked that "Virginia moves in a solid column, and the discipline of the party is as severe as the Prussian," while Oliver Wolcott became concerned for the first time with a persistent opposition. See Seth Ames, ed., *The Works of Fisher Ames*, 2 vols. (Boston: Little, Brown, 1854), I, 127–129; and George Gibbs, ed., *Memoirs of the Administrations of Washington and John Adams*, 2 vols. (New York: by subscription, 1846), I, 84–86.

2. The *Annals of Congress* show that excise and army bills afforded perennial opportunities for displays of libertarian rhetoric. These are discussed only briefly because the orators merely emphasized the expected warnings that professional armies could be used against the people and that excises were an expensive and insulting kind of tax. The English concern with army officers as parliamentary placemen was irrelevant in the U.S., where they were excluded from Congress. A very well done and thorough study of the army issue in the 1790s, though it is primarily concerned with Federalist ideas, is Richard H. Kohn, *Eagle and Sword: The Beginnings of the Military Establishment in America, 1783–1802* (New York: Macmillan, 1975).

3. The best short account of the campaign may be John C. Miller, *Alexander Hamilton: Portrait in Paradox* (New York: Harper & Row, 1959), 327–332.

Sometime in February 1793, Jefferson had prepared an agenda for his party. Including a division of the Treasury Department, abolition of the national bank, reduction of the impost, repeal of the excise, and the exclusion of public debtholders from Congress, every part of this agenda was aimed at the "Treasury system" and the supposed influence of that department in Congress.[4] Jefferson also took a leading part in the plan to censure Hamilton, drawing up the resolutions that William Branch Giles revised for presentation to the House on February 27.[5] For lack of something more injurious,[6] Giles's resolutions depended on an allegation that Hamilton had failed to "consult the public interest" and exceeded his legal authority in the handling of two loans. References in Jefferson's draft to a design to benefit speculators and increase the profits of the Bank were deleted before the presentation to Congress, and the Republicans confined themselves in debate rather strictly to the specific charges at hand. Still, the import of the resolutions was evident to all concerned. Their passage would have been sufficient to compel the Secretary to resign.

Technically, Hamilton had not followed the letter of congressional instructions in his handling of the loans, but he was guilty of little else.[7] Moreover, many congressmen believed that passage of the resolutions could reflect on Washington. In the event, the movers of the resolutions were unable to hold their followers in

4. Paul Leicester Ford, ed., *The Works of Thomas Jefferson*, 12 vols. (New York: Putnam, 1904), VII, 223–224.

5. Jefferson's original draft is presented alongside the resolutions as actually introduced in his *Works*, pp. 220–223.

6. Republicans repeatedly tried and always failed to find any evidence that might implicate Hamilton in speculation in the funds or other misuse of public office. This was, for example, the real significance of the Reynolds Affair. Hamilton was, in fact, lax in the supervision of sometimes-dishonest subordinates such as William Duer. Miller (pp. 274–276, 302) also concludes that the Secretary's attempts to promote the Society for Useful Manufactures involved the Treasury in a questionable relationship with the Bank of New York. There is no evidence, however, that Hamilton profited personally from his office.

7. In 1790, Hamilton had mixed together two loans that Congress had meant to keep separate, applying monies intended for payment of the foreign debt to domestic operations and domestic monies to the foreign debt. He exercised this discretion in the public interest.

line, and all of Giles's proposals lost by large majorities. Jefferson consoled himself with the reflection that he had expected failure all along and with the hope that the attempt had shown the people how affairs were run. It was clear to him that one-third of the members of the House were "bank directors and stock jobbers" who had voted "on the case of their chief," while another third were "persons blindly devoted to that party" or simply too ignorant or indulgent to understand.[8] He also hoped that the next Congress would alter the result, for he had detected in the elections and in the limited victory over influence earlier in the session signs that the tide was beginning to turn.[9] He may also have been heartened by the appearance in the press of some of the most effective and important contributions to the long campaign against the Hamiltonian system.

In January 1793, opening the effort that would culminate in presentation of Giles's resolutions, Republicans in the House had flooded Hamilton with demands for reports on Treasury activities. Understandably annoyed, the Secretary had complied, but not without a biting indication of what he thought of the harassment. His reply to the House offended legislative sensibilities and generated at least as much support for Giles's resolutions as his handling of the loans. It also provoked a reinvigorated barrage from the Republican press. With the strictures of "Franklin," "Decius," "Timon," "An American Farmer," and others on the Secretary's reply to the House, the *National Gazette* reached the crescendo of its criticisms of the Federalist scheme.[10]

Although they addressed themselves particularly to Hamilton's alleged misapplication of funds and to the insulting style of his reply to the House, the critics of 1793 were not primarily concerned with personal irregularities. Their criticisms rose out of the general framework of a neo-opposition language that had

8. *Works of Jefferson*, VII, 253–254.
9. Ibid., pp. 191–192.
10. "Franklin" was John Taylor of Caroline. "An American Farmer" was George Logan. Both writers are discussed at length later in this chapter.

been developed in the past two years. The method of attack was markedly consistent from one writer to another. "As far as the situation of the United States would admit," "An American Farmer" wrote, "we have introduced the form of the British government." The meritorious patriots of the Revolution had opposed Britain's designs without imagining that "the corrupt and wretched system of British politics and finance would ever become the favorite object of an American government." Yet the Hamiltonian system assured that the labors of the patriots' posterity would be for the advantage of "a few useless characters of our own day . . . whose wealth and disorderly lives tend to corrupt the government and undermine . . . liberty."[11]

Making it clear that they, too, blamed the economic program, others agreed with the "Farmer's" condemnation. "Franklin" argued that the national bank had been intended to accelerate what funding introduced, namely "an accumulation of great wealth in a few hands, a political monied engine," and a reduction in the powers of the states. "The whole original design, then, of this system was to destroy the Constitution."[12] "Franklin" was not ready to concede, with "An American Farmer," that the Federalists had managed to revive the "form" of the British government, but he did insist that "an administration literally copied from the monarchical system of Britain" had managed to reproduce its substance.[13]

A host of writers in these months, encouraged by reports from France to revive the old suspicions of aristocratic inclinations, proved able to fit their hostilities to the Federalists' social style into the same general framework. Honorific titles of address, pretentious Presidential levees, robes of office for the federal judiciary, and celebration of the President's birthday were all duly noted as evidence of a plot to corrupt the people's minds and

11. "An American Farmer," six numbers, *National Gazette*, Feb. 2–March 16, 1793. Quotations from numbers 2, 1, 6.
12. "Reflections on Several Subjects," ibid., Sept. 11, 1793. This passage reappeared word for word in John Taylor's *Enquiry*, which is discussed below.
13. Ibid., Feb. 20, 1793.

prepare them for the reintroduction of hereditary forms.[14] "The least innovation," "Valerius" warned, "becomes a step for other encroachments until the great barriers of their liberties are entirely levelled."[15] And "Timon" spoke for all his comrades and for Jefferson as well when he said that Hamilton had been exonerated in the vote on Giles's resolutions by the votes of stock jobbers and directors of the Bank of the United States.[16]

With these blasts at Federalism in the first months of 1793, the *National Gazette* attained a peak and then relinquished its creative leadership in the formulation and dissemination of Republican ideas. News of the European war arrived in April, and Freneau became increasingly preoccupied with the cause of France and the activities of her minister to the United States. Increasingly, his pages only rallied the convinced. Gradually, he alienated many of the faithful with his dogged defense of all the doings of Citizen Genet. The editor's personal courage in the face of the yellow fever epidemic failed to save his paper from financial disaster. Later in the year, publication ceased.

Contributors to other newspapers carried on the work begun by the publicists of the *National Gazette*. The remainder of the decade would see many other essays presenting the Republican critique in an extended, systematic form. By 1793, however, there were few newspapers that were not identified with one side or the other of the national political dispute. Readerships were generally established, and editors and writers were less interested in persuading the unaligned than in encouraging the party faithful. For the latter purpose, short but loaded condemnations of a Federalist conspiracy were usually enough. Long and systematic explication of Republican ideas was better left to pamphleteers.

14. In the *National Gazette*, see "Gracchus," March 9, 1793; "Valerius," Feb. 27, 1793; "Mirabeau," March 13, 1793; "A Farmer," Feb. 2, 1793; and "Thoughts on Several Subjects," Jan. 30, 1793. Contributors to the *Independent Chronicle*, the *New York Journal*, and even to Benjamin Franklin Bache's heretofore impartial Philadelphia *General Advertiser*, disguised as Mirabeau, Condorcet, Equality, and Sidney, also played heavily on this theme.

15. *National Gazette*, Feb. 23, 1793.

16. Ibid., March 29, 1793.

II

Between 1763 and 1776 the pamphlet had been the most important vehicle of American political ideas.[17] Although *The Federalist*, along with *Letters from a Federal Farmer*, which was the best production of the other side, appeared originally in newspapers, pamphlets retained their importance through the ratification debate. For reasons still unclear, they declined in importance in the years immediately following the establishment of the new government, only to recover their preeminence after 1792. As ways to reach a less restricted readership with fuller presentation of ideas, pamphlets had advantages unmatchable by the periodical press.

From October 1791 through the early months of 1793, the *National Gazette* led all other sources in the development of a cohesive opposition ideology. For the entire decade, the periodical press is the best source for an understanding of the enormous importance of the heritage of English thought in the development of a Republican persuasion. Swimming in an ocean of received ideas, however, newspaper writers could communicate whole series of connected thoughts with loose analogies or a suggestive word. During the 1790s, the great burden of the most telling and ideologically most fundamental criticism of Federalist government was carried by a cryptic code. A reference to congressional debtholders as placemen, a suggestion that the Plan for Manufactures envisioned the creation of a set of privileged corporations, a brief mention of Treasury influence, or the employment of a single word such as "corruption" conveyed to friends and enemies alike an entire language about social and governmental degeneration. The ramifications of this code are easily lost to minds formed in a different age. For the years after 1793, therefore, the best source for a comprehension of the content of the Republican attack on Federalism is the occasional

17. As Bernard Bailyn has reminded us in his introduction to *Pamphlets of the American Revolution, 1750–1776* (Cambridge: Harvard University Press, 1965), I, 3–8.

pamphlet in which the author commonly expounded his ideas at greater length.[18]

George Logan was the first important opposition pamphleteer. Heir to the country estate and fine library of his grandfather, who had been the secretary and political agent of William Penn, Logan was in style of life and in intellectual pursuits a Pennsylvania counterpart of John Taylor of Caroline. Educated as a physician in Edinburgh, Logan became a Whig relatively late in the Revolution and a radical later still. A Quaker disowned for bearing arms, an advocate of limited government who supported internal improvements and a federal university, a francophile of the 1790s who opposed the War of 1812, a radical Republican who opposed Thomas Jefferson in the years after 1801—Logan's career was as erratic, to a modern eye, as any in his age. Like Taylor's, it seems consistent only if we understand his underlying loyalty to an egalitarian and agricultural society, which seemed to him repeatedly threatened by the developments of his time. Defense of this ideal was the central purpose of Logan's life and work.[19]

Logan began his political career as a conservative. He was elected to the Pennsylvania legislature on the Anti-Constitutionalist ticket in 1785 and supported the federal Constitution. Yet he was never a good party man, gradually coming to oppose the Bank of North America and even to reconsider his original opposition to Pennsylvania's democratic constitution. After 1787 he was further influenced in a radical direction by his friendship with Benjamin Franklin, who may have introduced

18. A virtually complete bibliography is Charles Evans, *American Bibliography: A Chronological Dictionary of All Books, Pamphlets, and Periodical Publications Printed in the United States of America, 1639–1820*, 13 vols. (Chicago: Columbia Press, 1903–1959). In combination with the American Antiquarian Society's microfilm edition of the works listed by Evans, this bibliography gives scholars ready access to the pamphlets and election broadsides of the 1790s.

19. Frederick B. Tolles, *George Logan of Philadelphia* (New York: Oxford University Press, 1953), pp. x-xii. Unavoidably thin and conjectural in spots, because little of Logan's correspondence from the years before 1800 has survived, this is still a fine biography.

him to the physiocratic philosophers.[20] Having supported William Maclay for the Senate, he completed his political transformation in 1790 by opening a newspaper attack on Federalist policy. A series of letters published in Oswald's Philadelphia *Independent Gazetteer* between March 13, 1790, and January 8, 1791, were reprinted in the latter year as *Letters Addressed to the Yeomanry of the United States*, the first of three important pamphlets in which Logan publicized his growing alarm with the policies of the new government.

Originally, Logan was not concerned with administrative influence and made no use of the eighteenth-century criticism of governmental corruption that others were beginning to Americanize in the press. His suspicions of federal measures were prompted, instead, by his understanding of French economic thought (though that owed something, in turn, to the neo-Harringtonian ideas about society and politics that Penn and his grandfather had known so well).[21] With the physiocrats, Logan disapproved of governmental interference in a free economy. He believed that regulation of agriculture, manufacturing, and commerce exposed a country to ruinous commercial wars and created internal antagonisms by "sacrificing the interest of one class of citizens to another." Britain was to him the most terrifying example of the effects of a flood of regulations. "The independent yeomanry of England are almost annihilated," he explained, because the country gentlemen had been "duped" into believing that "to grant the demands of the commercial and manufacturing classes was the best way of promoting their own interests."[22] A

20. Ibid., pp. 76–111.

21. Too much can be made of French influence on the Republicans, particularly in view of the English sources of physiocratic thought. With the possible exceptions of Logan and Taylor, virtually all the Republican writers can be understood without any reference to French sources. Even in their cases, the English libertarian and opposition traditions were of surpassing importance. Much of Logan's political development, for example, took place in public in a series of eight essays in the *Pennsylvania Mercury* between March 18 and Sept. 6, 1788, significantly signed "Cato." It seems equally significant that Logan named his son, born in 1791, Algernon Sidney Logan.

22. *Letters, Addressed to the Yeomanry of the United States* (Philadelphia: Eleazer Oswald, 1791), pp. 14, 6.

similar prospect threatened the yeomen of America. Repeating the physiocratic doctrine that farming is ultimately the only productive work, Logan objected especially to the economic perils of taxes such as the excise. Indirect taxes could easily exceed the farmers' surplus over subsistence and thus destroy society's only source of wealth. They are oppressive, expensive to collect, and disproportionately burdensome to the poorer classes, on whose prosperity a nation's happiness depends.[23]

Inspired by hostility to the excise, the burden of condemnation in the *Letters To The Yeomanry* was economic. Logan attacked the introduction of programs that threatened to depress the agricultural population and produce economic ruin. Already, though, he tended to attribute the trouble to a band of citizens "infatuated with the false principles of the government of Great Britain [and] anxious to adopt her wretched system of policy."[24] Not the excise only, but the whole financial program was cause for alarm:

Public credit, which our politicians esteem of the greatest importance to government, should be regarded as the most unjust and ruinous invention of modern times. It is only useful and convenient to serve the ambitious projects of governments and to add to the wealth of monied men. [It requires governments to use] every artifice and deception . . . to draw money from the people to satisfy the demands of men who, living upon the blood of their fellow citizens, insult them with an ostentatious parade of their ill-gotten wealth. . . .

Your legislators, not daring openly to violate your rights, effect their purpose under the pretext of necessary commercial regulations; this point being once established, they will follow the example of Great Britain and interfere in every action of your lives, til, at length, like the people of that devoted country, you will not deserve the name of freemen.[25]

A year later, this suspicion of conspiracy was more obvious in Logan's thought, as were the neo-Harringtonian origins of some of his concerns. Another pamphlet, directed this time at Hamil-

23. Ibid., letters 3–4.
24. Ibid., p. 14.
25. Ibid., pp. 36–38.

ton's proposals for manufactures, voiced the Pennsylvanian's fear of the creation of an aristocratic society that would inevitably crush the agrarian interest and destroy American liberty. "The measures of the general government," Logan now asserted, "are tending . . . to undermine the liberties of our country" and destroy the influence and importance of the laboring classes.[26] Again, his argument began with a warning that governmental regulations tend to create separate interests in a society and sacrifice the most valuable portion of the people to "the wealthy few."[27] But now he explained the danger in a manner that was clearly neo-Harringtonian and strongly reminiscent of Madison's complaint in the newspaper piece entitled "Parties." "The accumulation of that power which is conferred by wealth in the hands of the few is the perpetual source of oppression and neglect of the mass of mankind." Republican laws should resist a concentration of wealth and power. Instead, Hamiltonian laws have encouraged the wealthy to combine into a compact body. "The American aristocrats have failed in their attempt to establish titles of distinction by law, yet the destructive principles of aristocracy are too prevalent amongst us and ought to be watched with the most jealous eye."[28]

For Logan, economic and social developments, not government, were still the foremost concern, and he remained less interested in the methods by which antirepublican policies became dominant than in detailing the consequences of the economic program. His target was not an ambitious administration operating through corruption toward political ends, but the aristocratic tendency of the laws. By his own route, nevertheless, he was moving closer to the systematic reintegration of eighteenth-century opposition ideology that others were developing into a fundamental critique of the Federalist system.

---

26. *Five Letters, Addressed to the Yeomanry . . . on the Dangerous Scheme . . . to Establish National Manufactories* (Philadelphia: Eleazer Oswald, 1792), p. 8.

27. Ibid., pp. 19–20, 9, 26.

28. Ibid., pp. 11–12. Madison's "Parties" appeared in the *National Gazette*, Jan. 23, 1792.

Widely published and sufficiently influential to be of interest in themselves,[29] Logan's pamphlets of 1791 and 1792 can also be studied as a record of the transformation of a Federalist of 1787 into a Republican stalwart of the 1790s. In print and at great length, Logan went through a course of intellectual development similar to that which carried many men from support of the Constitution to opposition to the Federalist administration. Some men traveled it more slowly, some more quickly; all went by individual routes. But the rivulets converged in a single stream.

Logan's route may well remind us of the gradual transition of Jefferson and Madison into an irreconcilable opposition to Hamilton's plans. Like Logan, the two Virginians were alarmed, at first, by a growing conviction that the federal laws were inequitable to their state and a serious threat to agrarian interests. Like Logan, they also proved susceptible to a democratic uneasiness with the tone and tendency of the Federalist social style. The union of their sense of a growing danger to the societal foundations of republican life with worries about executive influence on the legislature, which men such as Maclay and Jackson had expressed since 1789, gave rise to the connected constellation of ideas about society and government that could be called the Republican persuasion. Reunited by the irrepressible American habit of finding conspiracies in political life, social and governmental concerns came together in a close imitation of the eighteenth-century English pattern of opposition to a government in power. The process in individual minds was not unlike the gradual joining of several streams of criticism in the national press.

Logan, who had not participated in the revolutionary use of opposition ideology, was slower than some in arriving in the mainstream of the Republican attack on Federalism. He had arrived there, nonetheless, by 1793. Perhaps he had the benefit

29. The *Five Letters*, for example, originally appeared in Oswald's *Independent Gazetteer* in February. They appeared in pamphlet form on Aug. 21, 1792, and Freneau, who had already reprinted the whole series, again printed excerpts in August and September. Mathew Carey also reprinted the whole in the *American Museum*.

of personal attention from others who had gone before. By 1792, Stenton, Logan's estate six miles from Philadelphia, was a frequent meeting place for critics of Federalist policy. Jefferson himself was often there, and Logan's biographer sees reason to believe that the Republican leader may have helped inspire Logan's third attack on the administration.[30] Its appearance in the *National Gazette* at the height of the congressional criticism of Hamilton's conduct would also hint at a role in a concerted campaign.

While he remained less concerned with the internal workings of the government than with the social effects of Federalist policy, Logan had now developed his tendency to detect conspiratorial motives into a basic history of the new government. His third pamphlet owed as much to the neo-opposition arguments that were appearing all about as it did to the physiocratic principles with which he had begun. Logan charged that the new government "owed its existence to the influence and artifices of a few men who had taken advantage of the distresses of the country" by speculating in the public debt.[31] To assure themselves full payment of the debt, these "few aristocratic characters" had erected a funding system, which assured that the original creditors would become servants of a monied interest. They had succeeded in introducing the same "corrupt and wretched system of British politics and finance" that Americans fought a Revolution to escape, and they deserved the same opposition.[32] Logan's target now was the common conspiratorial villain of the Republican press:

To satisfy the ambition of one class of men and the avarice of another, the Americans have submitted to a second revolution by which they

30. Tolles, pp. 122–123, 126–127. The third letter of the series in particular made use of Jefferson's favorite dictum that the earth belongs to the living and his adaptation of Buffon's mortality tables.

31. "An American Farmer," *Letters Addressed to the Yeomanry of the United States, Containing some Observations on Funding and Banking Systems* (Philadelphia: n.p., 1793), p. 3. This work had appeared in six issues in the *National Gazette* between Feb. 2 and March 16.

32. Ibid., pp. 4, 7–8.

have bartered their domestic rights, liberty, and equality for the energy of government and the etiquette of a court. After having wrested the sceptre from the hand of a British tyrant, they have suffered it to be assumed by a monied aristocracy, where it will be found more oppressive and more injurious to the people.[33]

III

With the second session of the Second Congress, it would seem, the Republicans brought their entire arsenal to bear on the citadels of Federalism. We can suspect, if not precisely prove, that the reinvigorated barrage of criticism in the *National Gazette* was not merely coincidental with the congressional attempt to force Hamilton from office. Logan and other contributors, perhaps meeting with one another, with party leaders, and with editors to exchange ideas and plans, may have been doing a party job with ideological weapons that had met with the approval of the party as a whole. There is evidence that the Republicans proceeded in this manner at this time. At least one of the pamphlets of John Taylor of Caroline, the most interesting and important Republican publicist of the decade, was in timing, in preparation, and in content an all but official expression of party views.[34]

Having served in both the Continental Army and the Virginia Militia during the Revolutionary War, Taylor made his fortune by means of a happy marriage and the practice of law. By 1790 he was a great planter in Caroline County, already beginning the experimentation and study that would make him one of the best known agriculturalists in American history. He entered national politics in 1792, taking the Senate seat left vacant by the death of

33. Ibid., p. 24.
34. Since the publication of Charles A. Beard's *Economic Origins of Jeffersonian Democracy* (New York: Macmillan, 1915), most students of the Republicans have recognized the importance of Taylor's pamphlets, although no one has recognized their dependence on English opposition thought. For examples, see Cunningham, p. 57, and Charles Maurice Wiltse, *The Jeffersonian Tradition in American Democracy* (Chapel Hill: University of North Carolina Press, 1935), pp. 218–222. Unfortunately, the best-known study of Taylor's thought, Eugene Tenbroeck Mudge, *The Social Philosophy of John Taylor of Caroline: A Study in Jeffersonian Democracy* (New York: Columbia University Press, 1939), rests overwhelmingly on the works of the period after 1800 and neglects the pamphlets of the 1790s.

Richard Henry Lee. A lifelong friend of the other Senator from Virginia, James Monroe, he was immediately privy to the inner councils of the Republican party, and he quickly took a hand in the campaign against Hamilton with a number of contributions to the *National Gazette*.[35]

Taylor, however, was primarily a pamphleteer, the first Republican to write specifically for that form of publication. This may have been a matter of necessity as much as of choice, for Taylor was perfectly conscious of his notoriously prolix style. However that may be, the three pamphlets he produced during his first two years in the Senate are probably the most important source for an understanding of Republican thought in the middle 1790s. They comprise the most extensive and systematic of all the Republican attacks on Federalism, and they reveal more obviously than any others the Republicans' debt to English opposition thought.

The first of Taylor's pamphlets, a reworking of the arguments of "Franklin's" letters to the *National Gazette*, appeared immediately after the adjournment of the Second Congress. It was the most careful presentation to date of the neo-opposition attack on social and governmental corruption. More systematically than was customary in newspaper essays, Taylor began by asserting the crucial importance of an independent and responsible legislature for the preservation of liberty. Revealing his Antifederalist background, he argued that a popular watch on legislative servants was particularly necessary in federal America, where large congressional districts, huge constituencies, and the great distance of the capital combined to lessen the representatives' immediate responsibility to the people. He was not above suggesting that these inherent weaknesses in the American system were not wholly accidental. He was sure, in any case, that they had been compounded by the policies of the new government.[36]

Constitutionally defective to begin with in matters concerning

35. Henry H. Simms, *Life of John Taylor* (Richmond: William Byrd Press, 1932).
36. *An Examination of the Late Proceedings in Congress Respecting the Official Conduct of the Secretary of the Treasury* (Richmond: n.p., 1793), pp. 3–6.

the independence of its various branches and their responsibility to the people, the federal government had been further weakened by the accumulation of a huge debt into a nearly perpetual fund that was heavily dependent for its value on the Secretary of the Treasury. The dealers in this fund, Taylor pointed out, had a common interest not only distinct from, but contrary to, the rest of the public. "Having one common interest, which consists simply in the imposition of high taxes and their rigid collection, they form a compact body and move always in concert. Whilst the administration finds the means to satisfy their claims, they are always devoted to it and support all its measures." Fundholders, in brief, were a "ministerial corps," and a particularly dangerous one because much of the public considered their possession of the funds to be unjust.[37] Allied with them and even more subservient to the Secretary of the Treasury were stockholders in and directors of the national bank. The bank was dangerous both because it tied together with closer bonds "the members of the fiscal corps" and because its loans, in conjunction with the administration's power to control the prices of the funds, could powerfully influence some legislators' votes.[38]

Taylor believed that the union of the monied interests with an ambitious Secretary of the Treasury explained the measures of the federal government from its inception to the present day. "A faction of monarchic speculators seized upon its legislative functions in the commencement and have directed all its operations since." This faction quickly found "an apt instrument" in Hamilton, who has directed all his measures to its "emolument and advancement."

If the public debt has been accumulated by every possible contrivance, buoyed up by means of the sinking fund, made in a great measure perpetual, and formed into a powerful monied machine dependent on the fiscal administration, to this combination it is due. If . . . a dangerous inequality of rank has been created, . . . thereby laying the foundation for the subversion of the government itself by undermining its true

37. Ibid., p. 8.
38. Ibid., pp. 9–10.

principles, to this combination it is due. If those sound and genuine principles of responsibility which belòng to representative government and constitute its bulwark . . . have been annulled or weakened, if a practicable means of influence whereby the members of the legislature may be debauched from the duty they owe their constituents has been found, if by implication and construction the obvious sense of the Constitution has been perverted and its powers enlarged so as to pave the way for the conversion of the government from a limited to an unlimited one, to this combination they are due.[39]

The defeat of Giles's resolutions by congressional stockholders and bank directors was only the most recent consequence of this conspiratorial combination.

Taylor's cure for this corruption was as obvious and as traditional as his diagnosis of the disease. If the ailment could be traced to a new sort of ministerial influence and new varieties of privileged corporations, then the corrective had to be a new program of exclusion and a renewed dedication to the abolition of privilege. Like Jefferson, Taylor urged the exclusion of speculating stockholders from Congress, detachment of the national bank from the government, and reform of the Treasury Department to reduce the Secretary's swollen power. The *Examination of the Late Proceedings in Congress* was a brilliant presentation of the criticisms and reformist program that dozens of lesser publicists and party leaders had developed during the past two years. And Taylor was by no means through.

A year after the *Examination*, Taylor published at the capital the decade's most important statement of his party's neo-opposition creed. Edited and approved in advance by party leaders, its publication planned by them for greatest political effect, *An Enquiry into the Principles and Tendency of Certain Public Measures* was the decade's nearest approach to an authorized statement of the Republicans' reasons for opposing the Federalist system.

With the help of his kinsman and old guardian, Edmund Pendleton, Taylor had composed a draft of the pamphlet by May

39. Ibid., pp. 11–12.

1793.[40] In June, after discussing it with Monroe, he sent it to Madison with a letter asking the congressional leader to decide whether or not it should be published, to freely make corrections, and to consider when and how it could be printed for greatest effect.[41] In August, Madison sent the manuscript along to Jefferson with a note of commendation, and Jefferson replied in an enthusiastic tone.[42] The two leaders arranged for its publication just before the meeting of the Third Congress, in which the Republicans were planning to open an offensive against the national bank. Giles, Monroe, and Abraham Venable also saw the manuscript and approved its publication.[43]

In the *Enquiry*, too, Taylor opened his defense of the opposition by recurring to the first principles of representative government, this time reaching back to the classical axiom that demanded a "frequent recurrence to fundamental principles." To him as to other Republicans, strict interpretation of the Constitution was more than a convenient rationalization of party needs, more than a necessity to defend the powers of the states. It was an integral part of an entire ideology which assumed the degeneration of governments over time. Like others, he was particularly concerned that principles be kept sound through this "epoch of experiment. Corrupt morals in a state of infancy forebode a licentious manhood and a wicked old age."[44]

For Taylor, the most fundamental principle of the American Constitution was the dependence of the government on the

40. Taylor to Madison, May 11, 1793, in William E. Dodd, ed., "Letters of John Taylor of Caroline County, Virginia," *The John P. Branch Historical Papers of Randolph-Macon College*, II, nos. 3, 4 (1908), 253–254.

41. Taylor to Madison, June 20, 1793, ibid., pp. 254–257. Madison evidently did suggest some changes. See ibid., p. 259.

42. Madison to Jefferson, Aug. 11, 1793, Gaillard Hunt, ed., *The Writings of James Madison*, 9 vols. (New York: Putnam, 1900–1910), VI, 140–141; Jefferson to Madison, Sept. 1–9, 1793, *Works of Jefferson*, VIII, 12, 14, 32. These exchanges identify Taylor as the author of the "Franklin" letters. See also Madison to Monroe, Sept. 15, 1793, *Writings*, VI, 198: "Mr. J. is in raptures with the performance of our friend in C--l--n--e."

43. Taylor to Madison, June 20 and Aug. 5, 1793, "Taylor Letters," pp. 257–259.

44. *An Enquiry into the Principles and Tendency of Certain Public Measures* (Philadelphia: T. Dobson, 1794), p. 2.

people, which assured that the laws would be made in the general interest. The maintenance of a government in which the people legislate through representatives who are impelled to seek the general good was the most important test of an administration. By this test, the Federalists failed, and, though he was advocating representative democracy instead of balanced government, Taylor explained the danger inherent in their failure in a manner very similar to the eighteenth-century analysis of the subversion of balanced government by executive influence.[45]

For reasons much like Logan's, Taylor considered the national bank to be the keystone of the Federalist system. "A gift . . . of so much public property to private persons," a sort of indirect tax payable to a few individuals who could control most of the circulating medium of the country, the bank was the most dangerous kind of monopoly.[46] "Its chief design was to make the rich, richer and the poor, poorer."[47] It was the best evidence that a "design for erecting aristocracy and monarchy is subsisting, that a money impulse and not the public good is operating on Congress.[48] Indeed, if the national legislature remained at all independent and concerned with the public good, Taylor continued, it was only "by courtesy of a corporation."

If a number of the members of Congress are stockholders or bank directors, then an illegitimate interest is operating on the national legislature, then the bank hath seduced away from their natural and constitutional allegiance the representatives of the states, and then even

45. Ibid., p. 6. As Taylor's thought developed, he came to insist ever more strongly that the American system of divided powers, where every governmental agency depended on a sovereign people, was fundamentally different from systems where governmental estates were mixed and balanced, and he was concerned with the maintenance of responsibility rather than with the maintenance of balance. He was one of the first Americans to concern himself systematically with this distinction, and, as Mudge argues, the philosophical importance of his best known work, *An Inquiry into the Principles and Policy of the Government of the United States* (1814; rpt. New Haven: Yale University Press, 1950), depends partly on insights made possible by this distinction.

46. *Enquiry*, pp. 13, 22. "America has defeated a nation but is subdued by a corporation. She defended her property against open violence to be cheated of it by private fraud."

47. Ibid., p. 15.

48. Ibid., p. 7.

foreigners . . . have obtained an influence on our national councils so far as they have obtained bank stock. . . . When paper men get into Congress or members are metamorphosed into paper men after they get there, it is obvious that they will be influenced by their personal private interest . . . rather than the public good.[49]

Numerous "paper men," Taylor argued, have been in Congress, and it has been their personal interest to keep taxes high in order to increase the public money in the bank, to support the Secretary of the Treasury so that he will support the bank, and to provide the ministry with the means of influencing other legislators. Seeking to impel representatives to seek their constituents' good, the Constitution tried to assure "a similitude of interests, of burthens, of benefits, and even of habits between the people and their representatives."[50] This attempt was defeated by the admission of stockholders to Congress, where they really represent a corporation.

If the bank, the paper system, and the minister can influence a majority of . . . Congress . . . where are the representatives of the states? . . . Even school boys ridicule and contemn the corruption which guides the British parliament according to the will of a minister. . . . Compare the two cases and point out, if you can, a difference.[51]

49. Ibid., pp. 24–25.
50. Ibid., p. 35.
51. Ibid., pp. 39–40. Compare these passages with his later condemnation of Hamiltonianism in the *Inquiry into the Principles and Policy of the Government of the United States*, pp. 65–67. "Whatever destroys an unity of interest between a government and a nation infallibly produces oppression and hatred. Human conception is unable to invent a scheme more capable of afflicting mankind with these evils than that of paper and patronage. . . . A legislature in a nation where the system of paper and patronage prevails will be governed by that interest and legislate in its favor. It is impossible to do this without legislating to the injury of the other interest, that is, the great mass of the nation. Such a legislature will create unnecessary offices, that themselves or their relations may be endowed with them. They will lavish the revenue to enrich themselves. They will borrow from the nation that they may lend. . . . As grievances gradually excite national discontent, they will fix the yoke more securely by making it gradually heavier. And they will finally avow and maintain their corruption by establishing an irresistible standing army."
Comparison of the *Inquiry* with the earlier work and examination of Mudge will reveal that Taylor's essential concerns changed little after 1801. Mudge's work, though written before the rediscovery of eighteenth-century opposition thought, is as good an analysis of Taylor's ideas as could have been achieved at the time. On page 191, its author says of the works written after 1800: "The leading idea of Taylor's economic

The national bank, as Taylor saw it, was the capstone of an entire financial system deliberately designed to gradually reinstate the ruinous government of king, lords, and commons.[52] Having explained its corrupting effect on the government in a manner plainly borrowed from English oppositionists, he then examined its broader consequences in terms equally reminiscent of "Country" derivatives of Harringtonian thought. An aristocracy, he reasoned, is the forerunner of monarchy, and the Hamiltonian system creates an aristocracy in substance: "names or wealth united with exclusive privileges." "Money in a state of civilization is power," he put it in an aphorism. "A democratic republic is endangered by an immense disproportion in wealth. . . .Tyrants and slaves, an aristocracy enormously rich and a peasantry wretchedly poor, approximate in morals."[53]

Taylor himself could not have listed all the sources of his thought. Like Jefferson writing the Declaration of Independence, he did not consult the works of individual thinkers as he wrote, but an entire body of opinion he had absorbed from the political atmosphere of his youth. Still, *An Enquiry into the Principles and Tendency of Certain Public Measures* did owe a special debt to one English thinker. Beginning with a dedication urging Washington to override his wicked minister—to act, in effect, as a patriot king—it ended with an analysis of political parties strikingly similar to the one in Bolingbroke's *Dissertation upon Parties*.[54]

Like Bolingbroke condemning the "Robinocracy," Taylor tried to identify the administration as a party dedicated to selfish and partial interests. "Party," properly defined, must

---

thought is that the pure political and economic principles of the Revolution have been supplanted by an imported, nonproductive, monopolistic, paper system which has destroyed the security and freedom of the agricultural class." It might be wise, however, to add that Taylor was concerned in these arguments with much besides economics and that he was engaged in something rather different from a class attack on capitalism.

52. *Enquiry*, pp. 41–47.

53. Ibid., pp. 29–31.

54. Indeed, the whole structure of Taylor's argument, which judges an administration by how well it supports the constitution, seems modeled on Bolingbroke's work. And a year after the *Enquiry*, Taylor wrote his own *Definition of Parties*.

signify a confederation of individuals for the private and exclusive benefit of themselves and not for the public good. . . . Not only stockholders themselves but public officers who wish for higher salaries, paper men and speculators who will gain by an increase of the public debt and by dissipation of the finances, and all who languish after aristocracy and monarchy have enlisted under the auspices of a chief. And hence the industrious and vociferous cry in favor of the measures of the administration.

Like Bolingbroke defending the opposition to Walpole, Taylor also said of the Republicans, who opposed this interested faction within the government, that they deserved "rather the appellation of a 'band of patriots' than the epithet of 'a party.' "[55] It was Taylor's purpose, as he saw it, to enlist the "natural interests" of the country and the honest part of its people with these patriots in an attempt to exclude public creditors and bank directors from Congress. "The people," he insisted, "are the only safe guardians of their own liberty," and they can assure the protection of their liberty only "by cautiously electing members of Congress of a familiarity of interests, of burthens, and of habits" with themselves.[56] When, instead, a private interest governs a portion of the representatives, liberty is seriously endangered. "When a majority of such representatives is thus seduced, liberty is theoretically annihilated."[57]

IV

With *An Enquiry into the Principles and Tendency of Certain Public Measures*, the Republican attack on Federalism approached as closely as differences between the two nations would permit the eighteenth-century English criticism of social and political degeneration. In his social philosophy and in his political criticism, John Taylor was an American Bolingbroke, speaking

---

55. *Enquiry*, pp. 85–87. Compare "Paradox," *National Gazette*, Oct. 13, 1792, another piece that could have come from Taylor: "I believe that a man may . . . be a sincere friend to the . . . Constitution and an enemy to . . . the government . . . as also that a man may be a decided enemy in his heart to republican principles . . . and a zealous friend withal to measures and objects pursued by the government."

56. Ibid., pp. 53–54.

57. Ibid., p. 60.

for an American "Country" party. He applied in his attack on Hamiltonian finance virtually every aspect of the traditional critique of an administration which was seen to be subverting both the governmental institutions and the social structure on which liberty must rest.

It seems surprising, at first glance, that the ideology of English "Country" oppositions should have continued to exert so thorough and profound an influence on the politics of the republic. Taylor was among the first to see that the American Constitution rested on a major revolution in governmental thought. And yet the Constitution had not made the world anew, had not erased what seemed to be the universal lessons of the past. Taylor's allegiance to a political system that divided the power of a sovereign people rested, like the older theory of mixed government, on an assumption that the force of selfish interest had to be controlled in order to secure the good of all. Power had to be pitted against power to prevent its abuse. American liberty, like English, could be destroyed by an amalgamation of the separate powers of its governmental parts.

Reasoning from similar assumptions, the framers of the Constitution had made a conscious effort to avoid the weaknesses to which Americans attributed the decline of English freedom. The Federalists of the 1790s believed they had succeeded. There could be no conflict of estates in democratic America. There was no room for a grasping ministry in an executive headed by a responsible first magistrate. There were no rotten boroughs, and Article I of the Constitution barred placeholders of the British sort. Nevertheless, the assumption of human selfishness, the very principle that required a government of divided powers, induced in America as in England an expectation of constitutional decay. Hardened in the furnace of a great Revolution, this expectation helps explain the immediate insistence of some of the harshest critics of the new Constitution that the finished document be guarded carefully against constructions or developments that might alter the original foundations and bend the government into a different shape. More specific expectations about the likely course of constitutional decay are also an essential part of any explanation of the rise of the peculiar kind of opposition that appeared in the United States: an opposition that would quickly elevate the Constitution to the character of sacred text, assuring both its triumph and a party warfare that endangered its success.[58]

No one's thought is altogether free. No one sees reality first hand. Instead, reality is filtered through a screen of cultural conditioning, so that perceptions are a combination of the happenings outside with tools for understanding them which lie within. Once we have grasped the nature of the tools available in 1789, it seems almost inevitable that what transpired within the next few years would generate the kind of opposition that would claim to be more loyal to the Constitution than the government itself.

Sporadic applications of well-established tests of social and political stability, developed in the eighteenth century and used repeatedly in revolutionary days, were certain to occur when the new government went into effect. From its first months, some men displayed a tendency to stand on the strict words of the organic law, an inherited preoccupation with the dangers of executive influence, and an obvious concern for the social and moral health of a republican people. That all the separate tests (or all the different fears) should have combined so faithfully to re-create the old critique of an ambitious ministry, depended, though, on the ability of discontented men to identify the effects of the Hamiltonian program with the effects of ministerial influence and government by money. Despite the novel character of the American executive, despite the constitutional exclusion of placemen from the Congress, this was far from difficult to do. For years, Americans remained uncertain of the nature of the new executive. The veneration of George Washington combined with Hamilton's great influence so that it was not entirely obvious that

---

58. What follows is a restatement of my argument in "Republican Ideology and the Triumph of the Constitution, 1789–1793," *William and Mary Quarterly*, 21 (1974), 167–188.

the President controlled executive affairs.[59] And the inherited critique of officeholders had never depended exclusively on a condemnation of bribery. It had concentrated on the placeman's dependence for his living on the continuance of executive favor and his consequent inability to exercise an independent judgment of the public good.

Summarizing the classical idea of citizenship that had entered English thought through the works of Harrington, Algernon Sidney had remarked that a dependent man could not be trusted with the liberty of others.[60] Later critics of the rise of cabinet government had condemned the subservience to executive favor both of legislative officeholders and of extraparliamentary dealers in the public funds. American critics of the 1790s simply found that the targets of the English criticism of government by money had moved inside the legislature, where, as Taylor pointed out, the only difference between subservient placemen and dependent stockholders was the more violent opposition of the latter's interests to those of the public as a whole. In either case, the presence of executive dependents subverted the proper division of governmental powers and destroyed legislative responsibility. In either case, the influence of dependent men outside the legislative halls could spread debilitation into every corner of the land.

With the sources of their thought more firmly in our minds, it is less difficult to understand why the Republicans were condemned as levelers by their opponents or why historians were once inclined to see them as opponents of capitalistic interests. These characterizations approach an important truth. Criticism of dependent legislators was linked from the first with a heavy emphasis on the creation of a privileged group of new aristocrats,

59. Taylor's appeal to Washington to veto the measures of his minister was extreme, but it should also be recalled that Thomas Jefferson, who served in the cabinet and knew very well how decisions were made, was still most reluctant to attribute disagreeable policies to Washington, long assigning the responsibility to Hamilton's demonic influence on the great man.

60. The persistence of the classical identification of full citizenship with economic independence, by the way, helps explain the recurrent desire of many genuine democrats of this period for property qualifications for holding political office or exercising the franchise. Republicanism was not altogether consistent with universal suffrage.

seen not as passive tools of an ambitious ministry, but as full partners in an oppressive plot. Conscious appeals to democratic sentiments and agrarian interests, present also in the English criticism of government by money, were always more apparent in the American critique. Republicans *were* levelers, at least to a degree. Classical-republican analyses of the social foundations of a proper government taught them to prefer modest means to great. Poverty itself was not to be preferred, because the desperately poor could not afford the independence of mind that citizenship required. Great wealth, however—along with the preoccupation with the private life which the accumulation of great wealth required—was traditionally condemned as a discouragement to cultivation of the personal virtues associated with the pursuit of a living and the political virtue of submission of private interests to the general good. Since Aristotle, advocates of republican government had preferred a social majority of men of modest means. Harrington had codified this preference in his principle of the balance of property, and, from the first days of the new government, followers of his followers had expressed their concern with the balance of wealth in the United States. America had come to be defined, in part, in terms of its relatively equal, agrarian balance of property. Republicans held it as a first principle that private morality and public virtue depended on the maintenance of this distribution of wealth, a distribution profoundly threatened in their minds by the rise of the monied favorites of a Federalist administration.[61]

Ideologically, the Republicans were an agrarian party, but their rationalization of agrarian interests—if that is what it was—gained adherents among men of every social class and every interest group. And it would be an error to conceive of the

61. Douglas Adair made some of these points in "The Intellectual Origins of Jeffersonian Democracy: Republicanism, the Class Struggle, and the Virtuous Farmer" (Ph.D. thesis, Yale University, 1943). Insisting, against Beard, that the Republican commitment to an agrarian commonwealth was more ideological than economic, Adair traced its origins to the classical idea that a society of independent farmers, whose life was a virtuous mean between riches and poverty, insured a republic some immunity to ruinous struggles between economic interests.

Republicans as foes of either capital or wealth. The objects of their condemnation, like the objects of the English critique, were not merchants or manufacturers, but speculators, bank directors, and holders of the public debt. The target was not business enterprise, not wealth itself, but a particular variety of paper wealth that seemed too closely tied to governmental favor. It was not property, not even personalty, that the Republicans feared, but a peculiar kind of personalty that threatened the balance of the Constitution and destroyed in its owners that bar to the pursuit of purely private ends without which a republic could not endure.

Like its eighteenth-century predecessor, the Republican critique of Federalism could gather all manner of social and political discontents into its conspiratorial thesis, appealing to all sorts of men. Republicans could concentrate their criticisms on any one of a variety of ills. They could introduce a broader argument from any one of several starting points. Still, the spectre of a government whose branches were no longer independent, as liberty required, but united by a common interest in milking the people and subverting their authority, was the centerpiece without which we cannot explain the origins or limits of the Republican critique. Endemic visions of conspiracy, touched off by the unfolding of an "English" system of finance, forced early stirrings of uneasiness about the policies of the new government into familiar patterns of perception. These patterns of perception were the necessary catalyst to transform discontent into persistent opposition. They were necessary, too, to lead the rising opposition to a re-creation of an explanation for its role which was so thoroughly familiar as to guarantee wide popular appeal.

Since the middle of the eighteenth century, in both parts of the English-speaking world, persistent legislative minorities had reconciled their status with society's commitment to majority decisions by means of an established ideology that explained their situation as a consequence of constitutional corruption. Unable to control the legislature, they claimed, nevertheless, to represent a genuine majority of the people, the expression of whose will had been deflected by the influence of the executive on legislative affairs. Like them, Republicans were virtually compelled to call upon this ideology in order to place their opposition on acceptable grounds.

In an age when political factions were universally condemned, when persistent opposition to the government in power aroused suspicions of disloyalty to the state, resistance to constitutional degeneration—and that almost alone—could transmute members of a political faction into patriotic defenders of the common good. Men who joined together to resist a threat to liberty, who stood against a governmental plot, were something other than a band of factious politicians. From the first days of the federal government, persistent "Country" worries pushed opponents to resist administration plans. With equal force, the traditional necessities for a determined opposition pulled the critics toward a thorough reconstruction of the old ideas.[62]

Once begun, this reconstruction would neglect few elements of the received critique. But opposition to the progress of social and political corruption traditionally required an ancient constitution against which it could measure the degeneration of the present day. Lacking an ancient constitution, the Republicans instinctively settled for the next best thing, developing the inclination to insist on strict construction present from the start. Symbolically speaking, they made the Constitution old. In the process, they assured its quick apotheosis.

Revolutionary France tried six constitutions in fifteen years. Most of a century of civil strife lay behind the constitutional consensus of eighteenth-century England. In America, as early as the spring of 1791, within two years of its adoption, the Constitution was accepted on all sides as starting point for further

---

62. In *The Idea of a Party System: The Rise of Legitimate Opposition in the United States, 1780–1840* (Berkeley: University of California Press, 1969), Richard Hofstadter shows that a modern justification of party competition did not appear in America until well into the new republic. He does not fully explore the older justification for formed opposition.

debates. Here, the influence of a universe of classical political perceptions demanded that the opposition have a settled constitutional standard on which it could rely. The appearance of a deeply felt repugnance to the policies of the first administration assured the quick acceptance of the fundamental charter. But consensus of this sort did not prevent—in fact, it guaranteed—a conflict that would be no less ferocious for the fact that it occurred within the camp.

CHAPTER 8

The French Revolution

As long as party controversy concentrated on the disagreement over Hamiltonian finance, the argument was fierce; it
was profound. But it was not a potent danger to domestic peace.
To the participants, what was at stake in their increasing disagreement was the fundamental shape of the American Republic,
the survival and success of revolutionary dreams. Accordingly,
both parties struggled hard for popular support. Both succeeded
to a sizable degree. By the end of 1792, hundreds of ordinary
citizens in every section of the country had enlisted in the party
war. And yet the largest portion of the people was unmoved.
Times were prosperous. Leaders of heroic stature occupied the
seats of power. It was difficult to listen to inflated accusations that
the nation's liberty was once again at risk.

The proclamation of the French Republic, followed quickly by
the spread of European war, radically transformed the public
mood.[1] Through the early years of revolution, most Americans

Portions of this chapter appeared in somewhat different form as "Jeffersonian Ideology and the French Revolution: A Question of Liberticide at Home," *Studies in Burke
and His Time*, 17 (1976), 5–26. They are reprinted by permission of the editors.

1. Joseph Charles, *The Origins of the American Party System: Three Essays* (New
York: Harper & Row, 1961); Noble E. Cunningham, Jr., *The Jeffersonian Republicans*
(Chapel Hill: University of North Carolina Press, 1957); John C. Miller, *The Federalist
Era, 1789–1801*, (New York: Harper & Row, 1960); William Nesbit Chambers, *Po-
litical Parties in a New Nation* (New York: Oxford University Press, 1963). Two of the
most effective demonstrations of the polarizing effects at the local level are Paul Good-
man, *The Democratic-Republicans of Massachusetts* (Cambridge: Harvard University
Press, 1964); and Alfred F. Young, *The Democratic Republicans of New York* (Chapel
Hill: University of North Carolina Press, 1967).

had seen events in France as a product of their own example, promising the benefits of liberty and written constitutions to all mankind. Now, however, pride in the international influence of America's example (or a minority's disgust with French perversions of republican ideals) had to be mixed with practical considerations of the proper means of protecting national interests during a conflict that was rapidly becoming a worldwide war. Gratitude toward the French, with whom the new republic was still allied, was suddenly pitted against residual affection for the homeland of American culture and libertarian ideas. As the greatest trading neutral of the age—and yet a very minor power—the United States was caught between the clashing might of giants who were trying to deny their enemy the benefits of neutral commerce. Even in the absence of conflicting sympathies about the European states, Americans could scarcely have avoided sharp disputes about the nation's proper course. As it was, the two emerging parties made conflicting sympathies their own, and disagreements over foreign policy, reinforced by powerful emotions, clarified the differences between them in a way that earlier disputes had never done. Given issues that were less abstruse than arguments about finance, large portions of the people were aroused. Indeed, the bitterness of the division of the next few years has been exceeded only once in American history, and that resulted in a civil war.

I

The French Revolution was a seminal event in the history of the world. The wars of the Revolution were a profound test for a commercial people only ten years removed from a war for independence that had involved the same contestants. For Americans, however, responses to developments abroad were not a product of conflicting sympathies alone. Domestic divisions did not reach an unexampled level of intensity as a direct result of the intrinsic nature and importance of the Revolution and the wars. Instead, developments abroad and on the seas meant what they meant in the United States because they occurred in the context of an internal disagreement that was already shaping American perceptions of the history of the world. Foreign policy decisions assumed additional dimensions of significance because the issues raised in 1793 were defined in terms created by a preexisting argument. Both parties to a preexisting contest saw in what was happening abroad a larger version of a struggle long since underway at home. Both interpreted the larger struggle in a manner molded by existing understandings of domestic disagreements. They substituted a dramatic vision which originated in internal controversy for objective truths about the situation overseas and used the European drama to define more clearly what was happening at home. They looked to Europe as a stage on which the characters were distorted images of themselves.

For friends of the administration, as the Adamses had shown, there was a crucial difference between the American Republic and the riotous democracy that had been given reign in France. Though most had watched the early stages of the Revolution with bright hopes, growing numbers of Americans hesitated and then became appalled by rising violence, attacks on traditional religion, and a war in which the French would pit both armies and a revolutionary ideology against the old regimes.[2] In time, the radicalization of the Revolution and the successes of French armies seemed to threaten the advance of universal empire, the spread of social anarchy, and the collapse of civilization as it had been known, while Britain, with its ancient, stable liberty, became the dam that stood between the world and a barbaric flood. The European situation was momentous. More momentous still

---

2. Charles Downer Hazen, *Contemporary American Opinion of the French Revolution* (Baltimore: Johns Hopkins Press, 1897), marked 1793 as a turning point. Compare "Of France," *Gazette of the United States*, Nov. 6, 1790—an essay that nicely captures the early Federalist mixture of doubt and optimism—with "A Correspondent" in the same newspaper, April 20, 1793: "The Revolution in France, while it appeared to have for its object the destruction of the ancient despotism and the securing of the equal rights of man under a free and a just government, was exulted in by every friend of mankind in America and Europe. But when assassinations, murders, levellings, and depredations desolated the country and the foul fiends of anarchy and convulsion seized the reins of government, Hope depressed her towering crest and Widsom shed another tear."

was the analogy between that situation and developments at home. The Federalists had been preoccupied with the excesses of democracy and concerned with the leveling spirit of a part of the American people long before they found those evils in France. Thus, the Revolution overseas was always less a subject for objective study than a turmoil in which they could see a prophecy of what might happen here. Persistent admiration of the Revolution and attacks on the administration suggested that too many Americans were ready to follow the disorganizing course of France. For the friends of order, French influence and the French example endangered republican liberty in the United States. But their concern rose, not in conjunction with radicalism in France, but in close apposition to the activities of enemies at home.[3]

Meanwhile, Jeffersonian Republicans continued to associate the French Revolution with their own. To them, the victories of revolutionary armies were successes in a worldwide cause.[4] Republicans were blind for years to the reality of the French drive for universal empire and to the subversion of liberty in the Republic overseas. They had shaped an understanding of their quarrel with the Hamiltonian program by revising an opposition ideology whose proponents had long viewed the world as the scene of an unending contest between liberty and encroaching power. The European war, like the American Revolution, seemed another stage in this unending struggle. Republicans had already identified the domestic conflict as an effort to defend America against corrupting English ways, and it was easy now to see administration policy as an attempt to ally the country with England and the league of despots against liberty and the French. Close connections with the old regimes would be logical extensions of the plot to put an end to liberty at home.

Shortly after news arrived of the European war, Republican

3. Especially Gary B. Nash, "The American Clergy and the French Revolution," *William and Mary Quarterly*, 22 (1965), 392–412, an effective demonstration that clerical opinion of the Revolution turned condemnatory only after the most antireligious phase was over in France and the Republicans had begun to make significant gains at home.

4. This much is clear from the works cited in note 1.

writers began to connect the cause of France with the survival of liberty at home. "We have among us a particular class of men . . . inimical to the equal rights of the people, and, provided the British should succeed against the French, they would exert their influence to establish a monarchy within the United States."[5] On April 22, 1793, when Washington announced that the United States would pursue a "friendly and impartial" conduct toward the belligerent powers, the Republican press was furious. Neither duty nor interest called for neutrality. "The cause of France is the cause of man, and neutrality is desertion."[6] "The present war in Europe is a war of principles; it is a war between liberty and despotism."[7]

There was justice in the reply of the *Gazette of the United States* to blasts such as these. "It is too apparent that the enemies of the public credit of this country, despairing of success in their machinations to overthrow the funding system, are now attempting to implicate the United States in the war raging between France and the combined powers."[8] The Federalist editor at once identified the foes of neutrality with the enemies of the economic program. In this, he only recognized the immediate tendency of Republican writers to connect the foreign and domestic plans of the administration. Outrage at neutrality was less a product of concern for France than of fears for the security of liberty at home.

With the Proclamation of Neutrality, Republicans everywhere began to link their hostility toward the administration's foreign policy with their earlier condemnation of a domestic conspiracy against liberty. The Democratic Society of Pennsylvania issued a circular that explained its organization as a consequence of friendship for France *and* of fears for republicanism at home:

5. *Independent Chronicle*, April 19, 1793.
6. *National Gazette*, May 15, 1793. For attribution of this article, which proceeded to recommend an American attack on Canada, to the author of *Modern Chivalry*, see Claude Milton Newlin, *The Life and Writings of Hugh Henry Brackenridge* (Princeton: Princeton University Press, 1932), p. 132, note 17.
7. "An Old French Soldier," *General Advertiser*, Aug. 27, 1793.
8. May 1, 1793.

Should the glorious efforts of France be defeated, we have reason to presume that . . . this country, the only remaining depository of liberty, will not long be permitted to enjoy in peace the honors of an independent and the happiness of a republican government.

Nor are the dangers arising from a foreign source the only causes . . . of apprehension. . . . The seeds of luxury appear to have taken root in our domestic soil; and the jealous eye of patriotism already regards the spirit of freedom and equality as eclipsed by the pride of wealth and the arrogance of power.[9]

A meeting of citizens in Caroline County, Virginia, with Edmund Pendleton in the chair, resolved

that a dissolution of the honorable and beneficial connection between the United States and France must obviously be attempted with a view to forward a plan of a more intimate union and connection of the former with Great Britain as a leading step towards assimilating the American government to the form and spirit of the British monarchy.[10]

The New York Democratic Society agreed. "We most firmly believe that he who is an enemy of the French Revolution cannot be a firm republican and . . . ought not to be entrusted with the guidance of any part of the machine of government."[11]

Firmly committed to a policy of noninvolvement in the war, Republican leaders were less extravagent in their response. But they were neither content with a policy of impartiality nor immune to the tendency to see a connection between the foreign and domestic policies of their foes. Alexander Hamilton's vision of a great republic, able to assume an equal place among the powers of the world, required a good relationship with Britain. Britain, with her famous fleet and powerful economy, was the only nation that could gravely wound America in war or greatly

9. *General Advertiser*, July 13, 1793. One of the best studies of the impact of the French Revolution on American politics, Eugene Perry Link's *Democratic-Republican Societies, 1790–1800* (New York: Columbia University Press, 1942), emphasizes that these clubs began to organize before the arrival of Genet in Philadelphia and owed their origins to suspicion of the Federalists as well as to friendship for France.

10. *National Gazette*, Oct. 2, 1793. This was based upon a set of model resolutions drafted by Madison and sent to Pendleton and others. Gaillard Hunt, ed., *The Writings of James Madison* (New York: Putnam, 1900–1910), VI, 188–193. Throughout the 1790s both parties orchestrated public meetings in a similar way.

11. *Address to the Republican Citizens* (New York, May 29, 1794).

help it with investments in the new economy if good relations could be maintained. Moreover, British goods, in normal times, comprised approximately ninety percent of the foreign imports from which ninety percent of the federal revenues derived. Disruption of the British trade could wreck the whole financial plan.[12]

The Virginia leaders of the rising opposition were fully conscious of the links that bound America to Britain. But they had long ago concluded that the interests—if not, indeed, the sovereignty—of the United States demanded more diversification of her trade. Jefferson, while minister to France, and Madison, while still a member of the Confederation Congress, had both allowed themselves to hope that the alliance with France would make it possible to reach commercial agreements that would lessen the dangerous dependence on the British and encourage other European states to enter on a freer trade. Both favored constitutional reform, in part, because it might create a government that would be strong enough to undertake a policy of commercial confrontation to force the British to modify their restrictive navigation laws. In 1789, Madison made the first of several attempts to discriminate against the British in the tonnage and impost laws, while some of Jefferson's first disagreements with his cabinet opponent rose from differences about commercial policies and needs.[13] As time went by, it was increasingly apparent to the opposition leaders that Hamilton's vision of national greatness entailed, in the short term, foreign policies that would perpetuate a demeaning dependence on Great Britain, and, in the end, a course of national development designed to make it possible for the United States to enter as an equal in the rivalries and competitions of Atlantic states. From

12. Gerald Stourzh, *Alexander Hamilton and the Idea of Republican Government* (Stanford: Stanford University Press, 1970), can be supplemented on these points by Jerald A. Combs, *The Jay Treaty* (Berkeley: University of California Press, 1970).

13. Links between domestic politics and foreign-policy ideas are particularly well handled in Merrill D. Peterson, *Thomas Jefferson and the New Nation* (New York: Oxford University Press, 1970); and Ralph Ketcham, *James Madison* (New York: Macmillan, 1971).

the temporary object of good understanding with the British to the ultimate ideal of national development along the British line, Hamilton's means to greatness were irreconcilable with their vision of a virtuous republic.[14]

From the first days of the federal government, disputes about specific issues had been thoroughly entangled with a quarrel over the meaning of republicanism itself. From the first, moreover, different visions of the American Republic had been inseparably connected with contrasting calculations of the nation's needs and situation in the world. The European war soon brought these jarring calculations to the surface, confirming the enormous depth of party disagreements. Seeking to perpetuate a government which, in their minds, must rest on a society of independent men of virtue, the Virginians hoped that France would be a counterweight to an expensive and demeaning link with Britain. They hoped the old alliance could be used as lever to assure a wider outlet for the farmers' goods. Accordingly, in April 1793, Jefferson fought fiercely with his rival over the executive's response to Franco-British war. He won at least a draw. Washington decided to receive the first ambassador from the Republic, which was equivalent to recognition that the French alliance would continue in effect, while issuing a warning to the people that the government intended to maintain a neutral course.

Jefferson was satisfied at first. But Madison reacted to the Proclamation of Neutrality by expressing the dismay of good Virginians over the violation of treaty obligations inherent in a policy of strict impartiality. He also charged that the administration's action was a usurpation of the legislative power to decide on peace or war.[15] Quickly, Jefferson retreated from his satisfac-

14. An excellent short discussion of the coherence between foreign policy objects and domestic ideology is Drew R. McCoy, "Republicanism and American Foreign Policy: James Madison and the Political Economy of Commercial Discrimination, 1789–1794," *William and Mary Quarterly*, 31 (1974), 633–646. McCoy's "The Republican Revolution: Political Economy in Jeffersonian America, 1776 to 1817" (Ph.D. dissertation, University of Virginia, 1976), perhaps the finest dissertation I have ever read, fully develops dimensions of revolutionary thought and controversy that others have scarcely touched.

15. To Jefferson, June 13, 1793, *Writings of Madison*, VI, 130–132.

tion with the Proclamation, and, as he carried on his diplomatic work, he wondered at the motives of administration colleagues, who seemed disposed to reject every overture from France. He was, at first, more optimistic than before about the nation. "Parties," he told Monroe,

seem to have taken a very well defined form in this quarter. The old tories, joined by our merchants who trade on British capital, paper dealers, and the idle rich of the great commercial towns, are with the kings. All other descriptions with the French. The war has kindled and brought forward the two parties with an ardor which our own interests merely could never excite.[16]

Yet, as the year wore on and popular opinion moved behind the Proclamation, Jefferson, as well as Madison, grew more alarmed.

Two developments promoted a reconciliation of public opinion to administration policy in the last half of 1793. Probably the lesser in importance was the appearance of an able defense of the policy by Federalist spokesmen, particularly by Hamilton himself. The *Letters of Pacificus*, which defended neutrality and the President's authority to issue the Proclamation, were not the most impressive controversial pieces that Hamilton ever wrote. Their legalistic dismissal of any obligation to France must have infuriated those Americans who believed the cause of liberty to be at stake, and their ad hoc rationalization of the executive's conduct invited further development of Republican fears of their author's constitutional opinions.[17] They were sufficiently impressive, though, to provoke Jefferson's famous protest to his friend. "Nobody answers him, and his doctrines will therefore be taken for confessed. For God's sake, my dear Sir, take up your pen, select the most striking heresies, and cut him to pieces in the face

16. June 4, 1793. Paul Leicester Ford, ed., *The Works of Thomas Jefferson* (New York: Putnam, 1904), VII, 361–362 and *passim*.
17. These seven letters appeared originally in the *Gazette of the United States* between June 29 and July 20, 1793. Much more representative of Hamilton at his best were the shorter "Letters of Americanus," which reviewed the same subjects at the beginning of 1794. Both series can be found in Henry Cabot Lodge, ed., *The Works of Alexander Hamilton* (New York: Putnam, 1904), IV, 432–489, and V, 74–96.

of the public. There is nobody else who can and will enter the lists with him."[18]

Madison did take up his pen, responding to Jefferson's appeal with his *Letters of Helvidius*. Taking issue, not with the Neutrality Proclamation itself, but with the constitutional interpretations Hamilton has used to defend it, Madison's quarrel with "principles . . . which strike at the vitals of [the] Constitution" was one of the decade's best examples of the union of strict constructionism with the broader Republican criticism of governmental degeneration. Hamilton's generous interpretation of executive authority was derived, in Madison's opinion, from the theory and practices of monarchical Britain. It was "pregnant with . . . consequences against which no ramparts in the Constitution could defend the public liberty or scarcely the form of republican government."[19] Its nature and consequences were of a piece with other forms of corruption undermining American liberty. For, should Hamilton's interpretations become general,

every power that can be deduced from them will be deduced and exercised sooner or later by those who may have an interest in so doing. The character of human nature gives this salutary warning to every sober and reflecting mind. And the history of government in all its forms and in every period of time ratifies the danger. A people, therefore, who are so happy as to possess the inestimable blessing of a free and defined constitution cannot be too watchful against the introduction nor too critical in tracing the consequences of new principles and new constructions that may remove the landmarks of power.[20]

More influential, though, than the arguments of Hamilton or Madison were the popular veneration of the President and the misconduct of Citizen Genet. Criticism of Washington was still quite rare in 1793, but the Federalists bent every effort to make it appear that attacks on neutrality or the Proclamation were at-

18. To Madison, July 7, 1793, *Works of Jefferson*, VII, 436.
19. *Writings of Madison*, VI, 151–152. "Helvidius" appeared in the *Gazette of the United States* between Aug. 24 and Sept. 18, 1793.
20. Ibid., VI, 171–172.

tacks on their author.[21] Meanwhile, Jefferson complained that the outrageous conduct of the French ambassador had allowed the enemies of France and liberty to come forward as they had never dared before.[22] In a deliberate attempt to subvert American neutrality, Genet plotted filibusters by American citizens against British and Spanish territory and commissioned Americans as privateers to attack British shipping. His undisguised expressions of disdain and contempt for the administration came to a head in August, when he demanded a special session of Congress to decide between the administration and himself and threatened to appeal to the people if Washington refused to call it.[23] The Frenchman's madness damaged his American friends to the point where Madison cried out that "the Anglican party" was using his conduct and the veneration of Washington to inflame the people against the French and "to lead them from their honorable connection with these into the arms and ultimately into the government of Great Britain."[24]

Sound Republicans, of course, were not deceived. Those who did not choose to defend Genet were at least able to distinguish the ambassador from his country. They continued to attack Genet's opponents and, with Hamilton's entry into the public scrap, they were able to bind the issue of foreign policy more tightly to their original critique of Federalism. "Certain individuals who cannot be considered friendly either to this country or France," one author charged, had constantly tried to inflame relations between Genet and the executive and to weaken the popular attachment to France. Among them were "Pacificus" and other "inveterate enemies of our Revolution, whose prejudices are still alive to France for their assistance to America, . . . who are opposed to the republican principles of our constitution

21. In fact, a very few critics did venture to impugn Washington as a result of the Proclamation. For a representative criticism see the reprint from the Charlestown *Daily Advertiser* in the *Independent Chronicle*, Aug. 8, 1793.

22. To Madison, Sept. 1, 1793, *Works of Jefferson*, VIII, 11–12.

23. The most convenient account is Harry Ammon, *The Genet Mission* (New York: Norton, 1973).

24. To Jefferson, Sept. 2, 1793, *Works of Madison*, VI, 191.

and are desirous to incorporate in their stead those of monarchy and aristocracy.[25]

It was an important challenge for Republican writers to assess the motives of "Pacificus" for seeking to weaken the attachment to France, since it was assumed that they might reveal "the basis of a system which, thro' the influence of the author, may ere long become the operative principle of the government."[26] One early critic believed he had found the key in the administration's policy of obtaining loans from Holland, a British satellite. The national bank and the system of foreign loans were "so interwoven with the politics and finances of our government that there is a danger that the country from whence the loans are obtained will in time have an undue control in our public measures."[27] Another agreed that the Federalists were a party of self-interested men completely "within the operation of a system of finance that depends principally on our connection with England and Holland."[28] That being the case, it was easy to account for their partiality in foreign affairs. "The only peg which now holds together the aristocratic machine is the revenue which arises from our commercial connection with the British. Many in this financeering connection . . . are governed in all their measures solely by this baneful influence."[29] In defense of the economic system and in order to further their conspiratorial ends, the Federalists had drawn the country into "measures impolitic, pusillanimous, and partial."[30] To protect the British connection, which supported the domestic system of corruption, they seemed willing to sacrifice national honor and to court the hostility of France.

II

Foreign policy decisions in the spring of 1793 were greeted by the Republicans with a burst of rage that was linked with their op-

25. "A Republican," *Independent Chronicle*, Nov. 8 and Nov. 14, 1793. Compare "Republicanus," ibid., July 25.
26. "A Republican," ibid., Dec. 12, 1793.
27. Ibid.
28. "Moderation," ibid., May 26, 1794.
29. "Communications," ibid., July 7, 1794.
30. "A Farmer of the Back Settlements," *General Advertiser*, Jan. 3, 1794.

position to domestic policy mainly by the unconquerable inclination to detect conspiracies behind affairs. As their reaction grew in fury, though, it grew as well in rationality and in coherence with earlier ideas. Hamilton's public defense of administration policy encouraged a search for connections between the economic program, neutrality, and the criticism of Genet. Seizures of American shipping in the British blockade of France justified the party in their desire to distinguish between the belligerents' attitudes toward the United States. While the confrontation with "Pacificus" encouraged thought, events hurried party leaders in the preparation of an alternative to administration policy.

For several months, Jefferson and Madison had bolstered one another in the conviction that there was a clear disparity between French and British attitudes toward the United States.[31] Disgusted by a policy of equal treatment for an unfriendly monarchy and a republican ally, they were determined to attempt to shift the nation's course. In December 1793, as his last important act before retiring from his post, the Secretary of State sent Congress an exhaustive report on American commerce, in which he sought to demonstrate that French commercial policy was friendlier than British and condemned the great reliance on the British trade.[32] In January 1794, Madison presented more specific recommendations for a change of course in the form of a revival of his proposals of 1789 that America retaliate in kind for British limitations on her trade.

The first session of the Third Congress, which met from December 1793 to June 1794, was dominated by Madison's resolutions and other measures concerning the commercial policy of

31. The Republicans were most impressed by three contrasts between French and British policy. American ships could trade freely with the French West Indies while they were excluded by mercantilist policy from British possessions. By treaty, the French accepted American definitions of neutral rights, excluding provisions from the list of contraband of war and granting that goods carried in neutral ships were protected by the neutral flag, while the British condemned enemy goods carried by neutral ships and seized provisions headed for enemy ports. Finally, the French repeatedly offered to extend their commerce with America once the war had begun, while the British remained aloof.

32. *Works*, VI, 470–484.

the United States. Madison and his followers were pitted directly against Hamilton, who spoke through William L. Smith, in impressive debates on the economic interests of the nation, but these cannot detain us here. The Republicans were able to make a serious case for the country's interest in expanding the trade with France and for the wisdom of adopting a policy of coercion against Britain, but the Federalists realized that practical considerations were hardly the main concern. Uriah Tracy summarized debates in an attempt to call his Republican opponents back to practicality. The House, he protested, was not seriously deliberating upon "the welfare of our citizens but upon the relative circumstances of two European nations." Members were not debating "the relative benefits of their markets to us," but "which government is best and most like our own."[33] For Tracy, commercial interests may have been the foremost consideration. Republicans were more concerned for national dignity in relations with Britain and for the cause of international republicanism.

While Republicans made much of their embarrassment at the timidity of the administration's policy in face of British seizures, their opposition was directed primarily at the British connection itself. In part this resulted from their desire to cause America to lean to the republican side in the European war. In equal part, however, it resulted from an extension of their old concern with republican virtue at home. Madison expressed a fear of the effect on American manners and government of the extreme dependence on British trade. William Findley believed that British commercial credit promoted "a system of . . . influence dangerous to our political security," and William Branch Giles admitted that "he was inclined to think that an insensible foreign influence was operating at this time upon our councils."[34] Republicans were beginning to link their earlier critique of social and moral degeneration with a criticism of the corrupting influence that could spread through American society and government as a result of close association with Britain. They were also beginning

33. *Annals of Congress*, first session, Third Congress, p. 294.
34. Ibid., pp. 215, 234, 282.

to add the merchants trading on British credit to their list of corrupt, dependent men.

Madison's resolutions would probably have passed the House, where the Republicans were now more numerous than their opponents, if events had not taken away their sting. News arrived from the West Indies of massive British seizures of American ships, the public temper turned to stronger measures, and the Federalists themselves moved to increase the army, create a navy, and impose new taxes. Ironically, the party that had cried most loudly for coercion of the British now opposed these plans to strengthen national defense, supporting in their place proposals to sequester British property and to adopt a policy of nonintercourse with Britain.[35] The explanation for what seems a sharp reversal of direction can be found in the fears aroused by the Republicans' assessment of Federalist motives.

Only rarely did Republicans in Congress bother with elaborate explications of their ideas. In opposing an increase of the army or an additional excise, both traditional bogeys of opposition thought, they simply made it plain that they preferred the militia to a standing army and that excise taxes were dangerous to liberty.[36] But frequent remarks by members of both parties showed

35. Nonintercourse passed the House eventually and was defeated in the Senate by Adams' casting vote. In its place, a temporary embargo was placed on American shipping. Sequestration was undercut by the appointment of a special envoy to Britain.

36. Much of the second section of James Thompson Callender's *A Short History of the Nature and Consequences of Excise Laws* (Philadelphia: Stephens & Rivington, 1795) is a compilation of petitions, memorials, and speeches that appeared while the excise bill of 1794 was before Congress. Callender's own history of the excise in England concentrated on the general corruption induced by such a tax, and the American arguments were remarkably uniform. The general reaction to an excise, whenever it appeared, was summarized in a memorial of the Philadelphia snuff manufacturers to the Senate. The manufacturers, quoted by Callender on p. 86, expressed their belief that the proposed tax was "hostile to the morals and . . . odious to the feelings of a free people." They anticipated "for themselves the ruin of their trade and the impoverishment of their families and, for the public, the corruption of principles, the diminution of liberty, and the loss of manufactures."

For some typical press comment on the army bill see "A Calm Observer," *Argus*, May 12, 1795, and "From Correspondents," *General Advertiser*, May 21, 1795: "What this army was intended for, what to do and how to be employed ought to be the subject of investigation. . . . The liberties of every nation on earth have been destroyed by standing armies."

that each was aware of the ideological import of Republican thought. Speaking against the proposed excise on manufactured tobacco, Wilson Cary Nicholas said, "We are going on exactly in the steps of Britain. . . . What has degraded and annihilated the spirit of Britain? Public debts, taxes, and officers of excise. One half of the nation has been loaded with the plunder of the rest."[37] Opposing a naval bill, Giles reminded the House that in Britain "the people are oppressed, liberty is banished." The government there was so much extended that the productive part of the people had too many unproductive ones to support. In Giles's opinion, "the United States had already progressed full far enough into this system." It had a funded debt and an army, now a navy was proposed.

The system of governing by debts he conceived to be the most refined system of tyranny. It seems to have been a contrivance devised by politicians to succeed the old system of feudal tenures. . . . Its true policy is to devise objects of expense and to draw the greatest possible sums from the people in the least visible mode. . . . There is no device which facilitates the system of expense and debts so much as a navy.[38]

In great disgust with the Republicans' worries, Fisher Ames was finally driven to object that "excepting only the debate on the adjournment of Congress, there had not been a discussion of any length for a considerable time past where there had not been some pointed allusion to this paper bugbear."[39]

The Republicans wanted stronger measures against the British, yet their interpretation of the administration's motives made them fearful of adopting the usual measures for national defense.[40] Additional taxes and increasing public debts were tra-

37. *Annals of Congress*, p. 627.
38. Ibid., pp. 490–491.
39. Ibid., pp. 619–620. Similarly, Wadworth testified that "he was sorry for this little standing army, for it never comes before the House without meeting a rub" (ibid., p. 1221). And Oliver Wolcott complained to his father about "all the [congressional] cant about 'aristocracy,' 'interested measures,' and 'tendency to monarchical plans' " (George Gibbs, *Memoirs of the Administrations of Washington and John Adams* [New York: by subscription, 1846], I, 127).
40. See Monroe's striking admission of this difficulty in his letter to Jefferson of March 16, 1794. Stanislaus Murray Hamilton, ed., *Writings of James Monroe*, (New York: Putnam, 1900–1910), I, 286–288.

ditional agencies of constitutional decline. The transfer of a nation's wealth from the productive part of the people to speculators and government contractors prepared it for slavery. In the hands of a designing ministry, a standing army was the classic instrument of liberticide. The origins of the Republicans' staunch and ultimately disastrous belief in economic coercion as an alternative to active measures of defense lay partly in their attempt to escape the constitutional and social dangers traditionally associated with regular armies, high taxes, and preparations for war.

The Federalists, of course, had different fears. They believed that economic warfare with England would only provoke a shooting war for which America was ill prepared and in which domestic radicalism might gain the upper hand. Their alternative was John Jay's mission to attempt a diplomatic resolution of the differences with Britain.[41]

Jay's appointment as minister plenipotentiary to England only fueled the Republican fire. The notion of sending the Chief Justice on a mission abroad seemed in itself to be typical of the administration's disregard for the spirit of the Constitution, and a violation of the separation of powers was loudly proclaimed.[42] But the main force of Republican anger was directed at the prospect of negotiation itself and at the general timidity in relations with England of which it seemed a part. While decisions were being made in Congress, Hamilton continued his defense of neutrality in the *Letters of Americanus* and Noah Webster entered the lists with a thoroughgoing condemnation of events in

41. For Federalist reasoning see Hamilton to Washington, April 14, 1794, in *Works of Hamilton*, V, 97–115, and Wolcott to his father in Gibbs, I, 133–134.

42. For example, "Observations on Chief Justice Jay's Appointment," *General Advertiser*, April 29, 1794, an article which also objected to the appointment as impolitic in view of Jay's admission of 1786 that Britain was justified in its continuing occupation of the Western posts and in view of Jay's suspected insensitivity to the interests of western Americans, who had not forgiven him for his one-time willingness to trade American rights to navigation of the Mississippi for concessions to fishing interests. Critics also objected from the first that Jay's appointment was a deliberate executive attempt to frustrate the will of a majority in Congress, which preferred stronger measures—an objection in which they were entirely justified. See the correspondence in ibid., April 30, 1794.

France.[43] Republicans responded with further development of their attack on the Federalist conspiracy against liberty. The progress of Madison's proposals was carefully watched, and newspapers prayed for Republican success against "the British agents and their connections, . . . the combined power of Tories, aristocrats, [and] funding and banking gentry."[44] As the congressional quarrel proceeded, it became increasingly evident to Republican correspondents that the division over foreign policy was intimately connected with the earlier division over domestic affairs:

What means public credit? A readiness to get in debt, and what means a public debt? The means of causing a distinct interest from that of the whole community and enabling government to adopt systems and pursue measures which they could not, nor dare not attempt without this pretext. . . . A debt creates a party always at the nod of government, and the minister of a treasury has as absolute a command over it as the general of an army has the command of his soldiers. Why has opposition been made to every measure that would maintain the interest, the dignity, and the independence of the United States? Because of a public debt. Why is negotiation the darling substitute for efficient measures? Because we have a public debt. Why is there a certain party always united in ministerial plans and always opposed to anything like resistance to Great Britain? Because a public debt is to them a blessing and a rallying point to brave the influence of the people.[45]

The roots of Federalist pusillanimity in dealings with Britain were obvious to all who cared to see:

A funding system is to the United States what a nobility is to a monarchy. It has a separate representation, for, as it forms a phalanx of support, so it has the countenance and sympathy of government. It is a machine which sustains administration at all times and under all circumstances, and, like action and reaction, administration sustains it.

43. Noah Webster, *The Revolution in France* (New York: George Bunce, 1794), argued that the French should have been content with a constitutional monarchy, that France was now a barbaric despotism, and that the introduction of Jacobin principles and institutions into the United States would be a disaster.
44. "A Whig of 75," *Independent Chronicle*, Feb. 20, 1794.
45. A correspondent, *General Advertiser*, April 17, 1794. See also ibid., April 18, 1794; a letter from Philadelphia, *Independent Chronicle*, Feb. 10, 1794; and a letter from a Congressman, *Independent Chronicle*, Feb. 15, 1794.

The funding system is the Declaration of Neutrality, the parent of the present peace, the cause of our imbecility, the means of a submission to the most humiliating situation that freemen ever endured. It enters into competition with our liberties, interest, and independence—with our honor, dignity, and faith. Is there a question of even commercial regulation, it is opposed because of the funding system—is there a proposition to act with energy as a nation, why it will injure the funds and therefore is improper.[46]

In the years after 1793 other topics often were submerged beneath the furor over foreign policy. But it is critical to understand that the Republicans never faltered in their hatred of the economic program, never failed to use it as the starting point to which they periodically returned for comprehension of the ultimate significance of later events. The Hamiltonian system was the first cause of their existence as a party. Opposing it, they had found the fundamental principles of their opposition, the best legitimation of their role. They had constructed analytical machinery that could relate specifics to a broader comprehension of the nation's course, machinery that turned each later issue into a specific application of a general rule. Accordingly, new statements of the first grounds of their opposition appeared repeatedly whenever they needed to mold their creed to take account of different events.

John Taylor's *Enquiry into the Principles and Policy of Certain Public Measures* had appeared early in 1794. Later that year, the party's greatest publicist returned to his theme in a shorter pamphlet called *A Definition of Parties*. Again he asked why a Constitution designed to secure the common good was not achieving that end. Again his answer was completely classical. The legislature was corrupt. The principle of responsible representation had been destroyed by a "paper interest" that affected the decisions of Congress. The measures of the government had transferred the power of the people to a "paper junto." With the Secretary of the Treasury and the Bank of the United States, this junto comprised in embryo "a compact representation of king, lords, and

---

46. A correspondent, *General Advertiser*, March 24, 1794. The same argument was advanced by "An American Sans Culottes," ibid., April 3, 1794, and by many more.

commons." It threatened to destroy American liberty and to ally the country with the privileged orders of Europe in opposition to republican France.[47]

Another anonymous pamphlet of 1794 offered a new and thorough history of the conspiracy Taylor described. Building on the suggestions of earlier critics, the author maintained that secret monarchists had gotten into the Constitutional Convention, where they had deliberately created governmental infirmities that could be used by a designing administration to modify the constitutional form. The public debt provided the plotters with an opportunity "to aggrandize the Treasury Department, give scope to ministerial influence, and promote a new monied interest necessarily attached to the minister." Then, with Hamilton at their head, carefully guiding the legislature, and with Adams' apostate *Defense of the American Constitutions* as their ideal, this aristocratic party had proceeded with a "systematic plan for subverting the principles of the government." The economic program had created an oppressive aristocracy, corrupted the legislature, warped the sound principles of the Constitution, and "promoted a general depravity of morals and a great decline of republican virtue." Giles's resolutions and the reapportionment of the House were serious obstacles to their scheme, but still the conspirators persisted. Their intentions had been obvious when the administration provoked an Indian war in order to secure a standing army and when the Senate tried to institute titles. They were evident in the establishment of Fenno's "courtly gazette," judicial robes of office, and "courtly" Presidential levees. They were evident more recently in attacks on critical newspapers, popular societies, and the French.[48]

Because of the Whiskey Rebellion, the last months of 1794

47. *A Definition of Parties: or the Political Effects of the Paper System Considered* (Philadelphia: Francis Bailey, 1794). Quotations from pp. 5, 16.

48. *A Review of the Revenue System* (Philadelphia: T. Dobson, 1794), pp. 13, 45–48, 52. With the exception of Taylor's works, this pamphlet, which is usually attributed to William Findley, the radical Congressman from the whiskey country of Pennsylvania, was probably the most influential Republican pamphlet of 1794. See, for example, "Communications," *Independent Chronicle*, Sept. 1, 1794. In July and August the *Chronicle* had reprinted it in full.

were particularly fruitful in attacks on the economic program. The rioting in Western Pennsylvania was acutely embarrassing to the Republicans, and they were quick to join in the general condemnation of resistance to the laws. Still, the fact of resistance, along with the administration's powerful response to the insurrection, were opportunities too good to pass for renewed attacks on Federalist policies and motives. While they condemned the rioters, Republicans everywhere took pleasure in attributing the riots to "the arts, intrigues, and villanies of men in power." In one form or another, writer after writer maintained that "the insurrection may fairly be counted the first fruit of the blessed harvest sown by the advocates of the funding and banking systems."[49]

The excise tax was an integral part of the system of Hamiltonian finance, and Republican writers insisted on seeing the resistance to the excise in the entire context of national affairs:

Not only is our situation abroad critical and humiliating, but intestine divisions are taking place among us and the sword of civil war is about to be unsheathed. An odious excise system, baneful to liberty, engendered by corruption, and matured by the instrumentality of the enemies to freedom, has taken root among us.

Revolt against this system—resistance to republican laws—was evidence of a radical defect in the government:

This consists in men being appointed to legislative trusts who represent their own feelings and their own interests. . . . Congressional stockholders are marshalled in an impenetrable phalanx of opposition whenever their property is to contribute towards the general good, [but they exert every contrivance to] drain the laborer of his hard-earned pittance.

Either the corruption which has crept in among us must be eradicated or . . . a privileged order of men will be established among us who shall enjoy the honors, the emoluments, and the patronage of government, without contributing a farthing to its support. Whence are all the clamors and disquietudes among the citizens? They arise from a fund-

---

49. "S," *Independent Chronicle*, Aug. 13, 1794. See also "Communications," ibid., Sept. 1, 1794, and "A Correspondent," *General Advertiser*, Aug. 26, 1794.

ing system founded upon injustice, engendered in corruption, the offspring of the blood of our patriots.[50]

Time passed and events brought different issues, but the Republicans never tired of expounding their criticism of the economic program. New writers repeatedly proved themselves to be capable of as classic an analysis of its threat to American liberty as John Taylor had been. While Taylor had discussed the danger in terms of a threat to the principle of responsibility, some even returned to a more completely classic description of the degeneration of a balanced government. "In establishing every complex form of government," one of them wrote, "great pains are taken to preserve the powers of each branch distinct and the operations of each uncontrolled by the authority of any other." This, however, does not obviate the need for a continual watch against the "degeneracy or perversion" of the "original principles" of the constitution. Private interests will persist, and they will lead men to seek to increase the power of whichever branch of government may serve their ends. Usually, the danger comes from the executive:

The power of patronage, the gift of offices and emolument, the duration of authority rested in this branch renders the facility of intrigues, the extent of combination, and the number of dependents in it more formidable and influential than in any other. Hence the tendency of all governments to despotism. . . . The power which could form the only effective barrier to the executive will generally be the first to swell its encroachments. That influence which can operate on private individuals will operate also on individuals in the legislature. . . . All will have something to hope; and, in the prosecution of this hope, the principles of the constitution will be forgotten. By degrees, various powers which the legislature alone ought to exercise will be delegated to the executive.

Americans must awake to the danger of influence. Citizens must use their power in elections to choose officers "who have no separate interest from themselves and who have nothing to hope or fear from any government or any other officer." They must

50. "Franklin," *General Advertiser*, Aug. 22, 1794.

particularly refuse to elect public creditors, "a vast and formidable body united in a close phalanx by a tie of mutual interest distinct from the general interest." Public creditors cannot be expected to act impartially in questions that might affect the debt. They are necessarily subservient to the influence of an officer who can affect the value of the funds.[51]

It was unnecessary, after 1793, for any opposition writer to dwell for long on the fatal consequences of a system of executive influence. No literate American of these years could have remained unaware of the dire prophecies of the perversion of republican government and the approach of slavery. Republican publications were full of them, and Federalist publications occasionally reprinted them in order to attack Republican hysteria. Nevertheless, Republican critics periodically returned to lengthy examinations of the consequences of Hamiltonian finance. And with their rising inclination to identify the Federalists as an English party, they returned time after time to the story of English corruption in order to forecast America's fate.

While "An American" denied any concern with a sizable party who truly desired hereditary government, he found in the nature of the economic program and in the history of the English financial system a warning that American liberty could become a sham. He described how the ministers of William III had used loans to attach the public creditors to the crown and how similar expedients had followed until "the keys of the Treasury have been substituted in the place of the ancient prerogative . . . and it is now acknowledged by all parties that the operation of the government is a system of corruption." Reflection on this history, he warned, should alarm every American who considered "the imitative qualities of our politicians and their attachment to everything English." A "passion for fiscal enterprises . . . is the fatal rock on which our political navigators have nearly dashed to pieces the ship of state. . . . Almost every measure of government since that time has been influenced by that system."[52]

51. "For the General Advertiser," two parts, July 19 and 21, 1794.
52. "To the Citizens of New Jersey," reprinted from the *Centinel of Freedom* by the

As some of these examples show, the burden of continuing Republican criticism of Hamiltonian finance had by no means to be carried exclusively by the pamphleteers. A powerful source of neo-opposition ideology disappeared from the national scene late in 1793, when Freneau gave up the struggle to publish the *National Gazette*. But the void left by its passing was quickly filled by other party sheets.

From the early days of the new government, opponents of administration policy had had an important organ for their views in Boston's *Independent Chronicle*. In the late summer and fall of 1791, its publication of "The Watchman" and "The Ploughman" had contributed importantly to the early development of a neo-opposition critique of Hamiltonian policy. The *Chronicle* had also added an enthusiastic voice to the Republican chorus in the newspaper warfare of 1792. It had devoted considerable space to the controversy over Giles's resolutions in March of 1793. Throughout this period, it had reprinted many of the most important articles and series from the *National Gazette*. In all these ways, it helped to spread Republican ideology among its New England readership. With these exceptions, though, original articles in the *Independent Chronicle* rarely followed the main line of the anti-Hamiltonian critique in the years before 1793. Its Yankee contributors favored specific criticisms over more generalized attacks and concentrated more on the Federalists' "aristocratic" airs than on their economic policies.

Judging by the amount of space they gave the subject, neither the *Chronicle* nor Thomas Greenleaf's *New York Journal* had their hearts in national political controversy in the years before 1793. From the beginning of that year, however, foreign news began to occupy more space in both the papers, and defense of the French and Citizen Genet became by far the most frequent subjects of contributors. By 1794 the *Chronicle's* voice was much

---

Independent Chronicle, Jan. 16 and 19, 1797. Compare "A Member of Congress," *Aurora*, June 28, 1798, an essay reprinted in the *Independent Chronicle*, July 16, 1798, and quoted by John Allen in a speech supporting the Sedition Act, *Annals of Congress*, Fifth Congress, pp. 2100–2101.

more important in the national debate, and on May 11, 1795, Thomas Greenleaf, who had long since asked to be addressed as "citizen," began to supplement the *Journal* with the daily *Argus*, which rapidly became the second most important party organ in the land.[53] By that time, too, contributors to all three papers had adopted a consistent neo-opposition stance, aiming their rhetoric at Hamiltonians and concentrating on the debilitating influence of the Federalist system as a whole.

It was also in 1794 that Benjamin Franklin Bache added the name *Aurora* to the masthead of his *General Advertiser*, reflecting an even more important change in its political stance. Bache, who was Franklin's grandson, had founded his Philadelphia daily on October 1, 1790. Until 1793, he impartially admitted contributions from both sides of the slight amount of controversy that he published, and he maintained a personal position that might be characterized as moderately proadministration.[54] More space was given to controversy early in 1793, when Bache permitted a sizable campaign against titles, receptions, and celebration of the President's birthday (which some considered a kingly

53. Scholars generally confirm the judgment of William Duane in the *Aurora* of Sept. 21, 1799, that for five years, the *Aurora* was the great bulwark of Republicanism. Duane maintained, "scarcely . . . six public papers out of nearly 200 . . . maintained the principles of 1776." Second to the *Aurora*, he thought, was the *Argus*, followed by the *Independent Chronicle*. This "with a few more plagiary papers to the southward" completed the republican corps until the appearance late in the decade of the Albany *Register*, the Richmond *Examiner*, the Baltimore *American*, and the New London *Bee*. In line with this assessment, the *Argus* generally retained first spot among papers most frequently reprinted by the *Aurora*. In 1799, the *Examiner* replaced the *Chronicle* in second place. The Albany *Register* was next, followed by the *American*.

54. This disputes Donald H. Stewart, *The Opposition Press of the Federalist Period* (Albany: State University of New York Press, 1969), whose appendix simply characterizes the *Advertiser* as "Democratic." But see, for example, the editorial comment of July 7, 1791: "The administration of the general government has been conducted upon such liberal, just, independent, and successful principles that we shall seek in vain for a parallel to that acquiescence and applause which it has received from our citizens. The difference between the past and present circumstances of our national character, credit, and importance . . . ought to inspire . . . thanksgiving." And Bache long retained a capacity for considerable disgust with the opposition. On Jan. 16, 1792, he wrote, "Although the impartial foreign world resounds with applause for the revival of our public credit, . . . though our government is the frequent topic of the eulogies of the struggling patriot of the old world, the tongue of prejudice and error is incessantly recounting a different tale to the happy people of the United States."

custom). But the complexion of the *General Advertiser* changed
most significantly in the summer of 1793. By the end of that
year, the paper was strongly pro-French and antiaristocratic. It
became unmistakably partisan in 1794, rapidly assuming the
place once occupied by the *National Gazette*. Like the *Independent Chronicle*, the *Aurora* made its greatest contribution to the
propagation of Republican ideology after the French Revolution
and John Jay's Treaty with the British had become the most
exciting topics of debate.

III

Jay's negotiations with the British extended through the
summer and fall of 1794. Although a treaty was agreed upon in
November, its contents remained an official secret until June
1795, when a copy was leaked to the *Aurora* on the eve of the
Senate's ratification. During much of this interlude, national attention was redirected to events at home. The Whiskey Rebellion and its aftermath in the well-known congressional debate on
Washington's condemnation of the Democratic-Republican
Societies were quarrelled over primarily with the established
weapons of domestic controversy. Still, the activities of the popular societies assured new charges of foreign influence. By the end
of 1794, few questions could be discussed in isolation from the
international issues in which the country was increasingly absorbed. The evidence of private letters, public speeches, and the
press all show that leaders of both parties were coming to accept
the popular image of the political struggle as a contest between
"French" and "British" interests. Each side accused the other of
seeking, for domestic purposes, to involve the nation in the war.

During these same months, a general agreement on the
sources of administration policy had been achieved in numerous
scattered pieces in the Republican press. Quickly and easily in
the spring of 1793, Republican propagandists had identified
neutrality and criticism of France with a danger to republicanism
long evident at home. This identification did not depend exclusively on the spiritual affinity that Federalists felt for Britain as a

conservator of order in the world, not even on Federal willingness to identify the cause of civilization with the forces of hereditary power. Republican concerns were both deeper and more
specific. Before the war in Europe had become an issue in the
United States, the Republicans had identified themselves as opponents of a deliberate conspiracy to return to a constitution of
the British sort. In Federalist foreign policy, they inevitably detected a desire to preserve the financial sources of the domestic
system of corruption while moving closer to a concert, perhaps a
reunion, with the English fount of Federalist ideas. Jay's Treaty
came as the penultimate confirmation of their fears.

The Treaty of Amity and Commerce between the United
States and Britain was one of the least attractive in American
history. In exchange for British agreement to evacuate military
posts in the American Northwest and to admit small American
vessels to direct trade with the West Indian colonies (on conditions that the Senate would reject), the United States had to
forsake its position on neutral rights and grant Great Britain
most-favored-nation privileges in its ports. Boundary disputes,
American claims for British spoliations, and British claims
against American debtors were to be settled by joint commissions. There was no mention of settlement for slaves carried away
by the British at the end of the Revolutionary War or of the
matter of British impressment of American seamen, although the
British were protected against future sequestrations of their
property or discriminations against their trade.

Perhaps, as Hamilton argued in his *Camillus* papers, Jay could
not have obtained better terms.[55] Nevertheless, the first contemporary reaction was decidedly adverse. Washington hesitated for
four months before sending the treaty to the Senate. The Senate
ratified it without a vote to spare and only after it had rejected the
obnoxious Article XII, which would have forbidden American

---

55. This is the conclusion of the most recent students of the treaty. See Combs, *The
Jay Treaty*, and Charles R. Ritcheson, *Aftermath of Revolution: British Policy toward the
United States, 1783–1795* (Dallas: Southern Methodist University Press, 1969), chap.
16.

exports of any West Indian product. The people were absolutely enraged. With the first firm news of the treaty's terms, the nation erupted in mass meetings that appealed to Washington to refuse his consent.[56] Hamilton was mobbed in New York when he tried to speak in favor of the treaty; Jay was burned in effigy, threatened with impeachment, and physically attacked.[57]

The Federalists themselves were not entirely happy with the treaty, but they pushed it through the Senate on the strength of arguments that the alternative might well be war. And then they undertook to sell it to a most unhappy people. Meetings were organized around the country to produce addresses in support of the treaty, and its proponents began an exhaustive educational effort in the press. In collaboration with Rufus King, Hamilton, who had not resigned his interest in or influence over governmental affairs when he returned to private life in January 1795, again produced the most impressive defense. With their careful exposition of the necessity Jay had been under of compromising American with British interests and their brilliant explication of America's position in the world, the lengthy *Letters of Camillus* were as good a justification of Jay's Treaty as anyone has made. With Noah Webster's *Letters of Curtius* and lesser essays in defense, they heatedly maintained that there had been no choice except these terms or war.[58]

Slowly, the Federalist campaign began to split the opposition to the treaty. Many who had been disgusted by its terms were forced to recognize that it at least had ended an immediate danger of an English war. It was more than a year, however,

56. And the President seriously considered refusing his consent. He may have signed, in part, because he mistakenly believed that he had caught Secretary of State Randolph in an intrigue with the French.

57. Miller, *Federalist Era*, pp. 168–171.

58. *The Letters of Camillus*, which originally appeared in two New York newspapers, the *Argus* and the *Minerva*, are in *Works of Hamilton*, V, 189–491 and VI, 3–197. When Jefferson received a collection of writings on the treaty from John Beckley, he found that none of the Republican antidotes were strong enough to counteract the poison of "Curtius" and "Camillus," both of which he thought were Hamilton's. Again he appealed to Madison: "Hamilton is really a colossus to the antirepublican party. Without numbers, he is a host within himself. . . . When he comes forward, there is nobody but yourself who can meet him" (*Works of Jefferson*, VIII, 192–193).

before French attacks on American shipping caused opinion to reverse. Until then, the Republicans enjoyed a peak of popularity that they would not achieve again until the last year of the decade. It required no sophistication to interpret Jay's Treaty as an alliance with Great Britain and a betrayal of revolutionary France. Certainly, Republicans insisted that it was, and they were quick to take advantage of the opportunity presented by the treaty to persuade the people to consider their opponents' system as a whole. They found a willing response. In popular meetings across the country, they were able to produce addresses condemning the treaty as another stage in an old Federalist conspiracy against the rights of man. The report of a meeting at Plymouth denounced it in representative tone, calling the agreement a

business suspicious in its origins, dark and insidious in its progress, without reciprocity . . . , without policy, without gratitude to our best friends, violating the Constitution of the United States and prostrating the American character at the shrine of British arrogance, with no object apparent to us but to embarrass and distress the Republic of France and to break down the republican system of this country.[59]

In the summer and fall of 1795, the *Independent Chronicle*, the *Argus*, and the *Aurora* filled most of their space with similar addresses and with original essays and reprints attacking the treaty. With grim satisfaction and in surprising numbers, pamphleteers also joined in the attack.[60]

As "Camillus" remarked, the Republican reception of Jay's Treaty was predictable long before its terms were known. Dislike of its specific provisions was never more than a starting point

59. *Independent Chronicle*, Oct. 28, 1795. References are usually to "a very numerous meeting" or some such phrase. Occasionally, however, the level of involvement can be ascertained, and it was sometimes considerable. Thus, *The American Remembrancer* (Philadelphia: Mathew Carey, 1795), a collection of essays, speeches, and resolutions on Jay's Treaty, prints an address favoring the agreement which was signed by 413 "merchants and traders" of Philadelphia, along with a dissent from the vote of a meeting which condemned the treaty that was signed by 177 Bostonians and a dissent from an anti-treaty vote by 70 citizens of Trenton.

60. The briefest glance at Charles Evans' *American Bibliography* will show that the treaty prompted an outpouring of occasional pieces completely unexampled in the earlier 1790s.

for a broader condemnation of the treaty's place in the context of national affairs. Using the *nom de plume* "Franklin," under which so many Republican essays had appeared, one of the earliest and most widely reprinted critics objected that "if foreign connections are to be formed, they ought to be made with nations whose influence and example would not poison the fountain of liberty." Any treaty with Britain would have aroused this author's concern, "for a nation so debauched and corrupt must communicate her debauchery and corruption to those with whom her intercourse is easy and familiar."[61]

It was easy to argue that this was a bad, even a demeaning treaty, but the Republicans were most alarmed by the motives that had given it rise and by the consequences it could produce. Once again Hamilton's obvious hand in its defense permitted an easy connection of criticisms of the treaty with the fundamental grounds of Republican opposition. It also permitted a concerned explanation of the growing success of the Federalist campaign in the treaty's behalf. "The hero of the funding and excise systems," critics declared, had now assumed the lead of the treaty's advocates with his warnings of war. At one time, his scare tactics would have been without success, but "the instrumentality of a funding system aided by British influence and directed by another Walpole had not then ennervated us. We were strangers to corruption."[62]

Republicans were sharply aware that concern for the revenue system was an important consideration in Federalist opposition to any quarrel with Britain. This consideration had long been a

61. *Letters of Franklin on the Conduct of the Executive and the Treaty* (Philadelphia: Eleazer Oswald, 1795), pp. 11–12, 16. These letters had first appeared in Oswald's *Independent Gazetteer* between March 9 and June 6, 1795. They were published in pamphlet form with a preface in which Oswald, to whom they are attributed by Evans, specifically disclaimed any connection with the writer. This need not be taken at face value, but I cannot help speculating whether the author might have been John Taylor. Taylor had used this pseudonym before in this newspaper, and the argument and style were similar to his. Of course, Taylor could not have been responsible for every piece signed by "Franklin." Whoever he was, however, this "Franklin" was reprinted in full by all three of the most important Republican papers.

62. "Atticus," no. 6, reprinted from the *Independent Gazetteer* by the *Independent Chronicle*, Sept. 28, 1795.

key point of their attack, and critics continued to insist that retaliatory measures could have forced the British to better terms. "But alas! if we did not import British goods, what would become of all the mushroom men of fortune who live by the impost?" To prevent retaliatory measures, "all the funded gentry and all the British party contrived to form the egg of the treaty."[63] When the interests of the Tories, monarchists, aristocrats, British dependents, and funded gentry were carefully assessed, the treaty could be fitted readily into Federalist plans:

There seems to have been a deliberate plan to exterminate liberty, and this was to have been effected by throwing off the connection with France and consolidating ourselves with Great Britain—in the arms of despotism. . . . That the government of the United States has been making rapid strides towards aristocracy no unprejudiced man . . . will deny, and that a connection with Great Britain was sought for to facilitate this object, no one who has noticed the steps of our administration and has read the treaty . . . will controvert.[64]

IV

When the members assembled for the first session of the Fourth Congress early in December 1795, the Republicans had not abandoned hope of defeating Jay's Treaty. The House demanded the papers relating to Jay's instructions and to the course of the negotiations as a first step in a Republican plan to defeat the execution of the treaty by refusing to make the appropriations necessary for carrying it into effect. Washington's refusal to release the papers and his insistence that the House had no constitutional part in the treaty-making power established the issues that dominated the session until April 29, 1796, when Speaker Frederick Muhlenberg cast a tie-breaking vote for carrying the treaty into effect.[65]

63. "Millions," *Independent Chronicle*, Oct. 26, 1795.

64. "Atticus," no. 6, ibid., Sept. 28, 1795. Compare "Hancock," no. 5, *Aurora*, Sept. 12, 1795, and *Aurora*, Sept. 9, 1795.

65. Earlier, the House had voted 57 to 35 that it had the right to refuse appropriations, but Republican support had waned in the face of growing public support for the

In Congress, there was remarkably little ideological exchange on the treaty. Proponents stressed commercial gains, while the Republicans insisted that America had given up essential economic weapons without obtaining real concessions in return. Still, the congressional conflict helped to keep the treaty near the center of attention in the press. There, the level of debate was sliding down the alley of vituperation toward the nadir it would reach within the next few years. On both sides, editors and correspondents vied to demonstrate new talents for rhetorical abuse. One day, the *Aurora* would slap at the Federalist editor of the New York *Minerva*:

It is amusing to observe the puerilities to which Noah Webster stoops and the absurdities of which he is guilty in the prosecution of his daily task of calumniating the French. Having exhausted those sinks of party lies, the British ministerial papers, to prove the barbarity and tyrannical disposition of the French, he begins to pick a quarrel with their cockade.[66]

A few days later, another volley would seek a different mark:

The editor of the United States Gazette, Johnny Fenno, having long since abandoned all pretensions to candor and character, his insensibility to shame and remorse are so notorious that the defamatory effusions of his press have become the strongest testimonies of patriotism and true worth.[67]

Most despised and villified of all the Federalist writers was the English immigrant, William Cobbett, who supplemented his scurrilous Philadelphia newspaper, *Porcupine's Gazette*, with an inexhaustibly foul stream of vitriolic pamphlets abusing the American Jacobins. "Peter Porcupine" and his correspondents

---

treaty and the Senate's threat to withhold ratification of the pending treaty with Spain, which secured a right to navigate the Mississippi. The Senate had opened its doors to reporters at the beginning of the Fourth Congress, but its debates were not reported at any length.

66. *Aurora*, Nov. 12, 1796.

67. Ibid., Nov. 24, 1796. This single day's issue saw Fenno referred to as a "tool of despotism" and his supporters characterized as "lottery gamblers," "lick-spits of government," and "toad-eaters of administration." Exchanges of this sort eventually led to a street fight between Bache and Fenno.

identified the Republicans with the worst excesses of the French Revolution and directed their poisoned quills at French hirelings, atheists, and "cannibalistic" anarchists. Republicans returned them in kind with accusations that the "hedgehog" was a lickspit of the monarchical system which had driven him to the United States, a sordid hireling of the British interest, or an English spy.[68]

Perhaps because they sold well among a heavy-humored populace, abusive denunciations of this sort filled newspapers and pamphlets to the partial exclusion of more rational debate and debased the quality of public rhetoric as a whole. Not even in the war of abuse with Peter Porcupine, however, did the Republicans lose sight entirely of the more serious reasons for their concern. The very presence in America of this vitriolic English traducer of the rabble and the French was additional evidence of Federalist contempt for the people and the spread of a corrupting British influence:

There cannot be a doubt that there exists a disposition in certain characters in the United States to assimilate our government to that of Great Britain—monarchy is the idol of these men and republicanism of course their abhorrence. . . . The writings of Peter Porcupine . . . go to this point, and hence the patronage which he has received from certain characters. . . . There is a deliberate design to filch the people of this country of their liberties.[69]

68. In addition to the newspapers, a representative sampling of gutter ideology might include, by Cobbett, *A Bone to Gnaw for the Democrats* (Philadelphia: Cobbett, 1795), and *History of the American Jacobins* (Philadelphia: Cobbett, 1796). On the same side see [John Lowell], *The Antigallican* (Philadelphia: Cobbett, 1797). Some representative replies are [John Swanwick], *A Rub from Snub* (Philadelphia, 1796); *A Congratulatory Epistle to the Redoubtable Peter Porcupine* (Philadelphia: Thomas Bradford, 1796); and [Samuel Fisher Bradford], *The Imposter Detected* (Philadelphia: Thomas Bradford, 1796).

Porcupine's Gazette was a Philadelphia daily founded on March 4, 1797. It was always in disrepute among all but the most extreme Federalists for its vituperation, but it persisted until 1799, when a libel judgment in favor of Benjamin Rush forced Cobbett to flee the state.

69. *The Imposter Detected*, pp. xii-xv. Compare the more vitriolic presentation of the same charges in *A Pill for Porcupine*, pp. 81–83: "If a t-rd, much less a knave, came from England, by my soul I believe either would smell sweet to the nose of Alexander Hamilton, John Jay, and many of the well born here."

Publication of Jay's Treaty in July 1795 had resulted in a huge increase in the volume of attacks on the Federalist conspiracy in the *Aurora*, the *Argus*, and the *Independent Chronicle*. Until the end of 1796, when other subjects were subordinated to the election campaign, the nature and consequences of the treaty remained the focal point for most Republican demonstrations of the reality of the plot. To growing numbers of the rising party, the treaty and a desire to involve the nation in an alliance with Great Britain had joined and, to a degree, displaced the economic program among the instruments that Federalist conspirators employed to move the country toward their end. But the origins and goals of the conspiracy, as described by the Republicans, had changed only marginally since Confederation days.

Typical of the depiction of the history of Federalism was a pamphlet by a rising leader of Republicans in Congress, written in 1796 and published early in 1797. It had become clear, Albert Gallatin wrote, that the object of Washington's administration was "to prepare us for a war with France and to provoke her to a declaration of it, . . . to couple our country with the league of despots."[70] From the time of the Neutrality Proclamation, the administration had pursued a conduct so partial to England and hostile to France as to give the latter every cause for war. No government could have submitted to the "outrages" and "barbarities" ours had suffered at the hands of England "without being in secret combination with the nation committing them."

The spirit which animated our country to resist British tyranny and to declare independence is, alas, paralyzed by systems artfully contrived to render the mind pliant to the views of an insidious and ambitious administration. Funding and banking systems, with the speculations which have grown out of them have substituted an avarice of wealth for the glory and love of country. Had America in the year 1775 been what she is now, a nation governed by stock jobbers, stock-holders, and bank directors, we should have hugged the fetters which Great Britain had then forged for us.[71]

70. *An Examination of the Conduct of the Executive . . . towards the French Republic* (Philadelphia: Francis & Robert Bailey, 1797), p. v.

71. Ibid., pp. 65, 68.

Long before the Neutrality Proclamation, Gallatin reasoned, the administration began to pursue a systematic plan to subvert republicanism. Under the guidance of Alexander Hamilton— "apostle of monarchy," "high priest of slavery," "crusader against republicanism," "this Judas Iscariot of our country"—

we have had a government of individual will instead of that of the people, for the executive had but to say let there be, and there was. Virtually, Congress have been a committee of ways and means, a parliament somewhat after the ancient regime of France, to register edicts. . . . The aim is to assimilate our government to a monarchy. Every measure seems to squint towards this darling object, and hence irredeemable debts, excise systems, national banks, loans, federal cities, reports for raising revenue by an officer unknown to the Constitution and dependent on the executive—hence the plan to excite the Western Insurrection to increase the national debt, to furnish a pretext for a standing army, and to supply arguments against the cause of republicanism.[72]

Hence, a connection with Great Britain and provocation of a war with France.

As always, Hamilton was villain of the play, yet Gallatin no longer hesitated to attack George Washington as well.[73] By this time, the father of his country was enduring a merciless beating in the Republican press. In the fall of 1795, irritated by the Federalists' appeal to his prestige to defend the treaty, John Beckley, Benjamin Franklin Bache, William Duane, and others had deliberately set out to destroy the President's reputation.[74] Writing over pen names of "Belisarius," "Pittachus," "Valerius," and so on, they filled the *Aurora* with venemous attacks on Washington, sometimes even advocating his impeachment. The *Argus* and the *Independent Chronicle* reprinted many of these essays and soon began to bolster the campaign with original assaults of their own. From France, Thomas Paine joined with domestic pam-

72. Ibid., pp. 39–41.
73. Will Washington "become the tyrant instead of the savior of his country?" (ibid., p. 44).
74. Mathew Carey, *Autobiography*, (Brooklyn: Eugene Schwaab, 1942), p. 39. Carey realized that this campaign ultimately damaged the Republicans more than it did Washington himself.

phleteers in its support, calling Washington a man who could "desert a man or a cause with constitutional indifference," a "hypocrite" whose public life revealed him either as "an apostate or an imposter."[75] Jefferson himself became involved in condemnations of the President when a Federalist newspaper published his letter to Philip Mazei, with its often-quoted accusation that "men who were Samsons in the field and Solomons in the Council . . . have had their heads shorn by the harlot England."[76]

Occasioned by Jay's Treaty, the assaults on Washington focused on the President's betrayal of the country's interests and the people's will on that occasion. Yet nearly all of them attempted to arraign the hero's motives from the Revolution on. Most insisted that Washington's administration had conspired against liberty from the start, and they no longer absolved the President from responsibility for the plot. Addressing Washington directly, "Belisarius" listed in order the measures they condemned. Your administration, he accused, has entailed upon the country "deep and incurable public evils" culminating in a treaty "deeply subversive of republicanism and destructive to every principle of free representative government." Including the creation of a distinction between the people and the executive through monarchical pageantry, sanctioning the plunder of the veterans by speculators, mortgaging the revenue to an irredeem-

75. "Letters to George Washington," in Philip S. Foner, ed., *The Complete Writings of Thomas Paine*, 2 vols. (New York: Citadel Press, 1945), II, 689–723. This attack was comprised of three letters written during 1795 and inspired by Jay's Treaty and by personal suffering in France which Paine attributed to Washington's connivance. Although it was concerned primarily with foreign policy, it attacked Washington's character from the Revolution forward and accepted most of the opposition's interpretations of Federalist motives. Another important pamphlet attributing the Federalist conspiracy to the President himself was *Remarks Occasioned by the Late Conduct of Mr. Washington as President of the United States* (Philadelphia: B. F. Bache, 1797), probably the work of Beckley.

76. *Works of Jefferson*, VIII, 238–241. This excerpt on politics from a longer letter was first printed in a Florentine newspaper. From there, it was translated from Italian into French for the Paris *Moniteur* and thence into English for Webster's New York *Minerva*. The version which appeared in the *Minerva* is given in a footnote to ibid., pp. 237–240. Despite Jefferson's protests to the contrary, it is a surprisingly faithful translation of the original condemnation of "an Anglican monarchical and aristocratical party . . . whose avowed object is to draw over us the substance, as they have already done the forms, of the British government."

able public debt, and creation of a national bank, administration measures have established "a monied aristocracy whose baneful power has greatly influenced all the principles of the government." They have begotten submission to Britain, an Indian war, a standing army, excises and consequent rebellion, denunciation of the popular societies, a proclamation encroaching on the powers of Congress, and an unconstitutional appointment of an agent to unconstitutionally negotiate an unconstitutional treaty.[77]

Only if we forget the shower of abuse with which his opponents ushered Washington from office need we be surprised that the accession of John Adams to the Presidency was greeted by the Republicans as a considerable change for the better. Election propaganda in the campaign of 1796 had not been disconnected from the broader context of partisan dispute. Adams' books had been raised again to haunt him, and Republican newspapers and pamphlets had presented the election as a clear choice between a republican and a monarchist.[78] To a remarkable extent, however, the Republicans had proven willing to ignore the candidate in favor of attacks on Hamilton and Washington and the policies of the past eight years. Adams had never been identified with Hamiltonian economics—in fact, he had a known dislike for banks and standing armies and the like—and the Republicans saw cause to hope that anger over Hamilton's attempt to slip Thomas Pinckney into the Presidency would combine with Adams' undeniable independence of mind to make his administration less subservient to Britain than Washington's had been.[79]

77. "Belisarius," no. 1, *Aurora*, Sept. 11, 1795. Compare "Pittachus," no. 5, ibid., Sept. 28, 1795, and "Cassa," ibid., Oct. 16, 1795. For as extreme a condemnation as appeared at the time, including an appeal for impeachment, see also "Casca," reprinted from the *Petersburgh Intelligencer* by the *Independent Chronicle*, Oct. 29, 1795.

78. Some representative samples are "To the Citizens of the United States," *Independent Chronicle*, Oct. 17, 1796; "Franklin," ibid., Nov. 3, 1796; ibid., Nov. 17, 1796; election broadsides signed "A Republican" (Philadelphia, Oct. 3, 1796) and "Americanus" (Boston, 1796); and [Tench Coxe], *The Federalist* (Philadelphia: Mathew Carey, 1796). Even Benjamin Rush, a good friend of Adams, adopted this assessment of the contest. See Rush to James Currie, July 26, 1796, in Rush's *Letters*, II, 779.

79. The fullest study of the election, Steven Kurtz, *The Presidency of John Adams: The Collapse of Federalism, 1795–1800* (Philadelphia: University of Pennsylvania

Jefferson insisted that he felt no hesitation in accepting second place to Adams in a new regime.[80] Washington, in any case, had left the nation with a crisis Jefferson had no desire to handle. In the fall of 1796, following the ratification of Jay's Treaty, French privateers had begun to prey on American shipping in the West Indies. To the Republicans, who had been predicting French hostility since 1793, these depredations seemed an overdue response to policies that had consistently favored Britain. After all, the French had only declared that they would treat American ships in the same manner as the United States "suffered" the British to treat them. Federalist policies had courted French hostility.

Under the mask of professional friendship they have concealed the most deliberate enmity. It cannot be believed that the Executive Directory will be amused with fine professions when they are possessed of such a flood of facts that our administration is in secret combination with Great Britain against them. . . . May the Father of mercies soften the just anger of an injured friend, that the iniquities of the administration may not be visited upon the people.[81]

As the crisis grew through the fall of 1796, Republican insistence that French actions were a just retaliation for administration conduct and a plea to the United States for an impartial course gave way to urgent warnings of the dangers that must follow a collision. "It is a part, no doubt, of the plan of the administration to make war upon France, and why? Because it will establish British influence and British politics in our country. Because it will assist in assimilating our government to that of Great Britain."[82] John Adams was accepted with unfeigned relief because his private statements and his inaugural address promised to keep the peace with France.

Press, 1957), emphasizes the extent to which the Republicans ignored Adams in order to attack Hamilton or Washington.

80. Peterson, pp. 545, 557–558; Dumas Malone, *Jefferson and the Ordeal of Liberty* (Boston: Little, Brown, 1962), pp. 290–294.

81. *Aurora*, Nov. 15, 1796.

82. "A Correspondent," ibid., Dec. 22, 1796. Compare "A Correspondent," *Independent Chronicle*, Dec. 8, 1796.

CHAPTER 9

The Principles of Ninety-Eight

A useful analysis of politics in the 1790s distinguishes four stages in the party struggle, concurrent with the four great issues that dominated national debate. From 1790 to 1793, party controversy centered on Hamilton's economic program. In 1793, the issue of neutrality pushed to the front, and, between 1794 and 1798, national attention focused on Jay's Treaty and America's course in a world at war. The decade ended with the great argument over the crisis powers assumed by the Federalist government in the emergency of 1798 and 1799.[1]

Each of these shifts in national attention brought significant changes in the content and emphasis of Republican accusations against the Federalists. At each stage of the struggle, however, Republican reactions were shaped by the stages that had gone before. A powerful set of expectations and a useful collection of analytical tools had been created in the Americanization of eighteenth-century opposition ideology, which was complete in its essentials by the end of 1792. As events raised different issues, the Republicans simply added new rings of criticism to the original core of their critique. Gradually and subtly, the content of the message changed, but the conjunction of external happenings with the internal needs of the developed ideology was such that changes followed as coherently from one another as the ripples

1. Joseph Charles, *The Origins of the American Party System: Three Essays* (New York: Harper & Row, 1961).

started by the dropping of a stone into a pool. The principles on which the party stood in 1800 were the logical conclusion of a neo-opposition start.

I

The administration of John Adams opened with the first Presidential honeymoon. Openly relieved that Washington's retirement had removed the shield behind which enemies of freedom had pursued their schemes, the opposition courted Adams in the hope that they could separate him further from the Hamiltonians and in the expectation that he might avoid a clash with France.[2] The honeymoon was brief. On May 16, 1797, the President's address to a special session of Congress made it clear that new attempts to find a diplomatic resolution of the differences with France would be accompanied by further preparations for defense. By June, Congress was debating bills to fortify the harbors and construct a larger navy. Republicans revived their criticisms of the government's intentions.[3]

Little could be added, at this time, to the condemnation that had been developed through the past two years. Republicans still blamed the growing crisis on a foreign policy that favored Britain, still insisted that French seizures were a justifiable response to the betrayal of the old alliance. They continued to condemn Jay's Treaty as the source of present troubles with France and as the doorway through which British influence could extend cor-

2. Indeed, Madison found it necessary to persuade Jefferson to withhold a letter to Adams in which the new Vice President nearly offered an informal alliance against the Hamiltonians. Dumas Malone, *Jefferson and the Ordeal of Liberty* (Boston: Little, Brown, 1962), pp. 293–294.

3. The short special session, May 15, 1797 to July 10, offered no surprises and few debates of striking interest. Early in the session, the small Federalist majority in the House replaced John Beckley as Clerk. As attention turned to preparations for defense, Giles, Nicholas, and others freely expressed their suspicions that the Federalists were trying to provoke war, particularly with a bill to provide for the arming of merchant ships. Republicans, with help from moderates, were strong enough to defeat this measure and to resist increases in the army and navy with considerable success. They also carefully hedged the President's authority to employ the navy and torpedoed the creation of a provisional army by passing a bill to put the militia in a state of readiness.

rupting tentacles into the vitals of American society and habits.[4] They consistently maintained a bleakly pessimistic attitude about the prospects for a diplomatic resolution of the crisis. The French had justice on their side, as well as might, and the administration, with the Federalists in Congress, seemed to court hostilities with prideful rhetoric and preparations for defense.

Early in the second session of this narrowly divided Congress, though, a controversy did erupt which led the House of Representatives into as deep an exploration of the differences between the parties as the decade ever saw. John Nicholas touched off the argument by urging a reduction of the diplomatic corps. He argued that appointments had been used by the executive to reward its followers in Congress, establishing a "thirst for office" and a commitment to "executive infallibility" which tended to "produce a union and consolidation" of the different parts of government and to "destroy the Constitution."[5] Robert Goodloe Harper was next up with a reply that led the members into an intensive exploration of the principles of government and the effects of party. "The subject of foreign intercourse," he said,

> was never taken up without that gentleman or some other . . . advancing these opinions; they never failed to speak of the danger to be apprehended from executive influence. . . . Nor was this a doctrine confined to this country or this age. Whenever a set of gentlemen in any country found their views opposed by the measures of government, they became vexed and attributed the proceedings of those who differed with them in opinion to any motive rather than the public good. The desire of executive favor or executive office was an usual charge and it was at this day well understood. . . . The House was not afraid of executive influence.[6]

After listening to "Long" John Allen second Harper in a speech expressing fear of the effect of these chimerical anxieties

4. Additional examples seem superfluous. But [Richard Beresford], *Sketches of French and English Politics in America* (Charleston: W. P. Young, 1797) is an excellent example of the combination of an attribution of the crisis to Jay's Treaty and distress with the treaty's threat to republican virtue at home.

5. *Annals of Congress*, Fifth Congress, second session, pp. 849–852.

6. Ibid., pp. 852–853.

outside the House, Albert Gallatin, who had succeeded Madison in leadership of the Republicans, insisted that large numbers of rational people were "fully convinced that there was a faction existing within the United States and even within the walls of that House who wished to demolish the government." He might not agree with Nicholas that patronage or hope of patronage was an extensive evil at the present time, but he was certain that it could become an evil of the greatest magnitude. In Britain, corruption of this sort had swollen to such an extent that it had become "a part of the system itself, . . . without which, it is said, the government could not go on." Unless America could check the evil at an early stage, the same might happen here.[7]

Most leading members rose two times or more as arguments pushed ever closer to the center of concerns. Rising in response to Gallatin, Harper said: "As to all the idle declamation about executive influence, the danger of corruption, and the increase of patronage . . . which had been the constant topic of harangues in all governments constituted like ours from the days of James I till the present moment, he considered them as unworthy of answers or regard; . . . they . . . were thrown out merely *ad captandum vulgus*."[8] Seconding the charge that the Republican attack on influence was directed to the galleries, Roger Griswold argued that the executive was far too weak in the United States to pose this kind of danger, and Delaware's James Bayard followed him in thinking it absurd to rank the powers of the President with the enormous patronage of British ministries.[9] Several Federalists agreed with Bayard that the powers of the legislature posed the greatest threat to balanced government in the United States.[10] But Nicholas, with help from Edward Livingston and others, was not to be dissuaded. He insisted that "the example of England ought to be a sufficient warning to the people of this country," and he argued that America already suffered from "a

7. Ibid., pp. 856–859.
8. Ibid., p. 873.
9. Ibid., pp. 891–892, 895–896.
10. Ibid., pp. 897 ff.

description of persons . . . attached by interest to the executive, who formed a kind of standing army more powerful than if they had guns in their hands." He traced the origins of this connection to the funding scheme, which "was intended to produce a party . . . who would support the executive at all events."[11] Gallatin himself was willing to speak for three hours and a half in order to rebut the claim that danger was more likely to result from legislative usurpations. Whatever may have been the case in Greece or Rome, he reasoned, modern European history showed that the executive was the important source of danger. English government, most like our own, was the most relevant comparison. And there, since 1688, "a progressive patronage and a systematic, corrupting influence have sunk Parliament to a nominal representation, a mere machine . . . through which the executive reaches with ease the purse of the people."[12] What Harrison Gray Otis said still carried certain insight into opposition minds:

There are . . . men whose enjoyment of the present is always clouded by a gloomy anticipation of the future and who are never content with the most ample measure of present liberty and security but brood over the histories of kings and the oppressions of arbitrary power until their imaginations are heated by day and their visions disturbed by night by the spectre of tyranny stalking over the country. . . . These are the exclusive guardians of the public welfare, the sentinels who forewarn us of future danger, the political quacks who acknowledge the body politic to be in perfect health but at the same time foretell its untimely dissolution.[13]

As 1797 turned into 1798 without relief from French depredations and without news of success from the American envoys at Paris, Congress interrupted the debate on the diplomatic establishment to divert itself with the Blount Conspiracy and the Lyon-Griswold fight, displaying the frayed nerves and rising tempers that the heavy-handed humor of the press did not disguise. The revelation of Hamilton's affair with Mrs. Reynolds was a subject for satiric glee, and party pamphleteers continued

11. Ibid., pp. 928–929.
12. Ibid., pp. 1118–1143.
13. Ibid., pp. 1150–1151.

their running war of abuse with Peter Porcupine. But it was a time of old issues and stale rhetoric while everyone waited for news from France. In Congress and in the country at large, the opposition searched the foreign news for any hint of the expected breach with France that could doom the cause of liberty at home and in the world. On March 5, 1798, the day that Nicholas' proposal was defeated forty-eight to fifty-two, a message from the President announced that the American ambassadors no longer hoped to reach a resolution of the crisis.

II

Serious maritime difficulties with France originated in 1795, when Secretary of State Timothy Pickering estimated that 316 American ships had been seized. With the ratification of Jay's Treaty, the United States had reversed itself from a French to a British definition of neutral rights. In response, the French Directory loosed a horde of marauding privateers on American merchantmen in the West Indies and off the Atlantic coast. They calculated that damage to American commerce would assist their Republican supporters in the United States in reversing the policies that favored British interests. In this, they were seriously mistaken. Continuing French depredations and Republican attacks on Washington's policies may have contributed to the Federalist victory in the election of 1796. French seizures made it impossible for the Republicans to prevent the Federalists from combining diplomatic efforts to resolve the crisis with preparations for defense. In the end, French persistence in a policy of stubborn intransigence forced America into active hostilities and brought their American admirers to the brink of political ruin.[14]

Early in Adams' administration, nearly everyone had favored efforts to negotiate with France. In July 1797, John Marshall and Elbridge Gerry sailed from the United States to join Charles Cotesworth Pinckney as special envoys. For eight months there-

14. This paragraph and the next follow Alexander DeConde, *The Quasi-War: The Politics and Diplomacy of the Undeclared War with France, 1797–1801* (New York: Scribner, 1966).

after, the nation marked time in increasing tension while both political parties awaited the outcome of the mission. The first dispatches from the envoys, despairing of a reconciliation, did not arrive until March 1798. When they did, the fiery Adams was absolutely livid over the rebuff. His first inclination was to seek an immediate declaration of war, but, fearing for the safety of the envoys and believing that a little time would bring more popular support, he contented himself, on March 19, with an announcement of a state of limited hostilities and a request for additional measures of defense.

To the Republicans, this shocking blow at the cause of liberty in the world seemed literally insane. They could not believe that the administration was telling the truth about the progress of the negotiations and, suspecting that the Federalists were bent on war whatever the chances for peace, they insisted that the papers relating to the negotiations be submitted to Congress. Obligingly, the President sprung the trap into which they had stepped, transmitting the papers on April 3. On April 6, Congress voted to have them published. In this way, the whole sordid business of the XYZ affair was released to the public. America's ambassadors had waited weeks without a formal audience, to be approached, at last, by unofficial agents of the Foreign Minister—referred to in American dispatches as X, Y, and Z—who told them that negotiations could not start without a bribe for Talleyrand, a large American loan to the Republic, and an apology for certain comments in the President's address to Congress.

Republicans, of course, insisted that the publication of the diplomatic papers should be seen for what it was: "the last link in the systematic chain of measures pursued by the Tories to alienate this country from France, draw its connection with Britain closer, and, by strengthening the influence of that country here, pave the way for a subversion or total perversion of our Constitution."[15] The dispatches showed no more than that America's

15. "Sidney," no. 1, *Aurora*, April 14, 1798.

ambassadors had been approached by certain individuals who claimed to speak for Talleyrand. But

> attempts . . . are evidently making by men high in authority to widen the breach between the United States and the French Republic by holding up to the good people of these states the late unworthy propositions of certain unauthorized persons at Paris as the act of the French government. . . .
> We cannot but view the man . . . as inimical to the rights of the people . . . who shall by such means strive to involve us in all the calamities of a war with the most powerful Republic on earth.[16]

War, a public meeting warned, "burdens labor to support idleness and subjects virtue to vice. It exposes nations to the risk of slavery or leads them to the crime of conquest. War begets taxes; the people must pay them. War incurs debt; the people must redeem it. War makes a government stronger by making the people weaker. War makes individuals richer by making the people poorer."[17] It must be obvious, wrote "Nestor," that "the present state of things is artificial and has been contrived. . . . A standing army, a navy, immense debt, and extravagant taxes are admirable instruments to bow the neck to obedience, and these convenient engines could not have been obtained unless some pretext was instituted to give them legitimacy." Having failed in all their "well digested" efforts to infuriate the French, a set of men "who are not apostates from the course of the rights of man, but conspirators against them" had seized upon the XYZ Affair to goad Americans into a course of action that must "involve our rights, interests, and peace in one undistinguished ruin."[18]

Despite the opposition's efforts to defuse the popular reac-

16. Resolutions of Captain Bernard Magnien's Company of Grenadiers at Portsmouth, Virginia, May 5, 1798, reprinted from a Norfolk paper by the *Aurora*, May 16, 1798. Compare the address of the students of William and Mary to the Virginia Congressional delegation, ibid., June 18, 1798.

17. People of Caroline County, Virginia, ibid., April 18, 1798.

18. "The Catastrophe," 10 numbers, *Aurora*, April 14 to May 22, 1798. Quotations from numbers 4 and 10.

tion—if not, in part, because of them—there followed in the spring and summer of 1798 a patriotic furor of dimensions unexampled since the news from Lexington and Concord. Overnight, the public temper turned explosively against the French. New songs, "Hail Columbia" and "Adams and Liberty," replaced the "Marseillaise" in theatres. Patriotic mobs attacked the homes and offices of Republican editors. Benjamin Franklin Bache was brutally beaten on the Philadelphia docks. Old suspicions of a connection between the Republicans and the French flamed into a widespread belief in treasonous plots. Self-appointed spies followed the movements of Republican leaders, hoping to expose their French connections. Crowds wearing the black cockade of Federalism chased the French tricolor from the streets. A flood of patriotic addresses poured into Philadelphia, and the bellicose replies of President Adams, who had suddenly become a hero to rival Washington himself, encouraged the rising hostility against the French and their domestic sympathizers.[19]

On the crest of the popular hysteria, the Federalists in Congress launched a limited naval war with France. Money was appropriated to complete frigates that were already under construction, to purchase additional ships, to provide arms, and to fortify the ports. The French treaties were suspended, and American ships were authorized to engage and capture armed French vessels.[20] The regular army was tripled in size, and authorization was provided for the enlistment of a Provisional Army of ten thousand men, which would take the field in the event of an invasion.[21]

During June and July, at the peak of the patriotic fury, the

19. This "Black Cockade Fever" is described in most of the standard accounts of the crisis: DeConde, chap. 3; James Morton Smith, *Freedom's Fetters: The Alien and Sedition Laws and American Civil Liberties* (Ithaca, N.Y.: Cornell University Press, 1956), pt. I *passim*; and John C. Miller, *Crisis in Freedom: The Alien and Sedition Acts* (Boston: Little, Brown, 1951), chap. 1 and *passim*.

20. Republicans fought unsuccessfully to limit action to purely defensive measures. *Annals*, Fifth Congress, second session, pp. 1319–2186.

21. For the Federalist military program see Richard H. Kohn, *Eagle and Sword: The Beginnings of the Military Establishment in America* (New York: Free Press, 1975), chap. 8. On page 229 in particular, Kohn clarifies a multileveled structure of regular and provisional forces that has confused many historians.

Federalists also pushed through a thinning Congress a series of laws designed to suppress and intimidate domestic opposition. French and Irish immigrants tended to support the Republicans and to oppose the British in the struggle with France. Taking advantage of nativist hysteria and appealing to the need for internal security, the Federalists chopped at this source of Republican support by extending to fourteen years the period of waiting necessary for naturalization and by giving the President the power to deport any alien whose residence he considered dangerous to the United States. In a more direct blow at the opposition and its hated press, the Federalists also made it a criminal offense to incite opposition to the laws or to "write, print, utter, or publish . . . any false, scandalous, and malicious writing or writings against the government of the United States, or either House of the Congress of the United States, or the President of the United States, with intent to defame [them] or to bring them . . . into contempt or disrepute."[22]

Much of the political history of the next two years can be told in terms of the controversy over this legislation of the spring and summer of 1798. While the Alien and Sedition Bills were before Congress, the Federalists made it plain that they associated opposition to the administration with opposition to the government and that they identified resistance to their measures with a treasonable connection with France.[23] They meant, if possible, to bring this opposition to an end. Enforced by a partisan judiciary and a vigilant, High Federalist Secretary of State, the Alien and Sedition Laws established, in Jefferson's expression, a veritable "reign of witches" in the United States. Condemnation of this terror became the gravamen of the Republican indictment of Federalism in the years preceding the victory of 1800.

No one was actually deported under the Alien Friends Law, as

22. Smith's *Freedom's Fetters* is the most complete and careful history of the repressive laws, and I have followed it throughout. Also useful—and more readable—is Miller's *Crisis in Freedom.*

23. Among the grosser examples was John Allen's reference to Gallatin as a "foreign agent" (*Annals of Congress*, p. 1483). Kohn, chap. 10, is a recent and particularly effective discussion of Federalist motives, emphasizing the reality of Federalist fears of domestic subversion.

it was named, but the measure was not without effect. The threat of its passage and the possibility of a declaration of war, which would bring the Alien Enemies Act into effect, were sufficient to hurry shiploads of French immigrants out of the country. Aliens who stayed did so in the knowledge that the possibility of summary deportation hung over the head of any stranger who provoked the administration. There was ferocious controversy over the law. From the time it came before the House, Republicans considered it a federal usurpation of powers that belonged to the states, as well as a flagrant violation of the principle that all inhabitants of the United States were entitled to a judicial determination of their fate. "I have seen measures carried in this House which I thought militated against the spirit of the Constitution," Edward Livingston declared, "but never before have I been witness to so open, so wanton, and so undisguised an attack."[24] Never before, perhaps, but very soon thereafter. Opposition to the Alien Act was soon a corollary to the more intense hostility to the Federalists' attempt to repress American citizens.

The Sedition Law was enforced with partisan vengeance. Under its provisions, or under the common law of seditious libel, the Federalists attacked all three of the most important Republican newspapers, some of the lesser prints, and several of the most influential Republican pamphleteers. Benjamin Franklin Bache and William Duane of the *Aurora*, Mrs. Greenleaf of the *Argus*, Thomas Adams of the *Independent Chronicle*, James Thompson Callender, and Thomas Cooper all felt the sting of prosecutions.[25] Harried by the Federalists, the *Argus* and the *Time Piece*,

24. *Annals*, p. 2012, an excerpt from the longest and most eloquent speech against the Alien Bill.

25. While under indictment at common law, Bache died in the yellow fever epidemic of 1798. His assistant, William Duane, married Mrs. Bache and assumed the editorship, maintaining the stature of the *Aurora* as the leading Republican organ. Mrs. Greenleaf had continued to publish the *Argus* after her husband's death. Thomas Adams, like Bache, died while under indictment. Before his death, the *Independent Chronicle* was sold to James White, who changed its policy to one of impartiality for a time. On May 15, 1800, however, White sold the paper to its editor, Eliazer Rhodes, and to Abijah Adams, Thomas' brother, who quickly returned it to its Republican allegiance.

the only Republican newspapers in New York City, went out of business. Republican Congressman Matthew Lyon of Vermont—the "spitting Lyon" of the famous fight with Roger Griswold—was imprisoned for a publication incident to his campaign for reelection in the fall of 1798. Men were prosecuted under the Sedition Law for offenses as diverse and as trivial as circulating a petition for its repeal, erecting a liberty pole, and expressing a drunken wish that a cannon ball had hit the President in his behind.

The Sedition Law was a formidable threat to freedom of the press as it has since been understood in the United States.[26] Still, it never did the work the Federalists intended. Refusing to be gagged, the opposition publicists occasionally resorted to a satire that was difficult to prosecute.[27] More commonly, they simply wrote much as before. Soon after the enactment of the law, an extraordinary advertisement appeared in the *Aurora*:

Orator Mum takes this very orderly method of announcing to his fellow citizens that a Thinking Club will be established in a few days at the sign of the Muzzle in Gag Street. The first subject for cogitation will be:

Ought a free people to obey laws which violate the Constitution they have sworn to support?[28]

In the fright of the moment, a few Republicans mentioned secession or considered a forcible resistance to federal arms, but faith in the people and in their own political abilities ultimately prevailed. Far from splintering under the test, the Republicans

26. Leonard W. Levy has made an effective argument that the law actually incorporated the most advanced contemporary concept of freedom of the press, liberalizing the common law of seditious libel by making truth a defense and giving to juries the power to determine whether a libel had occurred. Levy's *Legacy of Suppression: Freedom of Speech and Press in Early American History* (Cambridge: Harvard University Press, 1960) finds the origins of the modern, absolutistic conception of the First Amendment's prohibition of interference with freedom of expression in the Republican opposition to the Sedition Law, pointing to the Congressional speeches and pamphlets noted below.

27. The Sedition Law may have been responsible, in part, for one of the best literary productions of the decade, Freneau's satiric "Letters of Robert Slender," which were published in the *Aurora* and can be found in Philip M. Marsh, ed., *The Prose of Philip Freneau* (New Brunswick, N.J.: Scarecrow Press, 1955).

28. *Aurora*, July 14, 1798.

pulled together to establish a party discipline more formidable than they had ever attained before and stuck at the repressive laws for being incompatible with representative government as it was understood and practiced in the United States.

Edward Livingston had sketched the theme of the Republican attack in his congressional condemnation of the Alien Bill. The crisis laws, newspapers soon agreed, "develop the system of the English faction in the United States." Republicans had always argued that "the first great object" of their Federalist opponents "was a change of our Constitution. . . . But it was not believed . . . that in the momentary delirium of fancied success these advocates of monarchy and war would so soon have deemed it unnecessary to mask the hideous features of their plan."[29] "England was under the process of corruption . . . above one hundred years before the nation was found sufficiently enervated to bear a sedition bill and the infringement of her bill of rights."[30] "To make an expected attack from abroad a pretext for attacking the principles of liberty at home has drawn aside the curtain and clearly illuminated all who are willing to see."[31]

To the Republicans, conditioned as they were by eight years of warfare with Federalism, the Quasi-War with France and the repressive legislation that accompanied it were logical progressions in a contest older than the Constitution. They had been implicit in the measures of 1786 and 1790. They "originated in a funding system and were perfected in a British treaty, the supporters of the one having been the uniform advocates of the other."[32] They were predictable steps in a conspiratorial design that followed a pattern cut out long before the independence of the United States. If they did not actually establish the mixed government or the reunion with Great Britain to which the outward evidence of a covert design had always pointed, they were certainly the final,

29. "Brutus," reprinted from the *Argus* by the *Aurora*, May 28, 1798.
30. *Aurora*, Nov. 30, 1798.
31. A memorial to the Virginia Assembly from a meeting of Sept. 24, 1798, in Orange County. *Aurora*, Dec. 1, 1798.
32. "Sidney," *Independent Chronicle*, Sept. 24, 1798.

overt steps toward that end. If the Federalists could succeed in suppressing the opposition to their plans, the way would be clear for permanent constitutional change. The same hostilities that were improved to justify domestic repression would provide the argument required to justify the instrument that could deliver the final blow.

There are many in power that have done all they could, under the fictitious name of Federalism, to enslave the people. Their first care hath been to form a treaty with Britain that was well calculated to injure the French. They then found that the treaty with England would not be sufficient to cause the French to declare war against us; they therefore, with their party, have endeavored to provoke and insult the French government as much as possible; their expectations are . . . that we shall form an offensive and defensive alliance with Great Britain . . . which would destroy the true principles of republicanism. They have endeavored to create as many salary men as possible, increasing foreign ministers, building a navy, and extending the power of the executive; the next thing in view will be to raise a standing army.[33]

The Republicans never admitted that it was necessary for America to engage in hostilities with France. Similar differences with an unrepublican state had been settled short of war, and the fact that Elbridge Gerry had stayed in Paris after Marshall and Pinckney came home seemed evidence that a reasonable attitude on the American part could effect a diplomatic resolution of the trouble. George Logan even left for France to see if a self-appointed Republican ambassador could end the disastrous confrontation.[34] Despite the evidence to the contrary, the Republicans continued to maintain that the President's bellicosity and the Federalists' determination to align themselves with Britain were the most important sources of the crisis. The Federalists needed war in order to further their antirepublican plans at home.

English opposition thinkers had traditionally maintained that war permitted an ambitious administration to advance its

33. "A Countryman," *Independent Chronicle*, Feb. 12, 1799.
34. Chapter 8 of Frederick B. Tolles, *George Logan of Philadelphia* (New York: Oxford University Press, 1953), is a good account of Logan's mission.

schemes in a manner not possible in peacetime. For the Republicans, this sort of argument was the essential explanation for the Quasi-War. Republicans believed "that we should not wantonly intermeddle with European politics or European wars," for that "will occasion standing armies and navies and introduce a host of placemen and Court dependents, which may involve us in all the miseries of ... European countries."[35] They believed that the dispute with France had "given an unnatural popularity to friends of aristocracy and monarchy. It has enabled them to propagate principles which were once heard with disgust and horror, and it has enabled them to accomplish designs which could not have been attempted two years ago without producing an immediate and universal insurrection of the people."[36] The Alien and Sedition Laws were the most obvious demonstration of these truths. With those laws, the Federalists had violated the Constitution boldly and contemptuously, as they had never dared before. The Republicans expended many pounds of paper in their attempts to awaken the people to this fact. But incompatibility with the provisions of the Constitution was not the only point they wished to make. More fundamentally, they sought to show that the Sedition Act struck at the very foundations of representative government by making criticism of the rulers and their measures a criminal offense.[37] Republican government was impossible without the creation and expression of popular opinion, which depended on freedom of the press.[38] Just as the Alien Act was the ultimate expression of the Federalists' habit of bend-

35. "A Freeman," *Independent Chronicle*, April 22, 1799.

36. "Curtius," no. 1, ibid., Dec. 31, 1798. This was the first of a five-part series attacking John Marshall.

37. This theme, too, was introduced by the Republicans in Congress during the original debates on the Sedition Bill. See the speeches of Gallatin and Nicholas, *Annals*, Fifth Congress, second session, pp. 2110, 2139–2145.

38. This Republican justification for an understanding of the First Amendment that would not confine the prohibition on restraint of freedom of the press to an injunction against censorship reached its fullest and finest expression in Madison's "Report of the Committee of the Virginia House of Delegates on the Replies of the States to the Virginia Resolutions of 1798," available in Gaillard Hunt, ed., *The Writings of James Madison* (New York: Putnam, 1900–1910), VI, 341–406. See also [George Hay], *An Essay on the Liberty of the Press* (Philadelphia: Aurora Office, 1799).

ing the Constitution in the direction of uncheckable executive power, so the Sedition Law was the conclusive demonstration of their lack of confidence in the people and their irreducible enmity to a representative regime.

To the Republicans, the repressive legislation of 1798 was not a temporary, wartime necessity, as the Federalists insisted. On the contrary, the war itself was an instrumental necessity, deliberately provoked in order to permit the Federalists to establish measures that would further their continuing design to destroy American liberty.[39] Federalist measures were not merely illiberal, not merely a violation of the Constitution and a danger to states' rights. They were modeled on the classic prototypes of liberticide.

War permitted the repression of domestic opposition and turned the people's minds away from their domestic discontents. Armies and navies were unmatchable objects of expense, at once the fountainheads of additional taxes and the guarantees that these additional expenses would become perpetual.[40] Military establishments drained a nation of its substance, impoverishing the people and destroying the spirit of sturdy competence necessary for freemen.[41] War increased the proportion of the nation

39. "External alarms are improved for the purposes of internal oppression and dangers from abroad are called in to further the work of injustice at home" (*Independent Chronicle*, July 16, 1798).

40. "People," ibid., April 8, 1799. Unlike English oppositions, the Republicans always opposed a navy nearly as strongly as an army. Perhaps America's geographic situation made it less obvious to the Republicans than it was to English "Country" politicians that regular forces of one sort, if not both, were indispensable in a world at war. The Republicans opposed a navy both as an unexampled object of expense and as an appendage of government, often going so far as to say that a sizable navy would cost more than American commerce was worth. Joel Barlow's objections were typical: "The navy system . . . is like the funding system. When once the funding system was adopted as a principle by your speculating legislators, it was necessary to create a debt to support it. . . . In like manner, the rage for a navy . . . is at last wrought into a system. They have created a new ministerial department adorned with all the pomp of patronage and ready to contribute its part to the splendor of the executive and the growth of the public debt. . . . These two systems . . . are certainly calculated for the destruction of liberty in the United States" (Joel Barlow, *To His Fellow Citizens* [Philadelphia, March 8, 1800], pp. 20–21).

41. An argument well phrased in the Orange County Memorial cited in note 31 above.

intimately connected with the government in power, turning independent merchants into war contractors, creating military officers, and requiring an enlargement of the civil establishment. It stretched the disparities of wealth that were so dangerous in a republic. In this war, in particular, bonds were floated at the exorbitant interest of eight percent, an enormous favor to the hangers-on of government, lifting the paper men another step above the mass. "While my farm is taxed for the war," one farmer complained, "these war-hawks are living on the public spoils."[42] Financing of this sort was obviously an aristocratic device.

More frighteningly, however, the war required an increase in the size of the regular army, and every Anglo-American knew that standing armies were the classic instruments of liberticide. As good oppositionists, the Republicans had always favored the militia over the regular army. They were neo-Harringtonians—classical republicans, in fact—who believed that a militia of independent freeholders was the backbone of a republic, the civic body in arms.[43] They consistently opposed the expansion of the regular army, insisted that America was safe in the hands of its militia even in the summer of 1798, when a French invasion seemed a remote possibility. Later, after Admiral Nelson's destruction of the French fleet had removed that threat, regular forces seemed even more unnecessary to meet any danger from abroad.

From the first, however, the Republicans had suspected that the army was not meant entirely for a foreign foe. "Whether it is to be raised from a real apprehension of foreign invasion (which

42. *Independent Chronicle*, Jan. 3, 1799.

43. I know of no better example of the persistence of the idea that the militia is the agency through which freemen express their virtue in arms than the famous speech for which John Randolph of Roanoke was threatened by a group of officers who objected to his characterization of them as "mercenaries" and "ragamuffins." Randolph had also said that "when citizen and soldier shall be synonymous terms, then you will be safe." Gentlemen who raise alarms against foreign dangers should listen to warnings "against standing armies—against destroying the military spirit of the citizen by cultivating it only in the soldier by profession, against an institution which has wrought the downfall of every free state and rivetted the fetters of despotism" (*Annals*, Sixth Congress, first session, p. 300). This is one of many reminders that there was nothing effeminate about the revolutionary concept of virtue.

the pacific disposition of France would seemingly preclude) or whether it is wanted to be at hand to support the authority and dignity of government independent of the voice of the censurers of the people, is a question we shall leave to our readers to determine."[44] Republicans began by saying that "a mercenary army . . . is the last verse in the chapter of expedients and the first in that of tyranny."[45] And when Alexander Hamilton, commissioned major general, was charged with organizing the expanded army, the suspicion that the swollen force was meant for use against domestic opposition became an article of faith. One pamphleteer spoke for his party:

This is, sir, an awful crisis for America, and he who disguises apprehensions which he conceives to be founded on a rational probability becomes an accessory to that political murder which I fear is meditated against the rights and liberties of the people. I most seriously apprehend the consequences of this army more than I do invasion. . . . When designing men contemplate the change of the republican system, external war has been the fatal result.[46]

Tying the increase of the army and navy closely to the problem of an immortal debt, Edmund Pendleton agreed that an army of "50,000 mercenaries at the devotion of some future enterprising President, aided by a sedition bill and other accumulated terrors, with the influence of hope from an enormous patronage, will subject America to executive despotism."[47] Jefferson himself wrote Charles Pinckney of his fear that "changes in the principles of our government are to be pushed till they accomplish a monarchy peaceably or force a resistance which, with the aid of an army, may end in monarchy."[48] Republicans worried seriously about this danger, and Federalists worried seriously about the

44. *Independent Chronicle*, Jan. 17, 1799.

45. A Memorial to the Virginia Assembly from a meeting of Nov. 13, 1798, in Caroline County, copied from a Richmond paper by the *Aurora*, Nov. 29. 1798.

46. *A Letter from Manlius to John Marshall* (Richmond: Samuel Pleasants, 1800), pp. 12–14.

47. *An Address . . . on the Present State of Our Country* (Boston: Benjamin Edes, 1799), p. 6.

48. Paul Leicester Ford, ed., *The Works of Thomas Jefferson* (New York: Putnam, 1904), IX, 87.

effect of the Republican charge. Men were prosecuted under the Sedition Act merely for suggesting that America *had* a standing army.[49]

III

Early in the 1790s, the Virginia legislature had put on record an explicit rationalization of the inherited concerns for the future of republican liberty which, consciously and unconsciously, had helped to spark the earliest opposition to Hamiltonian policy. Its remonstrance against funding and assumption had anticipated and helped to formulate a systematic ideology that justified a persistent opposition to Federalism and contributed to that opposition's growth from the dimensions of a congressional faction to those of a great national party. Near the end of the decade, the legislature of the Old Dominion served again as a vehicle for opposition ideas, giving them once more a visibility and impact they could not have attained through private channels alone.

It has long been recognized that the Virginia and Kentucky Resolutions of 1798 were opening shots in the campaign that carried the Republicans to victory in 1800.[50] Both sets of Resolutions have been studied for their striking revelation of the workings of the partnership of Jefferson and Madison and for their presentation of a compact theory of the Constitution, which prepared the way for the nullification experiments of later years. They have been placed with care and sensitivity in the context of the crisis of civil liberties brought on by the Alien and Sedition Laws. But the Virginia Resolutions, in particular, contained a passage that made it evident that the Republicans interpreted the current crisis in the light of a perspective that set the present crisis in a broader frame. Virginia denounced the uniform tendency of the federal government

---

49. Smith, *Freedom's Fetters*, p. 380.

50. The standard study of the preparation and purposes of the Resolutions is Adrienne Koch and Harry Ammon, "The Virginia and Kentucky Resolutions: An Episode in Jefferson's and Madison's Defense of Civil Liberties," *William and Mary Quarterly*, 5 (1948), 145–176.

to enlarge its powers by forced constructions of the constitutional charter . . . and . . . to expound certain general phrases . . . so as to destroy the meaning and effect of the particular enumeration which necessarily explains and limits the general phrases and so as to consolidate the states by degrees into one sovereignty, the obvious tendency and inevitable result of which would be to transform the present republican system of the United States into an absolute, or at best, a mixed monarchy.[51]

The legislature meant to frame its condemnation of the crisis laws in the context of a remarkable indictment of Federalist policy over the whole course of the decade.

In the preoccupation with the Resolutions themselves, it has often been forgotten that the Virginia legislature also published an "Address to the People," which explained and justified its course. Not content with further condemnation of the laws of 1798, the legislators asked their constituents to consider the Federalist system as a whole.

If measures can mold governments, and if an uncontrolled power of construction is surrendered to those who administer them, their progress may be easily foreseen and their end easily foretold. A lover of monarchy who opens the treasures of corruption by distributing emolument among devoted partisans may at the same time be approaching his object and deluding the people with professions of republicanism. He may confound monarchy and republicanism by the art of definition. He may varnish over the dexterity which ambition never fails to display with the pliancy of language, the seduction of expediency, or the prejudices of the times. And he may come at length to avow that so extensive a territory as that of the United States can only be governed by the energies of monarchy, that it cannot be defended except by standing armies, and that it cannot be united except by consolidation.

Measures have already been adopted which may lead to these consequences. They consist:

In fiscal systems and arrangements which keep an host of commercial and wealthy individuals embodied and obedient to the mandates of the Treasury.

In armies and navies which will, on the one hand, enlist the tendency of man to pay homage to his fellow creature who can feed or honor him,

51. *The Virginia and Kentucky Resolutions of 1798 and '99* (Washington: Jonathan Elliot, 1832), p. 5.

and, on the other, employ the principle of fear by punishing imaginary insurrections under the pretext of preventive justice.

In swarms of officers, civil and military, who can inculcate political tenets tending to consolidation and monarchy, both by indulgencies and severities, and can act as spies over the free exercise of human reason.

In restraining the freedom of the press and investing the executive with legislative, executive, and judicial powers over a numerous body of men.

And, that we may shorten the catalogue, in establishing by successive precedents such a mode of construing the Constitution as will rapidly remove every restraint upon federal power.

Let history be consulted; let the man of experience reflect; nay, let the artificers of monarchy be asked, what farther materials they can need for building up their favorite system.[52]

Virginia's "Address to the People," more fully than the resolutions it accompanied, announced the theme of the Republican campaign. In newspapers, pamphlets, and election broadsides, party publicists played heavily on rising discontent with recent measures: repressive laws enforced with growing rigor as the threat of an invasion eased and national elections rapidly drew on; a large standing army; a sizable navy; land tax; stamp tax; and loans at eight percent. But party writers seldom failed to represent the current measures as the culmination of a scheme that had been carefully pursued since the Confederation years, a scheme that aimed at nothing less than the subversion of the Constitution and its ultimate replacement by hereditary rule.[53] In the campaign of 1800, as in the campaign of 1792, the Republican quarrel with Federalism was a quarrel with this scheme.

How much did the ideology contribute to Republican success? Less, it may well be, than other things. Superior machinery and better legwork go at least as far to help explain the party's triumph. The crisis brought on by the Quasi-War encouraged the

---

52. Ibid., p. 8.

53. Some representative Republican listings of the measures they objected to, often prefaced by a brief history of the Federalist conspiracy, include: *Aurora*, March 8, 1799; an address "To the Republicans of the County of Philadelphia" from the County Committee of Conference, ibid., August 16, 1800; "Address to the Citizens of Bucks, Chester, and Montgomery Counties" by a meeting at Pottsgrove, ibid., Sept. 26, 1800.

Republicans to build an interlocking network of committees reaching from the leadership into the wards and organizing voters in a way that their opponents could not match.[54] While this was happening, moreover, events demoralized and split their foes.[55]

Confronted with hostilities they never really wanted, the French soon recognized that it had been an error to attempt coercion. Although Adams was determined to defend the nation's honor, he seized the chance for peace—and seized it in a way that may have been designed to damage the extremists in his party. The President had always shared some central concepts with the opposition. He was suspicious of the bank and funding system. He hated Hamilton for his intrigues and for his influence on the Cabinet and Congress. He was a navalist who lost all taste for war when Washington compelled him to accept the hated Hamilton as second-in-command of the extended army.[56] When he received assurances that France would treat new envoys with respect, he acted without warning to his Cabinet or the Federalists in Congress. His nomination of a minister to France and subsequent dismissal of Pickering and James McHenry left the Federalists with large and costly military forces, wartime taxes, and an effort to repress domestic opposition—all supposedly intended for a threat that was increasingly remote. They also opened an irreparable breach with the Hamiltonian members of his party, who had contemplated offensive military operations, who had sometimes seemed to beg a chance to use the army against their domestic opponents, and who were committed to the war with France as an instrument for maintaining their political supremacy. Eventually, the Republicans were able to publish a scathing attack on Adams that Hamilton had been

54. Noble E. Cunningham, Jr., *The Jeffersonian Republicans* (Chapel Hill: University of North Carolina Press, 1957), chap. 6.

55. Stephen G. Kurtz, *The Presidency of John Adams: The Collapse of Federalism, 1795–1800* (Philadelphia: University of Pennsylvania Press, 1957), and Manning J. Dauer, *The Adams Federalists* (Baltimore: Johns Hopkins Press, 1953).

56. Kohn, *Eagle and Sword*, chap. 12, is an excellent discussion of the pivotal role of the army question in Adams' split with the Hamiltonians.

circulating privately among his friends.[57] During the campaign of 1800, the dispute among the Federalists was nearly as intense as their common quarrel with the opposition.[58] The Republicans, who saw their enemies' discomfort as a falling out among the thieves—both factions "monarchists," but one more "English" than the other—enjoyed reprinting Federalist attacks on one another, worked undistractedly in order to perfect their own superior organization, and rode events to victory.

The triumph over Adams was relatively close, for all the opposition's efforts to persuade the people to a choice between the author of the Declaration and a monarchist.[59] Peace was popular, and Adams had successfully escaped association with the war. His party, though, was far less lucky. The Federalists lost forty seats in the incoming Congress, a blow from which they never would recover. The losses may have owed as much to wartime taxes and the Federalists' confusion as to anything the opposition said. To prove the opposite would be a hopeless task. And yet it also seems incredible to think that opposition charges were without effect.

We have approached as closely as is possible the political be-

57. "Not denying to Mr. Adams patriotism and integrity and even talents of a certain kind, . . . he does not possess the talents adapted to the administration of government . . . and there are great and intrinsic defects in his character which unfit him for the office of chief magistrate. . . . He is a man of imagination sublimated and eccentric, propitious neither to the regular display of sound judgment nor to steady perseverance in a systematic plan of conduct; and . . . to this defect are added the foibles of a vanity without bounds and a jealousy capable of discoloring every object" (Hamilton, "The Public Conduct and Character of John Adams, Esq., President of the United States," in Henry Cabot Lodge, ed., *Works of Alexander Hamilton*, [New York: Putnam, 1850–1851] VII, 310–311, 314).

58. The growing conviction of High Federalists that Adams' reelection would be nearly as bad as a Jeffersonian victory, along with protests against the Adamsites' use of opposition propaganda, is conveniently presented in the correspondence included in George Gibbs, ed., *Memoirs of the Administrations of Washington and John Adams* (New York: by subscription, 1846), II, 346–433 *passim*.

59. Dauer and Kurtz have been particularly influential in challenging older interpretations by emphasizing the popularity of Adams and the narrowness of the Republican victory. A Hamiltonian victory over Burr in New York City would have meant a Federalist success, and Pinckney might have become President by bargaining for South Carolina's electoral votes. Cunningham argues, however, that the close electoral vote of 1800 does not reflect the wide swing of the popular vote in Pennsylvania or the marked Republican success in the congressional elections.

liefs of common men during the 1790s. If we cannot say with certainty that newspapers, broadsides, and the resolves of public meetings were the products of average men, we can be sure at least that they were widely studied by the mass of voters. Those who wrote them thought that they could move the people by means of an argument that men in power were pursuing a familiar plot to subvert republican government and replace it with monarchy and aristocracy. The Republican party gained adherents as it developed this critique, and this was probably not a matter of coincidence alone. Republican attacks on Federalism appealed to the deepest fears and the highest aspirations in Anglo-American political thought. They appealed, at once, to the hesitations of agrarian conservatives as they experienced the stirrings of a more commercial age, to the desires of rising men who felt excluded by monopolists of privilege, and to a democratic people's confidence in itself.[60]

60. Dauer explained the triumph of the Jeffersonians as a consequence of the alienation of commercial-farming regions—the seat of the Adams Federalists—from a wing of the party that no longer represented their interests. The most important recent studies agree that such a neo-Beardian analysis of the social sources of political division in the 1790s is too simple: Richard Buel, Jr., *Securing the Revolution: Ideology in American Politics, 1789–1815* (Ithaca, N.Y.: Cornell University Press, 1972); David Hackett Fischer, *The Revolution of American Conservatism* (New York: Harper & Row, 1965), appendix 1; and Paul Goodman, "The First American Party System," in William Nesbit Chambers and Walter Dean Burnham, eds., *The American Party Systems: Stages of Political Development* (Oxford: Oxford University Press, 1967), pp. 56–89. Emphasizing the deferential character of politics in the period, Buel identifies Federalism as the ideology of established elites who were insecurely seated and challenged from below. This is consistent with Goodman's description of the Republicans as ambitious newcomers who were organized by an elite that was secure at home but felt excluded from federal power. Fischer agrees that established elites, outside the South, were generally Federalist, while their challengers were Jeffersonian, although his identification of Federalist regions as "mature, static, homogeneous, and ingrown" would seem to clash with Goodman and Buel. The resonances of party ideologies—the Federalists' preoccupation with order and the Republican appeal to antielitist sentiment—would seem in general to support the characterization of the party conflict as a struggle between social ins and social outs. Recognition of the English opposition sources of Republican ideology would strongly warn, however, against the common tendency to see the Republicans as a progressive party. A left-right argument is not a proper model to apply to the new nation. The social ideal of the Republicans was reactionary and antimodern in several respects. The stronghold and original home of the party was located in those regions which, if not the most egalitarian in social structure, were certainly the most homogeneous and agrarian.

Certainly, Republicans themselves believed that they had managed to arouse the people to their danger. On February 20, 1801, when Congress had resolved the tie between the party's first and second choices and the time for campaign rhetoric was through, the *Aurora* wrote that "the Revolution of 1776 is now and for the first time arrived at its completion. . . . On Tuesday last . . . the question . . . on the issue of which rested the liberty, Constitution, and happiness of America was terminated as every republican and honest man wished. . . . On that day the sun of aristocracy set, to rise no more."

"Inroads upon the principles of the revolution of 1776 were attempted without intermission," the editor explained, "from the dawn of peace to the close of John Adams' administration." A few years after independence, when "the spirit of avarice and corruption had taken place of the generous and noble passions," a "league" was formed "between avarice and . . . fell ambition." From this league came robbery of the veterans and "enrichment of a band of conspirators" in all the branches of the federal government. From it came an attempt to establish hereditary government, a standing army, "multitudes of unnecessary offices," incitement of insurrection, war, attacks on representative government, and a preference for Tories in places of important trust. Yet these were not the work of the nation, which was inexperienced and did not suspect that "the vices and depravity of the most corrupt governments of the old world should be imitated and adopted in the new." They were the work of "secret enemies of the American Revolution—her internal, insidious, indefatigable foes." Never, until now, had these conspirators been thoroughly discomfitted, their masks torn off, "the faction" sunk. At last experience had dissipated the delusion under which the nation suffered such encroachments on its rights. "The reign of terror and corrupt government is at an end." The public trust had been delivered to a party which defined its character in opposition to corruption and gave every indication of commitment to a sweeping change.

Epilogue

THE COUNTRY COMES TO POWER

By avoiding the course which other nations have steered, we shall likewise avoid their catastrophe.

Joseph H. Nicholson

CHAPTER 10

The Revolution of 1800 and the Principles of Ninety-Eight

THE final proof of principle is conduct. Accordingly, no study of the origins and nature of Republican convictions can avoid the question whether the persuasion that developed in the years of opposition exercised a central influence when the party came to power. The years of the Republican ascendency are properly the subject for another work. The present one, however, would be incomplete without some effort to address at least two crucial questions.

Were Republicans in power faithful to the principles they urged in opposition? As much so, I will argue, as almost any party we could name. Enough so that historians have made a strong beginning toward an understanding of the Jeffersonian ascendency that has, as one of its essential themes, a recognition of the lasting influence of the principles of 1798. In 1801, if my analysis is right, the "Country" came to power. A party that defined its character in terms derived from eighteenth-century British oppositions was entrusted, for the first time, with the guidance of affairs. Without insisting that Republicans were of a single mind, without suggesting that the most important leaders of the party were the helpless captives of their thought, it still seems possible to argue that the party's triumphs and its failures were the products, in large part, of its attempt to govern in accordance with an ideology that taught that power was a monster and governing was wrong.

If this is so, however, then a second question must be raised. If the party conflict of the 1790s was so largely a derivative of British arguments between the Country and the Court—if, in addition, we can see the history of the United States between 1800 and 1815 as the story of a party's effort to apply its Country principles to the direction of affairs—then when will it be possible to mark an "end of classical politics" and the emergence of a more genuinely indigenous mode of thought? At no point, I would think, before the finish of the War of 1812. Although the years in opposition had already carried the Republicans some distance from the British sources of their thought, there was no point before the months surrounding the conclusion of that war when it is possible to say that the ideas received by revolutionary thinkers from the English eighteenth century had ceased to exercise a guiding influence on American affairs.[1]

I

Thomas Jefferson wrote proudly of "the revolution of 1800," calling it "as real a revolution in the principles of our government as that of 1776 was in its form."[2] Many of his followers agreed. Today, however, most historians would probably prefer a different phrase.[3] Too little changed—and that too slowly—to justify the connotations present in that loaded word. There were no radicals among the great triumvirate who guided the Republicans in power, as they had led them through the years of opposition. The President was bent on reconciliation with the body of his former foes. "We are all Republicans, all Federalists," he said.[4] He wanted to detach the mass of Federalists from their former

1. Since writing this chapter, I have encountered Forrest McDonald, *The Presidency of Thomas Jefferson* (Lawrence: University of Kansas Press, 1976). Independently of my work, McDonald concludes that an ideology borrowed from English oppositions is the key to the policies of Jefferson's administration and the source of Jefferson's ultimate failure.

2. To Spencer Roane, Sept. 6, 1819, in Paul Leicester Ford, ed., *The Works of Thomas Jefferson* (New York: Putnam, 1904), XII, 136.

3. Exceptions include McDonald and Daniel Sisson, *The American Revolution of 1800* (New York: Knopf, 1974), but Sisson's work, which received some highly critical reviews, does not discuss the question of a revolution in terms of the policies followed after 1801.

4. In the inaugural address, *Works*, IX, 195.

leaders, and he knew that this was incompatible with an abrupt reversal of the policies that had been followed for a dozen years.[5] He had, in any case, no notion that his predecessors' work could be dismantled all at once. The Hamiltonian system might be hateful, but it had bound the nation to a contract it had no alternative except to honor.[6] Madison and Gallatin, who were by instinct more conservative than Jefferson himself, were not disposed to disagree.

From the beginning of the new administration, nonetheless, Republicans insisted that a change of policies, not just of men, was necessary to return the state to its republican foundations. In his inaugural address, Jefferson announced commitment to "a wise and frugal government which shall restrain men from injuring one another, shall leave them otherwise free to regulate their own pursuits of industry and improvement, and shall not take from the mouth of labor the bread it has earned." This kind of government, he hinted, would be guided by a set of principles that could be readily distinguished from the policies of years before. Among them were

Peace, commerce, and honest friendship with all nations; entangling alliances with none.

The support of the state governments in all their rights as the most competent administrations for our domestic concerns and the surest bulwarks against anti-republican tendencies. . . .

A well disciplined militia, our best reliance in peace and for the first moments of war, till regulars may relieve them. . . .

Economy in public expense, that labor may be lightly burdened.

5. "The greatest good we can do our country is to heal its party divisions and make them one people. I do not speak of their leaders, who are incurable, but of the honest and well-intentioned body of the people. I consider the pure Federalist as a republican who would prefer a somewhat stronger executive and the Republican as one more willing to trust the legislative power for many reasons. But both sects are republican, entitled to the confidence of their fellow citizens. Not so their quondam leaders, covering under the mask of Federalism hearts devoted to monarchy. . . . It is very important that the pure Federalist and Republican should see in the opinion of each other but a shade of his own . . . , that they should see and fear the monarchist as their common enemy on whom they should keep their eyes, but their hands off" (To John Dickinson, ibid., 281–282).

6. "It mortifies me to be strengthening principles which I deem radically vicious, but this vice is entailed on us by the first error" (To Dupont de Nemours, ibid., 343–344n).

The honest payment of our debts and sacred preservation of the public faith.[7]

Reform began while Jefferson awaited the assembly of the first Republican Congress. Pardons were issued to the few men still affected by sedition prosecutions. The diplomatic corps, a target for its costs and for the influence it was thought to give to the executive, was cut to barest bones. A few of the most active Federalists were purged from office, while the President withheld commissions signed by Adams after his defeat was known.[8] The evolution of a partisan appointments policy was too slow for some members of the party, who argued that "no enemy to democratic government will be provided with the means to sap and destroy any of its principles nor to profit by a government to which they are hostile in theory and practice."[9] But even the most radical were satisfied with the administration's purpose when the President announced his program to the Seventh Congress.

Jefferson's first annual message was "an epitome of republican principles applied to practical purposes."[10] After a review of

7. Ibid., 197–198. Compare the policies suggested by the inaugural address with the well-known statement of principle Jefferson made to Elbridge Gerry on January 26, 1799. "I wish an inviolable preservation of our present federal constitution . . . and I am opposed to the monarchising its features by the forms of its administration with a view to conciliate a first transition to a President and Senate for life and from that to a hereditary tenure. . . . I am not for transferring all the powers of the states to the general government and all those of that government to the executive branch. I am for a government rigorously frugal and simple . . . and not for a multiplication of officers and salaries merely to make partisans and for increasing by every device the public debt on the principle of its being a public blessing. . . . We never differed but on one ground, the funding system; and, as from the moment of its being adopted . . . I became religiously principled in the sacred discharge of it . . . , we are united now even on that" (ibid., 17–18, 20).

8. Chapter 2 of Noble E. Cunningham, *The Jeffersonian Republicans in Power: Party Operations, 1801–1809* (Chapel Hill: University of North Carolina Press, 1963) is a fine brief treatment of Jefferson's appointment policy. See also Carl E. Prince, "The Passing of the Aristocracy: Jefferson's Removal of the Federalists, 1801–1805," *Journal of American History*, 57 (1970), 563–575, though Prince's arguments should be considered with care.

9. William Duane in the *Aurora*, Feb. 27, 1801. Compare ibid., March 26, 1801: "To tolerate such men after such conduct would be to . . . bring republican government into contempt." Principle conveniently supported a desire for loaves and fishes in this case.

10. Duane again, ibid., Dec. 18, 1801.

foreign policy and Indian affairs, the President suggested abolition of all internal taxes. "The remaining sources of revenue will be sufficient," he believed, "to provide for the support of government, to pay the interest on the public debts, and to discharge the principals in shorter periods than the laws or the general expectations had contemplated. . . . Sound principles will not justify our taxing the industry of our fellow citizens to accumulate treasure for wars to happen we know not when, and which might not perhaps happen but from the temptations offered by that treasure." Burdens, he admitted, could only be reduced if expenditures fell too. But there was room to wonder "whether offices or officers have not been multiplied unnecessarily." The military, for example, was larger than required to garrison the posts, and there was no use for the surplus. "For defence against invasion, their number is as nothing; nor is it conceived needful or safe that a standing army should be kept up in time of peace." The judiciary system, packed and altered by the Federalists at the close of their regime, would naturally "present itself to the contemplation of Congress." And the laws concerning naturalization might again be liberalized.[11]

The Seventh Congress, voting usually on party lines, did everything that Jefferson had recommended. It also gave approval to a plan prepared by Gallatin, the Secretary of the Treasury, for the complete retirement of the public debt before the end of 1817. Along with its repeal of the Judiciary Act of 1800, it reduced the army to three thousand officers and men, while lowering appropriations for the navy in the face of war with Tripoli. Of all its measures, though, the abolition of internal taxes (and four hundred revenue positions) called forth the most eloquent enunciation of the principles on which the new majority thought it should act:

The Constitution is as dear to us as to our adversaries. . . . It is by repairing the breeches that we mean to save it and to set it on a firm and lasting foundation. . . . We are yet a young nation and must learn

11. *Works of Jefferson*, IX, 321–342.

wisdom from the experience of others. By avoiding the course which other nations have steered, we shall likewise avoid their catastrophe. Public debts, standing armies, and heavy taxes have converted the English nation into a mere machine to be used at the pleasure of the crown. . . . We have had no riot act, but we have had a Sedition Act calculated to secure the executive from free and full investigation; we have had an army and still have a small one, securing to the executive an immensity of patronage; and we have a large national debt, for the payment . . . of which it is necessary to collect 'yearly millions' by means of a cloud of officers spread over the face of the country. . . . Iniquitous as we deem the manner of its settlement, we mean to discharge; but we mean not to perpetuate it; it is no part of our political creed that 'a public debt is a public blessing.'[12]

Before the session ended, Jefferson could tell a friend that "some things may perhaps be left undone from motives of compromise for a time and not to alarm by too sudden a reformation," but the proceedings of the Congress gave every ground for hope that "we shall be able by degrees to introduce sound principles and make them habitual."[13] Indeed, the session was so good a start that there was little left to recommend in 1802. The effort of the next few years would be to keep the course already set.

"Revolution" may not be the proper word to characterize the changes introduced in 1801 and early 1802. "Apostasy," however, would be worse. Yet every study of the Jeffersonian ascendency must come to terms with the nagnificent and multivolumed work of Henry Adams.[14] Though now almost a century old, the scope and literary power of this classic give it influence that has lasted to the present day. And one of Adams' major themes was the abnegation of the principles of 1798 by the Republican regime. Jefferson had hoped to put an end to parties by detaching the great body of Federalists from their irreconcilable leaders. By 1804 he seemed to have approached this end.[15]

12. Joseph H. Nicholson of Maryland, *Annals of Congress*, Seventh Congress, first session, pp. 802–804.
13. To Dupont de Nemours, Jan. 18, 1802, *Works of Jefferson*, IX, 343–344 n.
14. Henry Adams, *History of the United States during the Administrations of Thomas Jefferson and James Madison*, 9 vols. (New York: Scribner, 1889–1890).
15. Jefferson's opponent, C. C. Pinckney, received 14 electoral votes. Republican

To Adams, though, his great successes were a consequence of Jefferson's abandonment of principle and single-minded quest for popularity.[16] If party lines were melting, it had been the Jeffersonians who had compromised their principles the most:

> not a Federalist measure, not even the Alien and Sedition laws, had been expressly repudiated; . . . the national debt was larger than it had ever been before, the navy maintained and energetically employed, the national bank preserved and its operations extended; . . . the powers of the national government had been increased [in the Louisianna Purchase] to a point that made blank paper of the Constitution. It was the Federalists, not the Republicans, who now upheld the states' rights principles of 1798.[17]

Every part of Adams' powerful indictment could be contradicted or excused. Thus, Jefferson abandoned scruple in the case of the Louisianna Purchase with reluctance and because there seemed some danger that the Emperor of France might change his mind about a bargain that could guarantee the nation's peace while promising indefinite postponement of the day when overcrowding and development might put an end to its capacity for freedom. Jefferson continued to distrust the national bank, but would not break the public's pledge by moving to revoke its charter.[18] The party *had* repudiated the Sedition Law, explicitly refusing to renew it in the session that had also seen a relaxation of the naturalization law. The national debt *had* been considerably reduced before the purchase of Louisianna raised it once again, and it would fall much further in the years to come.

It is necessary to admit, however, that the list of Adams' charges also could be lengthened. While Jefferson himself was

---

majorities increased in both houses of Congress. The party even captured the government of Massachusetts.

16. "He was a gentle leader, not a commander, who valued principle less than popularity and power" (Adams, II, 90–92).

17. Ibid., I, 204–205.

18. "This institution is one of the most deadly hostility existing against the principles and form of our Constitution. . . . An institution like this, penetrating by its branches every part of the union, acting by command and in phalanx, may, in a critical moment, upset the government" (To Gallatin, Dec. 13, 1803, *Works of Jefferson*, X, 57–58).

never reconciled, Gallatin and Madison eventually supported the Bank of the United States.[19] While Jefferson preferred to lead by indirection, he was in fact a stronger President than either of his predecessors ever tried to be. His public messages *suggested* measures, but his hints were often taken as commands by party members in the Congress. Informally or through floor leaders in the House, the administration made its wishes known and drafted most of the important legislation.[20] Finally, in 1808, in its progressively more stringent efforts to enforce the embargo, Jefferson's administration wielded powers over the daily life of Americans that far exceeded anything its predecessors' ever sought, even using regulars to help enforce the law.[21]

There were, without a doubt, occasions after 1801 when the warring parties come so close to switching sides that one might doubt that principle meant much to either group. The Federalists stood forth, when they could hope to profit, as defenders of states' rights. They shamelessly employed old opposition rhetoric to criticize the massive force of party loyalty and the influence of the President on Congress.[22] Nor was Henry Adams first to charge the Jeffersonians with a surrender to the principles of their opponents. Jefferson and his successor faced a swelling

19. In retirement, Madison defended himself against a charge of inconsistency by explaining that he had simply conceded that his original opinion that the bank was unconstitutional had been overruled by repeated actions of every branch of the government. Gallatin, who had not been closely involved in the original attack on the bank, was conscious from the first of its great services to the government. Counterbalancing these services, he told Jefferson (Dec. 13, 1803), "there are none but political objections, and those will lose much of their force when the little injury they can do us and the dependence in which they are on government are duly estimated. . . . Whenever they shall appear to be really dangerous, they are completely in our power and may be crushed" (Henry Adams, ed., *The Writings of Albert Gallatin*, 3 vols. [Philadelphia: Lippincott, 1879], I, 170).

20. Dumas Malone suggests that Jefferson's record as a legislative leader was unmatched until Woodrow Wilson, arguing that Congress passed "virtually no bills of any significance" without his approval. *Jefferson the President: First Term, 1801–1805* (Boston: Little, Brown, 1970), p. 110.

21. The most extensive recent criticism of the way Jefferson's conduct failed to match his professions is Leonard Levy, *Jefferson and Civil Liberties: The Darker Side*, rev. ed. (New York: Quadrangle Books, 1973).

22. Some excellent examples are quoted in Cunningham, p. 94, and in *The Revolution of American Conservatism: The Federalist Party in the Era of Jeffersonian Democracy* (New York: Harper & Row, 1965), p. 153, David Hackett Fischer says that the

discontent from a minority of purists among Republicans themselves.

In October 1801, before the meeting of the Seventh Congress, Edmund Pendleton had published a widely read consideration of the policies that would be necessary to make the revolution of 1800 complete. Jefferson's election, he began, had "arrested a train of measures which were gradually conducting us towards ruin." But the election victory did not permit Republicans to rest content. It merely opened up an opportunity "to erect new barriers against folly, fraud, and ambition and to explain such parts of the Constitution as have been already or may be interpreted contrary to the intention of those who adopted it." Liberty, said Pendleton, is the "chief good" of government, but "if government is so constructed as to enable its administration to assail that liberty with the several weapons heretofore most fatal to it, the structure is defective: of this sort, standing armies—fleets—severe penal laws—war—and a multitude of civil officers are universally admitted to be." Union is a great good, but union can "only be preserved by confining . . . the federal government to the exercise of powers clearly required by the general interest . . . because the states exhibit such varieties of character and interests that a consolidated general government would . . . produce civil war and dissension." A separation of powers is necessary, but the Constitution gives the Senate a part in the exercise of powers that belong to other branches "and tends to create in that body a dangerous aristocracy." Representative government must rest on the will of the people, but the people's will can "never be expressed if their representatives are corrupted or influenced by hopes of office." "Since experience has evinced that much mischief may be done under an unwise administration," it is time to consider several amendments to the Constitution. These should make the President ineligible for a second term and give the appointment of judges and ambassadors to Congress; end the Senate's role in

---

Federalists "came to terms with every major argument of the Jeffersonians—majoritarianism, individuality, the everbroadening concept of equality, states' rights, even agrarianism and Anglophobia."

executive functions and shorten the Senators' terms of office; make judges and legislators incapable of accepting any federal office; subject the judges to removal by the legislature; form "some check upon the abuse of public credit;" declare that treaties relating to war or peace or requiring the expenditure of money must be ratified by the whole Congress; and define the powers of the federal government in such a way as to "defy the wiles of construction."[23]

"The Danger Not Over" was a systematic effort to define the fundamental changes that seemed to be implicit in the principles of 1798. And as the years went by without a movement to secure the constitutional amendments it had recommended, without destruction of the national bank, without complete proscription of old Federalists from places of public trust, "there were a number of people who soon thought and said to one another that Mr. Jefferson did many good things, but neglected some better things," who came to "view his policy as very like a compromise with Mr. Hamilton's, . . . a compromise between monarchy and democracy."[24] Strongest in Virginia and including several of the most important party writers of the 1790s—George Logan and John Taylor as well as Pendleton himself—this band of "Old Republicans" soon found an eloquent, if vitriolic and eccentric, spokesman in the Congress. In 1806, John Randolph, who had led the party's forces in the Seventh Congress, broke with the administration and commenced a systematic opposition to the moral bankruptcy and "backstairs influence" of the government.[25] As Jefferson and Madison began to face the gravest crisis of their leadership, they were persistently annoyed by a minority of vocal critics from within their former ranks. In 1808, Monroe

23. Edmund Pendleton, "The Danger Not Over," Richmond *Examiner*, Oct. 20, 1801. The essay was widely reprinted in other Republican organs.

24. John Taylor to James Monroe, Oct. 26, 1810, in William E. Dodd, ed., "Letters of John Taylor of Caroline County, Virginia," *The John P. Branch Historical Papers of Randolph-Macon College*, II, nos. 3–4 (1908), 310–311.

25. The standard biography is William Cabell Bruce, *John Randolph of Roanoke, 1773–1833*, 2 vols. (New York: Putnam, 1922).

became the unsuccessful candidate for those expressing this variety of discontent.[26] The Old Republicans—in name as well as principle—should bring to mind the English faction to which revolutionary thinkers were indebted for so many patterns in their thought. In eighteenth-century England, too, Old Whigs insisted that they were the remnant of the larger party who had not abandoned principle for power.[27] In the same vein, John Taylor warned Monroe that if the latter ever won the presidential office, "it would probably be an irreparable breach with the republican minority . . . because you must in some measure suffer yourself to be taken in tow by an administration party, and I do not recollect in the history of mankind a single instance of such a party being republican." Taylor would himself do everything to aid in the election of Monroe, then join immediately with the minority who voted independently by conscience. "This is the sum total of what I understand by minority republicanism. Majority republicanism is inevitably, widely (but not thoroughly) corrupted with ministerial republicanism."[28]

The ideology of opposition days had undeniably considered party loyalty as one of several agencies that might corrupt the independence of the people's representatives and undermine the necessary separation of the branches of a balanced government. Each of Pendleton's proposals also had firm roots in neo-opposition thought. Still, we need not follow the minority or Henry Adams in concluding that abandonment of principle— or compromise, at least—should be a major theme for histories of the new regime. We need not grant the Old Republicans' conten-

26. Harry Ammon, "James Monroe and the Election of 1808 in Virginia," *William and Mary Quarterly*, 20 (1963), 33–56, is an admirable narrative of the development of discontent in the Old Dominion. Monroe was temporarily estranged from his colleagues in the aftermath of the administration's rejection of his treaty with the English.

27. Norman K. Risjord, *The Old Republicans: Southern Conservatism in the Age of Jefferson* (New York: Columbia University Press, 1965), on which I have depended heavily, does not remark these similarities, but it would be difficult to believe that contemporaries were not aware of them.

28. "Letters of Taylor," pp. 316–317.

tion that they were the sole legitimate defenders of the principles of '98.

Both Adams and the Old Republicans identified the principles of '98 with the Virginia and Kentucky Resolutions of that year. To both, the party's creed in years of opposition centered on allegiance to states' rights. But I have tried to show that such an understanding is too narrow. Even in the crisis introduced by the repressive laws, states' rights and strict construction of the Constitution were among the means to more essential ends. The means were taken seriously, indeed, but they were never held among the absolutes. The body of the party and its most important leaders never sought, as their essential end, to hold the federal government within the narrowest of bounds. They sought, instead, a federal government that would preserve the virtues necessary to a special way of life. Their most important goal had been to check a set of policies—among them loose interpretation of the Constitution—that Republicans had seen as fundamentally destructive of the kind of government and social habits without which liberty could not survive. To judge them only on the basis of their loyalty to strict construction and states' rights is to apply a standard they had never held.[29]

Minds changed when party leaders were confronted with responsibility. But they did not change thoroughly enough to justify the charge that they adopted principles of their opponents. The principles of the Republicans had not been Antifederalist. Republicans had traced the evils of the 1790s to the motives of the governors, not to the government itself. With few and brief exceptions, most had thought a change of policy, without a

29. On this point see Ralph Ketchum, one of several recent writers whose superior grasp of the principles of the 1790s informs their understanding of the years in power. In the 1790s Madison feared centralization and loose construction as parts of a larger theory and practice with "implications deeply hostile to Madison's understanding of the needs of republican independence. Debt, funding systems, banks, tariffs, English treaties, armies, navies, enlargement of the federal government, loose construction, and the Sedition Act—taken together and joined to the Hamiltonian vision of a splendid commercial nation led by a proconsul—had meaning far beyond that attached to any of the devices taken singly and in a less ominous context" (*James Madison: A Biography* [New York: MacMillan, 1971], p. 604).

change of structure, would effect a cure.[30] Moreover, in the last years of the decade, the development of party thought had probably persuaded many members to believe that a simple change of men might cure more evils than they once had thought. The Republican persuasion rose, in the beginning, under circumstances that conjoined to make a reconstruction of an ideology developed in a different time and place seem relevant for the United States. The revolutionary debt to eighteenth-century opposition thought was certainly sufficient, by itself, to have assured loud echoes of the old ideas in the first years of the new republic. But this is not the lesson of this work. Republican convictions were not simply reminiscent of the old ideas. Republicans revived the eighteenth-century ideology as a coherent structure, reconstructed it so thoroughly that the persistence of an English style of argument is easily as striking as the changes we might trace to revolutionary alterations of the American polity. At least three circumstances of the 1790s had to join with expectations prompted by the heritage of revolutionary thought to generate a reconstruction so complete. None of these circumstances persisted to the decade's end. First, popular respect for Washington and ambiguity about the nature of the new executive directed discontent at the first minister. Second, Hamiltonian finance was modeled on an English prototype. And finally, an opposition first appeared in the House of Representatives.

The Republican persuasion, in its early years, attempted to

---

30. See Merrill D. Peterson, *Thomas Jefferson and the New Nation* (New York: Oxford University Press, 1970), pp. 610–611. Peterson argues persuasively that Taylor and other old-line Virginia Republicans never fully overcame their Antifederalist beginnings. Believing the Constitution wrong in essentials, they traced evils to this source. Jefferson did not, although he may have wavered far enough in 1798 to lead Taylor to expect more than he was willing to deliver. See also Taylor to Monroe, March 25, 1798, "Letters of Taylor," p. 269: "I have for some time thought that yourself and other patriots were not entirely right in directing your efforts towards a change of men rather than of principles. . . . If the mischief . . . as I think, was done by the Constitution—if that established a form of government holding out to its administrators violent temptations to ambition and cupidity, is it surprising that they should have recourse to corruption, insincerity, and injustice?"

alert the nation to a ministerial conspiracy that was operating through corruption to secure the revival of a British kind of constitution. Ministerial influence would subvert the independence of the Congress, which would acquiesce in constitutional constructions leading to consolidation of the states and thence to monarchy.[31] Meanwhile, a decay of public virtue, spread by the example of the lackeys of administration and encouraged by the shift of wealth resulting from the funding plan, would ease the way for a transition to hereditary forms. With relatively minor changes, this was just the accusation that the eighteenth-century English opposition had traditionally directed at governments in power, and, like its prototype, it was, in the beginning, the weapon of a legislative group that had to reconcile its status as minority with its commitment to majority control. Legislative blocs were fluid, and the minority could understand its own position and appeal for popular support with the assistance of traditional assumptions that the influence of the Treasury, when added to an honest difference of opinion, was sufficient to account for policies with which they disagreed.

Images of conspiracy and accusations of corruption continued to provide the starting point for Republican analyses of Federalist policies, but it was not so many years before events and circumstances pushed Republican opinion away from its original foundations. First, circumstances undermined a logical necessity of neo-opposition arguments by making the Republicans a ma-

31. The clearest explication of the connection between monarchy and consolidation in Republican thought may be in Madison's report on the answers to the Virginia Resolutions, Gaillard Hunt, ed., *The Writings of James Madison* (New York: Putnam, 1900–1910), VI, 357–359. "That the obvious tendency and inevitable result of a consolidation of the states into one sovereignty would be to transform the republican system . . . into a monarchy is a point decided by the general sentiment of America." Two consequences must follow from consolidation. The sphere of executive discretion must be enlarged, since no legislature would have time or competence for so extensive and complex a job. And there must be an increase in "the offices, honors, and emoluments depending on the executive will. . . . This . . . increase of prerogative and patronage must evidently either enable the chief magistrate . . . by quiet means to secure his re-election from time to time and finally to regulate the succession as he might please or, by giving so transcendent an importance to the office, would render the elections to it so violent and corrupt that the public voice itself might call for an hereditary . . . succession."

jority in the House. Then, Hamilton resigned. Concurrently, however, Jay's Treaty and the foreign war became the major issues for dispute. In other words, just when the opposition might have savored the retirement of the archconspirator, just when their logic was endangered by their own success, events conjoined to redirect attention to the powers of the Senate and the actions of the President himself. British influence and affection for the cause of monarchy displaced attachment to the funding system as the leading explanation for administration policies. But the Republicans could see that the financial structure was dependent on the British trade, and thus the Federalists' foreign policy appeared to be a new means to old ends. In this way, the Republicans continued their conspiratorial analysis into the Adams years.

Only in the last years of the decade can we see a clearer movement of Republican concerns away from the inherited foundations of their thought and toward a style of argument that seems more native. The alteration might be traced to 1794, when the Republicans began to count on a majority of Representatives. From that point forward, we have seen, party writers focused somewhat less on the corruption of the lower house and somewhat more on dangers posed by enemies of the Republic in the several branches of the government and in the country as a whole. During the first years under Adams, critics concentrated their denunciations less on the "funding and banking gentry" or the Hamiltonian "phalanx" than on the "anglo-federal," "anglo-monarchical," or simply "tory" party.[32] The crisis of 1798—the popular hysteria, the Quasi-War, and the Sedition Law—strengthened this trend. Such a crisis in a polity that rested on a

32. The transition can be followed in microcosm in Jefferson's letters from the period between 1793 and 1798, *Works*, vol. VIII, or in the "Anas," *Works*, I, 163–430. By the time Jefferson began the "Anas" late in 1791, he was convinced that there had long existed a plot to reintroduce monarchy in America and that Hamilton was working toward this end with his systematic attempts to create a system of corrupting influence. But Jefferson also feared British influence from an early date, and his concern with the Federalists' motives in foreign policy increasingly replaced his preoccupation with influence after 1793. The "Anas" breaks off from 1794 through 1796, while Jefferson was in retirement. When it takes up again in 1797, the shift of concern is unmistakable.

large electorate made the administration's influence on the legislature seem less important than the efforts of a ruling party to mislead the people and destroy effective checks on Federalist abuses. Finally, the split among the Federalists confirmed the inclination to direct attacks, not at the link between the government and its dependents in the Congress—the characteristic target of the British critics of administration—but at a party that depended on its influence with the voters. During the last two years of the decade, Republican newspapers gave less space to criticism of the Congress or administration than they did to mockery of their Federalist competitors or efforts to assassinate the reputations of the leaders of the other party.[33] The scurrility of party sheets reflected their recognition that the enemy, in the United States, was not a governmental faction of the British type, but a party with its base among the people.

When Jefferson assumed the presidential office, he and the body of his party were prepared to believe that they had wakened a majority of voters and thereby put an end to the most immediate danger to the American Republic. Removal of the enemy from power and from public trust had come to seem sufficient, by itself, to safeguard liberty while friends of freedom worked toward gradual replacement of the Hamiltonian system with one better suited to republican ways. With the conspirators deposed, the country could afford to *ease* toward change—and change would come more certainly that way. Still, change it must—change as rapidly as possible according to a very different vision of the good society. Republicans were still persuaded that the debt must be retired as rapidly as preexisting contracts would permit, without internal taxes. It should not be clung to for its

---

33. Some representative examples from the *Aurora*, a few days apart: on Aug. 5, 1799, "Goodloe Harper, whom little Brown [editor of the Federal Gazette] calls *honorable*, is settled at Baltimore—as they say to pursue the law—but as we say to pursue a *white wife*;" on Aug. 11, 1800, "The great and *gallant* Major General—we do not mean the *brave*, but the *amarous* hero who has proclaimed his adventures with Maria—he, it seems, has said that he would lose his head or he would subvert the present government at the head of a triumphant army"; and on Oct. 8, 1800, "Long John Allen, this monarchical hero . . . has fairly come out in his thirteenth number of Burleigh and pointed out the object of his party—a separation of the union."

broader economic uses. It would not be used as an excuse to push the federal government into revenue resources better left to separate states. Even here, fanaticism was eschewed by a majority. Jefferson's administration did not hesitate to borrow more for the Louisianna Purchase. But the Republicans were willing to subordinate almost all else to the reduction of the debt. Every year the debt existed meant, to them, another year that taxes would inflate the rich, another year of the increasing gap between the rich and poor, which was potentially destructive to free states.[34] By 1812, Republican administrations had reduced the debt from $83 million, where it had climbed under the Federalists, to $27.5 million. They would have retired it completely in a few more years if war had not gotten in the way.

Reform did not go far enough to satisfy the Old Republicans. Change was incomplete enough—and leaders compromised enough—to make it possible for Henry Adams to support his accusation that the Jeffersonians surrendered to the principles of their opponents. Yet even Adams tried to have it several ways. Sometimes he condemned the Jeffersonians for lack of principle. Sometimes he accused them of a change of mind. At other times, however, he switched ground to level his attacks on their adherence to a set of principles that were ill-suited to the country's needs. The effort to retire the debt, he pointed out, committed the first $7.3 million of yearly revenues to payment of principal and interest. The remainder was too small to run the government and meet the costs of national defense. "The army was not large enough to hold the Indians in awe; the navy was not strong enough to watch the coasts. . . . The country was at the mercy of any Power which might choose to rob it."[35] "Gallatin's

34. As Jefferson put it, early in his successor's administration, "I consider the fortunes of our republic as depending, in an eminent degree, on the extinguishment of the public debt before we engage in any war; because, that done, we shall have revenue enough to improve our country in peace and defend it in war without recurring either to new taxes or loans. But if the debt should once more be swelled to a formidable size, its entire discharge will be despaired of and we shall be committed to the English career of debt, corruption, and rottenness, closing with revolution. The discharge of the debt . . . is vital to the destinies of our government" (To Gallatin, *Works of Jefferson*, XI, 124–125).

35. Adams, *History*, I, 242–243.

economies turned on the question whether the national debt or the risk of foreign aggression were most dangerous to America." The Republicans assumed the former.[36]

If we would choose among the different condemnations Adams made of the Republican regime, it would be better to prefer the last. Adherence to the principles of ninety-eight—a strikingly consistent effort to adopt and maintain policies implicit in the ideology of opposition days—is a better explanation for Republican actions during their years in power than any emphasis upon hypocrisy or change. The Old Republicans were worrisome beyond their numbers for no other reason than that they appealed to principles that still had the allegiance of large portions of the party.[37] And, as Adams saw, it was the party's loyalty to old ideas that brought the country to the edge of ruin in 1812.

II

The first years of the new republic were a time of unexampled prosperity and growth. The most important reason was the European war, which continued with few interruptions from 1790 to 1815. With France and Britain both preoccupied with warfare, a portion of the trade that they would normally have carried fell by default to neutrals. As the greatest trading neutral of the age, America had much to gain. It also risked involvement in the war, since both the European powers periodically attempted to deny the other neutral help.

During the 1790s, America's attempt to carry on a thriving commerce had nearly brought a war with Britain. The effort in fact resulted in a limited conflict with France. Thomas Jefferson came to the Presidency near the beginning of a brief respite in the European struggle, and the interlude of peace gave the Republicans a chance to apply their principles of governmental economy. In 1803, however, France and Britain resumed their

36. Ibid., 251.
37. In addition to Risjord, see Cunningham, chap. 9, who demonstrates that, in so far as Randolph attracted support from squabbling local factions, it was from the regular Republicans, not from "Quid" groups who cooperated with local Federalists.

titanic war. With Napoleon in power, Republicans had long since dropped their admiration of the French. But the commercial problems of the 1790s now returned with doubled force. After 1805, when Admiral Lord Nelson destroyed most of the French fleet in the Battle of Trafalgar, Britain was unchallengeable at sea, while Bonaparte was temporarily supreme on land. Both powers turned to economic warfare, catching the United States between.[38]

For America the situation reached its worst in 1807. In that year Napoleon's Milan Decree completed a "continental system" under which the Emperor threatened to seize any neutral ship that had submitted to a British search or paid a duty in a British port. Britain replied with Orders-in-Council that promised to seize any neutral trading with the continent *unless* that ship had paid a British fee. The combined effect of French and British measures was to threaten any vessel engaged in the continental trade. To make the situation worse, in the summer of 1807, near the mouth of Chesapeake Bay, the British frigate "Leopard" fired upon the American warship "Chesapeake," forced it to submit to search, and impressed four sailors into British service. By any standard, "Leopard's" action was a cause for war.

War might have been an easy choice. There was a storm of patriotic outrage possibly a match for that following the revelation of the XYZ Affair ten years before. Particularly in the Old Northwest, where British officials in Canada soon began to give assistance and encouragement to Tecumseh and his efforts to unite the western tribes against the progress of new settlement, demands for war rose steadily from that point on. But the Republicans did not want war. They were determined to face the present troubles in the way that they believed the Federalists should have responded to similar problems in the 1790s.[39]

38. The developments summarized here and below can conveniently be followed in detail in either of the biographies of Jefferson or in Marshall Smelser, *The Democratic Republic, 1801–1815* (New York: Harper & Row, 1968).

39. Again, I do not mean to suggest that the Republicans were monolithic, and I would not argue that specific responses to foreign policy decisions were dictated by ideology alone. In what follows, I simply mean to outline the ideological dimension of

Since the beginning of the party quarrel, Republicans had consistently expressed a fear of war and a profound distrust of normal preparations for defense. They were afraid of war's effects on civil liberties. They clung to the traditional distrust of standing armies. They had consistently opposed the frightful cost of navies. Their ideology identified high taxes, large armed forces, and the increase in executive authority that seemed inseparable from war as mortal dangers to republican society and government. Even preparations for hostilities would require abandonment of all the most important policies that they had followed since the triumph seven years before: low taxes, small armed forces, little governmental guidance of the nation's life, and quick retirement of the public debt.

In any case, Republicans had always argued that America possessed a weapon that provided an alternative to war, a weapon that had proven its effectiveness during the long struggle preceding independence. This weapon was its trade. Since opposition days, the party's leaders had maintained that the things America exported—mostly food and other raw materials—were necessities of life. The things America imported, on the other hand, were mostly manufactured goods and other "luxuries." In case of trouble, then, America could refuse to trade. Healthier than Europe, because it was not bound to large-scale manufacturing, America would win a test of wills, creating potent discontent and dislocation in the feebler state. Trade restrictions could secure the national interest as effectively as war and without the dangers to free government and social health that war would necessarily incur.[40] Trade was the weapon that the Madisonians had wanted to employ against the British back in 1794. It was the weapon

Republican conduct as it has been illuminated by several recent students and as it may be explained by the preceding chapters.

40. As previously noted, Ketchum and Peterson are especially perceptive in their analyses of the connection between the Republicans' domestic vision and their foreign policy. But they should be supplemented by Drew R. McCoy's excellent article, "Republicanism and American Foreign Policy: James Madison and the Political Economy of Commercial Discrimination, 1789–1794," *William and Mary Quarterly*, 31 (1974), 633–646, and the same author's "The Republican Revolution: Political Economy in Jeffersonian America, 1776 to 1817" (Ph.D. dissertation: University of Virginia, 1976).

that Republicans preferred when difficulties once again arose. Indeed, the party held to economic warfare, to its antiwar and antipreparation ideology, so long and so stubbornly that the result was nearly a disaster for the United States.[41]

In December 1807, Jefferson's administration responded to the French and British decrees by placing an embargo on American trade.[42] The embargo had a measurable effect in France and Britain. Unfortunately, the economic consequences for America were even worse. Under the embargo, all American sailings overseas were halted for more than a year. The country suffered a severe depression. In New England and upstate New York, noncooperation and illegal sailings rose to such proportions that the government resorted to repressive measures so severe as to endanger the Republicans' reputation as friends of limited government and guardians of civil rights.[43] To keep the peace within the country and to safeguard their majority, the Republicans relaxed their application of the economic weapon.[44] As Madison succeeded Jefferson, Congress started a long search for ways to hurt the Europeans more than the United States.[45] On the surface, this looked very like a gradual retreat. Inconsistent enforcement of changing regulations meant that pressure was repeatedly relaxed just as it began to have effect, and the Republi-

41. A most effective consideration of the ideological sources of the Republicans' resistance to more active measures of coercion and defense, informed by a sharp insight into the thought of the 1790s, is Roger H. Brown, *The Republic in Peril: 1812* (New York: Columbia University Press, 1964).

42. There was, however, by no means unanimous support for Jefferson's own concept of an embargo as a long-term alternative to war. Gallatin told the President from the first that, "in every point of view, privations, sufferings, revenue, effect on the enemy, politics at home, etc., I prefer war to a permanent embargo" (*Writings of Gallatin*, I, 368).

43. Levy, *Jefferson and Civil Liberties: The Darker Side*, is the most effective demonstration.

44. The embargo was repealed in the last days of Jefferson's administration and without the President's whole-hearted approval. Jefferson virtually abdicated his responsibilities as leader after Madison's election, but he continued to believe that the experiment should be prolonged or abandoned only for war.

45. Administration policy did not change when Madison succeeded Jefferson, but Congress did assume a larger portion of responsibility for the country's course. Principle and personality combined to make Madison a far less effective legislative leader than Jefferson had been.

cans' persistence simply led the warring powers to conclude that America would never fight. In 1809 the embargo was replaced with a measure confining nonintercourse to trade between America and French or British ports. In 1810 restrictions were removed completely, although it was provided that nonintercourse would be resumed against one country or the other if either of the powers would agree to end its violations of neutral rights.

Since the ending of American restrictions would benefit Great Britain, Napoleon made moves that it was possible to interpret as an exemption of American shipping from the Berlin and Milan Decrees. Madison announced that nonintercourse would be imposed against the British unless the Orders-in-Council were repealed. When they were not, restrictions were resumed.

The situation quickly passed the bounds of the absurd. By the winter of 1811–1812, four years of various experiments with commercial coercion had failed to force a change in European policies. During all that time the frontier trouble had continued, and Great Britain had persisted in its arrogant, humiliating practice of impressment. Meanwhile the Republicans had lost New England and were threatened in the middle states by the revival of a party that they still considered dangerous to the survival of a democratic way. With the people growing restless under policies that damaged their prosperity without securing change, it was increasingly apparent to most members of the party that commercial weapons would not work. The choice must be between submission to the British policies and war. Neither the people's sense of national honor nor the survival of the Republican Party—a party that believed that liberty would not be safe with its opponents—would permit submission. Madison reluctantly resigned himself to war, and younger representatives from the West and South—"war hawks" to their enemies—worked a declaration through the Congress. There were defections by Clintonians and Quids, but it was basically a party vote.[46]

46. I have followed the argument of Brown, *The Republic in Peril*, and Norman K. Risjord, "1812: Conservatives, War Hawks, and the Nation's Honor," *William and Mary Quarterly*, 28 (1961), 196–210.

III

To anyone inclined to balance gain with loss, the War of 1812 must seem a masterpiece of folly. The god who ruled its fortunes was decidedly perverse. Two days before the Senate completed a declaration of war, though not in time for news to cross the sea, the British government announced that the Orders-in-Council would be repealed. The battle at New Orleans was planned by generals who had not learned that peace had been agreed upon at Ghent on December 24, 1814, two weeks before. The slaughter on the Missisippi—nineteen months of warfare—ultimately went for naught. The Treaty of Ghent simply restored the situation that had existed before the war. Boundaries were unaltered. Disputes over neutral rights and impressment were left unresolved.

Contemporaries, however, were not disposed to make a practical calculation of this sort. After all, the war had not been fought for rational reasons alone. National honor, the reputation of republican government, and the continuing supremacy of the Republican party had seemed to be at stake.

National honor had been satisfied. Jackson's stunning victory at New Orleans more than redeemed earlier reverses in the field. And news of his triumph arrived in the East just before the news of peace. Americans celebrated the end of the struggle with a brilliant burst of national pride. They felt that they had fought a second war for independence, and had won. If little had been gained, nothing had been lost in a contest with the greatest imperial power on the earth.

Independence, of course, had never been literally at risk. For Britain the War of 1812 was an unwelcome outcome of a quarrel that had seemed a lesser evil than a relaxation of the struggle against Napoleon. Once Bonaparte was vanquished, little could be gained by further prosecution of the lesser war. British statesmen had no will whatever for the effort that would have been required to defeat, much less to subjugate, the United States. They preferred a quick renewal of the valuable American trade.

Nevertheless, a new American independence did follow the

Treaty of Ghent. The American Revolution was, at least in one respect, an effort to break connections with a corrupt Old World. But withdrawal from European involvements had been far from complete. Americans could not be indifferent when the republican revolution promised to convert Europe in the years after 1789, and the new American republic had continued an oceanic trade that inevitably weighed in the power calculations of European states. Independence from European involvements could not be more complete until the new nation had proven its ability to survive the great wars of the French Revolution.[47] The magnetic attraction of European developments would not be weakened until the United States stood once again as the preeminent republic in the world, its belief in European corruption once again confirmed.

In 1815 the Bourbon monarchy was restored in France. The conquerors of Napoleon met in Vienna to make arrangements that inaugurated a century of general peace. Peace on the Atlantic was the indispensable assurance that trade would not again become a vortex to suck young America into European war. The close of the democratic revolutions made it clear that the future of republicanism depended once more on developments at home. Only after 1815 did the great nations of Europe begin to take it for granted that the American Republic would persist, that it could not be made a satellite of any one of them. Only then could the United States turn its attention from the east to face a continental destiny beyond the Appalachian hills.

Only then, moreover, could Americans themselves begin to take it for granted that their experiment in republican government was going to endure. Through all the years since 1789, the American union had been a very fragile thing. Every serious difference over policy had seemed a difference over revolutionary

47. This discussion of the years around 1815 as the end of the revolutionary era owes much to Richard Buel, Jr., *Securing the Revolution: Ideology in American Politics, 1789–1815* (Ithaca, N.Y.: Cornell University Press, 1972). I am also indebted to Professor J. G. A. Pocock, with whom I collaborated closely while preparing the original version.

principle as well. Every difference over principle had tested the union of the states. Perhaps the passing years had strengthened national loyalties, yet the collapse of federal government had never seemed more imminent than during the troubles connected with the War of 1812.

After years of Republican experiments with economic coercion, the nation had entered the war with New England bitterly alienated from federal policy. During the struggle wealthy Yankees declined to lend money to a government that tottered near the edge of bankruptcy. Legislatures passed resolutions condemning the war. New England governors refused to permit their militia to be used outside the boundaries of their states. Too often, noncooperation shaded into disloyalty of several sorts: trade with the enemy, plots to disrupt the union, schemes for a separate peace.

Most New Englanders never carried noncooperation to such extremes. But enough of them were angry that in December 1814 they held a convention at Hartford, Connecticut, to consider the section's grievances against the nation. The majority of delegates overrode the few secessionist plotters, but the Hartford Convention did agree on a set of demands designed to protect New England from a Southern and Western majority in Washington. They called for constitutional amendments that would break Virginia's grip on the presidency by limiting the office to a single term and forbidding successive elections of men from the same state, that would reduce the number of Southern congressmen by ending the representation of three-fifths of the slaves, that would limit any embargo to sixty days, and would require a two-thirds majority in Congress to admit new states, provide for commercial retaliation, or declare a war. And the Convention sent a committee to Washington with a manifesto that promised a second convention and hinted at more drastic action if the demands should be refused.

Despite the New Englanders, of course, the federal government survived the war. Not only that, but the committee from Hartford reached the capital just in time for the celebration of the

news from New Orleans. As a result, the attempt to extort constitutional change under pressure of war appeared both foolish
and disloyal. James Madison and the Republican party finished
the war with more prestige than they had had at the start, while
the reputation of New England Federalism was damaged beyond
repair. The swelling national pride of the people moved behind
the party that had carried the nation through. Within a few
years—for practical purposes—the Republicans were the only
party left. Within a decade, John Adams' son was a Republican
President.

Survival in the War of 1812 had nonetheless required an
ample portion of good luck. Republican principles had combined
with a lack of planning, poor management, and the alienation of
New England to brew a bitter soup. For years, the principles and
beliefs that recommended commercial coercion as an alternative
to war had also bolstered many members of the party in their
inclination to refuse requests for normal preparations for defense.[48] Similar motives had encouraged Jefferson's first Congress to repeal internal taxes, and, in 1811, they had entered into
the refusal to renew the charter of the Bank of the United States.

In 1812, America challenged a great empire with sixteen war-
ships and a regular army of less than seven thousand well-trained
men. Congress provided for larger forces once it was clear that
war could not be escaped, but ships could not be built in time to
have an effect. Enlistment in the army was painfully slow, so that
regulars carried the largest part of the burden only in the northern campaign of 1814. Meanwhile, the British fleet drove the
American from the ocean, the finest American militia sat home in
New England, and Western soldiers enjoyed a very mixed success. Meanwhile, too, the government showed itself a financial

48. Beginning in 1805, Republican administrations sought increased appropriations
and preparations, but with little success. In 1805, for example, Jefferson asked for
additional harbor fortifications, reorganization of the militia, and consideration of the
construction of six ships-of-the-line. Congress refused the ships, returning the navy to a
peacetime establishment of three frigates and nine hundred men. The regular army
remained at three thousand men, mainly on western stations. See Peterson, pp. 832–
839.

cripple. When war became inevitable, Congress approved new taxes. But revenues were slow in coming in. Until they did, funds were difficult to find. Without a national bank, the Treasury had no dependable source of ready loans, no easy way to transfer the monies it had from one part of the country to another.[49] Against a less distracted, more determined foe, complete humiliation might well have been the result.

The administration learned its lessons. Early in 1815, President Madison recommended a peacetime army of twenty thousand men. In his annual message of December 5, 1815, the great architect of the old Republicanism called upon Congress to consider federal support for certain internal improvements, tariff protection for new industries which had been encouraged by the argument with England, and creation of a new national bank.[50] The implications of this message were profound. It might be said they mark the advent of a very different age.

In the first years of the new federal government, Alexander Hamilton had grounded his great plans on the assumption that the world was not the kind of place where republican purists could pursue their schemes in peace. Republicans had insisted that there was an alternative to the Secretary's system, one which could secure national respectability without the unacceptable risks to revolutionary accomplishments that Hamilton's seemed to entail. In the years after 1800, they had gradually dismantled much of the foundation on which the Federalists had meant to build an America that could compete with empires such as England's on English terms. They had substituted a different vision,

49. To a degree, moreover, the administration sought to conduct the war on Republican principles. In the aftermath of the "Chesapeake" Affair Gallatin had written to Joseph H. Nicholson that "the greatest mischiefs which I apprehend from the war are the necessary increase of executive power and influence, the speculations of contractors and jobbers, and the introduction of permanent military and naval establishments" (*Writings of Gallatin*, I, 339). His concerns were little changed by March, 1812, when he confessed to Jefferson that war was "unavoidable" and that he could only do his best to see that the United States "may be burdened with the smallest possible quantity of debt, perpetual taxation, military establishment, and other corrupting or anti-Republican habits or institutions."

50. The message is in *Writings of Madison*, VIII, 335–344.

in which a society of independent men of virtue would appear in arms when necessary to defend America's shores, but trust their influence on the course of history, more generally, to the moral force of republican example and the necessary demand for the raw materials they would produce for trade. Jefferson and Madison had also tried a different course in foreign policy. Under the pressure of Napoleonic wars, the Republican alternative had failed.

Hamilton had been right, at least in significant part. America did not have the capacity to force the great states of Europe to accept the kind of international order within which the new nation could pursue the Republican ideal, a society in which the virtue of independent farmers and craftsmen would not be threatened by great cities, large-scale industry, professional armed forces, and a polity committed to the mysteries and dangers of English-style finance. The choice did seem to lie between greater self-sufficiency and national humiliation or war. Now, implicitly, a Republican President admitted this truth.[51]

It was not an unconditional surrender to Hamilton's ideas. Madison could hope that vast expanses of western land and the continued leadership of genuine republicans would postpone to an indefinite future the debilitating corruption that Republicans had always feared. He still had no desire to see the land become a democratic England.[52] Yet he did suggest that old Jeffersonian principles might be tempered with a program that would resur-

---

51. As his predecessor also did. Thirty years ago, Jefferson told Benjamin Austin on Jan. 9, 1816, he might legitimately have been quoted in favor of a continuing dependence on England for manufactures. But no one then foresaw the great wars and the violations of freedom of the seas. Circumstances have changed, and we now know that "there exists both profligacy and power enough to exclude us from the field of interchange with other nations, that to be independent for the comforts of life we must fabricate them ourselves. . . . He, therefore, who is now against domestic manufacture must be for reducing us either to dependence on that foreign nation or to be clothed in skins and to live like wild beasts in dens and caverns. . . . Manufactures are now as necessary to our independence as to our comfort" (*Writings*, XI, 502–505).

52. Nor did Jefferson. Six months after endorsing domestic manufactures in the letter to Austin, Jefferson wrote to William H. Crawford: "The exercise, by our own citizens, of so much commerce as may suffice to exchange our superfluities for our wants may be advantageous for the whole. But it does not follow that . . . it is the interest of

rect an essential portion of the Hamiltonian state. In doing so, he legitimized the other side of a debate that had held the nation's attention since 1789. He hinted that America could build on an amalgam of Republican and Federalist ideas, and the majority of his party agreed. If we must mark a single point at which to write an end to the debate that traced back to the eighteenth-century argument between the English Country and the Court, we might select the second session of the Fourteenth Congress, which adopted all of Madison's proposals.

The ancient argument did not abruptly stop. The old ideas did not abruptly lose their influence. The United States has seldom had a less effective government than in the years between 1817 and 1829, not least because its chief executives did not believe in leading Congress and Republicans in Congress did not believe in being led. Presidential leadership and the effective use of patronage still smelled of influence and a danger to the public good. Allegiance to a party still seemed too much like corruption.[53] As the "American System" of Henry Clay, the Hamiltonian vision of a self-sufficient republic, where industrial development would provide a domestic market for agricultural goods and federal programs would tie diverse sections into an imperial whole, remained a central topic for political division and dispute.

---

the whole to become a mere city of London to carry on the business of one half of the world at the expense of eternal war with the other half. . . . Our commercial dashers . . . have already cost us . . . more than their persons and all their commerce were worth" (*Writings*, XI, 537–539). As Merrill Peterson points out, Jefferson still declined to embrace industrialization, still disliked the prospect of manufacturing cities, great companies, and masses of dependent workers. "What he embraced, then, was the household-handicraft-mill complex of an advanced agricultural society" (*Thomas Jefferson and the New Nation*, pp. 940–941).

53. Though objectionable in details, James Sterling Young, *The Washington Community, 1800–1828* (New York: Columbia University Press, 1966) is a remarkable contribution of a political scientist to early national history. While only hinting at the ideological configurations involved, Young provides an effective picture of the way in which the governing community at Washington formed itself into separate social enclaves centered on the Capitol and the executive mansion, enclaves with separate schools, separate stores, separate churches, separate cemeteries, and separate social diversions. Party affiliation proved far too frail a bond to overcome the aversion to executive leadership and the insistence on a separation of powers which was reflected even in the design of the capital city itself.

Jacksonians attacked "aristocracy" and "corruption." Whigs condemned "King Andrew." John C. Calhoun was intensely concerned with something strongly reminiscent of corrupting influence. The new Republicans who followed Lincoln celebrated virtue and the independent man.[54] As a consequence of revolutionary hopes and thought, proponents of American grandeur have always had to answer those who worry about a loss of innocence at home. In the years around 1815, however, the context of these controversies underwent a fundamental change. Experiments with economic coercion, followed by the War of 1812, had exposed an undeniable weakness in the principles on which the Republican party had based its rule. But the war had also made it easier to contemplate a change of course. Events destroyed one of the two great parties to the long dispute over the shaping of a society and government that could make republicanism lasting and complete. Doing this, they freed the other party to turn its attention to the needs of the future. Leadership passed increasingly to younger men, whose lives had not been molded by the great Revolution that had shaped the experience of the generation before. Arguments among the younger men would still be fierce, but the edges of hysteria grew blunt. For it was now the most appropriate means of national development that seemed to be at stake, not the very meaning of America itself.

54. See William H. Freehling, "Spoilsmen and Interests in the Thought and Career of John C. Calhoun," *Journal of American History*, 52 (1965), 25–42. Fred Somkin, *Unquiet Eagle: Memory and Desire in the Idea of American Freedom, 1815–1860* (Ithaca, N.Y.: Cornell University Press, 1967), is an effective demonstration of the persistence of a concern with virtue and a fear of prosperity beyond the Jacksonian period. Eric Foner's brilliant *Free Soil, Free Labor, Free Men: The Ideology of the Republican Party before the Civil War* (New York: Oxford University Press, 1970) may suggest that Lincoln's party could be characterized as men of old agrarian and even Harringtonian principles who had fallen in love with enterprise.

Index

The Jeffersonian Persuasion

Designed by R. E. Rosenbaum.
Composed by Graphic Composition, Inc.,
in 11 point VIP Monticello, 2 points leaded,
with display lines in Monticello.
Printed offset by Vail-Ballou Press on
Warren's No. 66 text, 50 pound basis.
Bound by Vail-Ballou Press
in Joanna book cloth
and stamped in All Purpose foil.

Library of Congress Cataloging in Publication Data
(For library cataloging purposes only)

Banning, Lance, 1942–
    The Jeffersonian persuasion.

    Includes bibliographical references and index.
    1. United States—Politics and government—1783–1809. 2. Jefferson, Thomas,
Pres. U. S., 1743–1826—Views on politics. 3. Representative government and representation—United States—History. 4. Democracy.
    I. Title.
    E302.1.B2   320.5′0973   77–14666
    ISBN 0–8014–1151–3